READY-TO-USE

LIFE SCIENCE ACTIVITIES

FOR GRADES 5-12

Mark J. Handwerker, Ph.D.

THE CENTER FOR APPLIED
RESEARCH IN EDUCATION
West Nyack, New York 10994

Library of Congress Cataloging-in-Publication Data

Handwerker, Mark J.
    Ready-to-use life science activities for grades 5–12 / Mark J.
Handwerker, Ph.D.
        p.   cm.—(Secondary science curriculum activities library)
    1. Life sciences—Study and teaching (Secondary)—Activity
programs.   2. Life sciences—Study and teaching (Middle School)—
Activity programs.   I. Title.   II. Series.
QH316.4.H35   1999
570'.71'2—dc21   99-10010
                                                                                                           CIP

Printed in the United States of America

10   9   8   7   6   5   4   3

ISBN 0-87628-439-X (spiral)   ISBN 0-13-029111-0 (lay-flat pbk)

ATTENTION: CORPORATIONS AND SCHOOLS

The Center for Applied Research in Education books are available at quantity discounts with bulk purchase for educational, business, or sales promotional use. For information, please write to: Prentice Hall Direct Special Sales, 240 Frisch Court, Paramus, NJ 07652. Please supply: title of book, ISBN number, quantity, how the book will be used, date needed.

**THE CENTER FOR APPLIED RESEARCH
IN EDUCATION**
West Nyack, NY 10994

On the World Wide Web at http://www.phdirect.com

About This Resource

Ready-to-Use Life Science Activities for Grades 5–12 is designed to help you teach basic science concepts to your students while building their appreciation and understanding of the work of generations of curious scientists. Although The Scientific Method remains the most successful strategy for acquiring and advancing the store of human knowledge, science is—for all its accomplishments—still merely a human endeavor. While the benefits of science are apparent in our everyday lives, its resulting technology could endanger the survival of the species if it is carelessly applied. It is therefore essential that our students be made aware of the nature of scientific inquiry with all its strengths and limitations.

A primary goal of science instructors should be to make their students "science literate." After completing a course of study in any one of the many scientific disciplines, students should be able to:

1. appreciate the role played by observation and experimentation in establishing scientific theories and laws,

2. understand cause-and-effect relationships,

3. base their opinions on fact and observable evidence—not superstitions or prejudice, and

4. be willing to change their opinions based on newly acquired evidence.

Scientific theories come and go as new observations are made. During the course of instruction, teachers should emphasize the "process" of science as well as the relevance of pertinent facts.

This volume of science activities was designed to accomplish all of the above, keeping in mind the everyday challenges faced by classroom instructors.

On Your Mark!

Begin by stimulating students' gray matter with basic scientific concepts through brainstorming and open discussion.

Get Set!

Kindle interest by making concepts real through demonstration and/or descriptive analogy.

Go!

Cement concepts into concrete form with exciting hands-on experience.

Each of the 15 teaching units in this volume of *Ready-to-Use Life Science Activities for Grades 5–12* contains *four* 40–50 minute lessons and follows the same instructional sequence so that your students will always know what is expected of them. Each unit comes complete with the following:

- a **Teacher's Classwork Agenda for the Week** and **Content Notes for Lecture and Discussion,**
- a student **Fact Sheet** with **Homework Directions** on the back,
- four 40–50 minute **Lesson Plans,** each followed by its own **Journal Sheet** to facilitate student notetaking, and
- an end-of-the-unit **Review Quiz.**

Each unit has been tested for success in the classroom and is ready for use with minimal preparation on your part. Simply make as many copies of the Fact Sheet with Homework Directions, Journal Sheets, and Review Quizzes as you need for your class. Also, complete answer keys for the homework assignments and unit quiz are provided at the end of the Teacher's Classwork Agenda for the Unit.

Mark J. Handwerker

ABOUT THE AUTHOR

Mark J. Handwerker (B.S., C.C.N.Y., Ph.D. in Biology, U.C.I.) has taught secondary school science for 15 years in the Los Angeles and Temecula Valley Unified School Districts. As a mentor and instructional support teacher, he has trained scores of new teachers in the "art" of teaching science. He is the author/editor of articles in a number of scientific fields and the coauthor of an earth science textbook (Harcourt Brace Jovanovich, *Earth Science*) currently in use.

Dr. Handwerker teaches his students that the best way to learn basic scientific principles is to become familiar with the men and women who first conceived them. His classroom demonstrations are modeled on those used by the most innovative scientists of the past. He believes that a familiarity with the history of science, and an understanding of the ideas and methods used by the world's most curious people, are the keys to comprehending revolutions in modern technology and human thought.

Suggestions for Using These Science Teaching Units

The following are practical suggestions for using the 15 teaching units in this resource to maximize your students' performance.

Fact Sheet

At the start of each unit, give every student a copy of the **Fact Sheet** for that unit with the **Homework Directions** printed on the back. The Fact Sheet introduces content vocabulary and concepts relevant to the unit. You can check students' homework on a daily basis or require them to manage their own "homework time" by turning in all assignments at the end of the unit. Most of the homework assignments can be completed on a single sheet of standard-sized (8½" × 11") looseleaf paper. Urge students to take pride in their accomplishments and do their most legible work at all times.

Journal Sheet

At the start of each lesson, give every student a copy of the appropriate **Journal Sheet** which they will use to record lecture notes, discussion highlights, and laboratory activity data. Make transparencies of Journal Sheets for use on an overhead projector. In this way, you can model neat, legible, notetaking skills.

Current Events

Since science does not take place in a vacuum (and also because it is required by most State Departments of Education), make **Current Events** a regular part of your program. Refer to the brief discussion on "Using Current Events to Integrate Science Instruction Across Content Areas" in the Appendix.

Review Quiz

Remind students to study their Fact and Journal Sheets to prepare for the end-of-the-unit **Review Quiz.** The Review Quiz is a 15-minute review and application of unit vocabulary and scientific principles.

Grading

After completing and collectively grading the end-of-the-unit Review Quiz in class, have students total their own points and give themselves a grade for that unit. For simplicity's sake, point values can be awarded as follows: a neatly completed set of Journal Sheets earns 40 points; a neatly completed Homework Assignment earns 20 points; a neatly completed Current Event earns 10 points; and, a perfect score on the Review Quiz earns 30 points. Students should record their scores and letter grades on their individual copies of the **Grade Roster** provided in the Appendix. Letter grades for each unit can be earned according to the following point totals: A ≥ 90, B ≥ 80, C ≥ 70, D ≥ 60, F < 60. On the reverse side of the Grade Roster, students will find instructions for calculating their "grade point average" or "GPA." If they keep track of their progress, they will never have to ask "How am I doing in this class?" They will know!

Unit Packets

At the end of every unit, have students staple their work into a neat "unit packet" that includes their Review Quiz, Homework, Journal Sheet, Current Event, and Fact Sheet. Collect and examine each student's packet, making comments as necessary. Check to see that students have awarded themselves the points and grades they have earned. You can enter individual grades into your record book or grading software before returning all packets to students the following week.

You will find that holding students accountable for compiling their own work at the end of each unit instills a sense of responsibility and accomplishment. Instruct students to show their packets and Grade Roster to their parents on a regular basis.

Fine Tuning

This volume of *Ready-to-Use Life Science Activities for Grades 5–12* was created so that teachers would not have to "reinvent the wheel" every week to come up with lessons that work. Instructors are advised and encouraged to fine tune activities to their own personal teaching style in order to satisfy the needs of individual students. You are encouraged to supplement lessons with your district's adopted textbook and any relevant audiovisual materials and computer software. Use any and all facilities at your disposal to satisfy students' varied learning modalities (visual, auditory, kinesthetic, and so forth).

CONTENTS

LS1   ACTIVITIES AND NEEDS OF LIVING THINGS / 1

Teacher's Classwork Agenda and Content Notes

Classwork Agenda for the Week . . . Content Notes for Lecture
and Discussion . . . Answers to the End-of-the-Week Review Quiz

Fact Sheet with Homework Directions

Lesson #1
Students will list the basic activities performed by all living things.
Journal Sheet #1

Lesson #2
Students will list the basic needs common to all living things.
Journal Sheet #2

Lesson #3
Students will explain how plants trap energy from the sun in a process called photosynthesis.
Journal Sheet #3

Lesson #4
Students will explain how plants and animals release trapped solar energy during a process called respiration.
Journal Sheet #4

LS1 Review Quiz

LS2   CLASSIFICATION OF LIVING THINGS / 15

Teacher's Classwork Agenda and Content Notes

Classwork Agenda for the Week . . . Content Notes for Lecture
and Discussion . . . Answers to the End-of-the-Week Review Quiz

Fact Sheet with Homework Directions

Lesson #1
Students will classify objects according to structure.
Journal Sheet #1

Lesson #2
Students will classify objects according to function.
Journal Sheet #2

Lesson #3
Students will use a binomial classification system to name objects classified according to structure and function.
Journal Sheet #3

Lesson #4
Students will contrast the major characteristics of the world's five living kingdoms.
Journal Sheet #4

LS2 Review Quiz

LS3 DESCENT AND CHANGE IN LIVING THINGS / 29

Teacher's Classwork Agenda and Content Notes

Classwork Agenda for the Week . . . Content Notes for Lecture
and Discussion . . . Answers to the End-of-the-Week Review Quiz

Fact Sheet with Homework Directions

Lesson #1
Students will compare and contrast the variety of organisms in the environment.
Journal Sheet #1

Lesson #2
Students will explain why species tend to overpopulate.
Journal Sheet #2

Lesson #3
Students will examine the adaptations of a variety of organisms in the environment.
Journal Sheet #3

Lesson #4
*Students will explain how mutation and natural selection result in the evolution
of structure in living things.*
Journal Sheet #4

LS3 Review Quiz

LS4 THE HISTORY OF LIFE / 43

Teacher's Classwork Agenda and Content Notes

Classwork Agenda for the Week . . . Content Notes for Lecture
and Discussion . . . Answers to the End-of-the-Week Review Quiz

Fact Sheet with Homework Directions

Lesson #1
Students will identify the organic molecules found in all organisms.
Journal Sheet #1

Lesson #2
Students will examine the role of extinction in the evolution of life on earth.
Journal Sheet #2

Lesson #3
Students will list and identify the predominant organisms of the precambrian and paleozoic eras.
Journal Sheet #3

Lesson #4
Students will list and identify the predominant organisms of the mesozoic and cenozoic eras.
Journal Sheet #4

LS4 Review Quiz

LS5   LEVELS OF ORGANIZATION IN LIVING THINGS / 57

Teacher's Classwork Agenda and Content Notes

Classwork Agenda for the Week . . . Content Notes for Lecture
and Discussion . . . Answers to the End-of-the-Week Review Quiz

Fact Sheet with Homework Directions

Lesson #1
Students will learn how to use a microscope.
Journal Sheet #1

Lesson #2
Students will identify different types of cells under a microscope.
Journal Sheet #2

Lesson #3
Students will identify different types of tissues under a microscope.
Journal Sheet #3

Lesson #4
Students will list familiar organs and organ systems.
Journal Sheet #4

LS5 Review Quiz

LS6   THE LIVING CELL: PART I / 71

Teacher's Classwork Agenda and Content Notes

Classwork Agenda for the Week . . . Content Notes for Lecture
and Discussion . . . Answers to the End-of-the-Week Review Quiz

Fact Sheet with Homework Directions

Lesson #1
Students will compare and contrast the organelles of plant and animal cells.
Journal Sheet #1

Lesson #2
Students will begin gathering information about the structure and function of cell organelles.
Journal Sheet #2

Lesson #3
Students will continue gathering information about the structure and function of cell organelles.
Journal Sheet #3

Lesson #4
Students will develop a cooperative plan for constructing a three-dimensional model of a plant or animal cell.
Journal Sheet #4

LS6 Review Quiz

LS9 INTRODUCTION TO GENETICS / 113

Teacher's Classwork Agenda and Content Notes

Classwork Agenda for the Week . . . Content Notes for Lecture
and Discussion . . . Answers to the End-of-the-Week Review Quiz

Fact Sheet with Homework Directions

Lesson #1
Students will construct a model of a protein molecule.
Journal Sheet #1

Lesson #2
Students will construct a model of a DNA molecule.
Journal Sheet #2

Lesson #3
Students will use models to show how DNA codes for the production of proteins.
Journal Sheet #3

Lesson #4
Students will use models to show how scientists manufacture recombinant DNA.
Journal Sheet #4

LS9 Review Quiz

LS10 MICROORGANISMS / 127

Teacher's Classwork Agenda and Content Notes

Classwork Agenda for the Week . . . Content Notes for Lecture
and Discussion . . . Answers to the End-of-the-Week Review Quiz

Fact Sheet with Homework Directions

Lesson #1
Students will compose a graphic organizer showing the relationships between different types of microorganisms.
Journal Sheet #1

Lesson #2
Students will contrast the structures and characteristics of viruses and bacteria.
Journal Sheet #2

Lesson #3
Students will compare and draw different species of protozoa.
Journal Sheet #3

Lesson #4
Students will contrast the structures and characteristics of molds and protozoa.
Journal Sheet #4

LS10 Review Quiz

LS13   VERTEBRATES / 169

Teacher's Classwork Agenda and Content Notes

Classwork Agenda for the Week . . . Content Notes for Lecture
and Discussion . . . Answers to the End-of-the-Week Review Quiz

Fact Sheet with Homework Directions

Lesson #1
Students will compose a graphic organizer showing the relationships among fish, amphibians, reptiles, birds, and mammals.
Journal Sheet #1

Lesson #2
Students will compare and contrast the adaptations of fish and amphibians.
Journal Sheet #2

Lesson #3
Students will compare and contrast the adaptations of reptiles and birds.
Journal Sheet #3

Lesson #4
Students will compare and contrast the adaptations of mammalian orders.
Journal Sheet #4

LS13 Review Quiz

LS14   BIOMES / 183

Teacher's Classwork Agenda and Content Notes

Classwork Agenda for the Week . . . Content Notes for Lecture
and Discussion . . . Answers to the End-of-the-Week Review Quiz

Fact Sheet with Homework Directions

Lesson #1
Students will use a map of the globe to identify the major biomes of the world.
Journal Sheet #1

Lesson #2
Students will create imaginary organisms adapted for life in the tundra and desert.
Journal Sheet #2

Lesson #3
Students will create imaginary organisms adapted for life in the forests and grasslands.
Journal Sheet #3

Lesson #4
Students will create an imaginary organism adapted for life in the deep ocean abyss.
Journal Sheet #4

LS14 Review Quiz

Teacher's Classwork Agenda and Content Notes

Classwork Agenda for the Week . . . Content Notes for Lecture
and Discussion . . . Answers to the End-of-the-Week Review Quiz

Fact Sheet with Homework Directions

Lesson #1
Students will diagram the relationships between organisms in an ecosystem.
Journal Sheet #1

Lesson #2
Students will examine the food chains in aquatic and terrestrial communities.
Journal Sheet #2

Lesson #3
Students will diagram the four major natural chemical cycles.
Journal Sheet #3

Lesson #4
Students will examine the effects of pollution on the environment.
Journal Sheet #4

LS15 Review Quiz

APPENDIX / 211

Alcmeaon

Aristotle

Roger Bacon

William Bateson

Louis de Broglie

Martinus Willem Beijerinck

Marie François Xavier Bichat

Stanely Cohen

Francis H.C. Crick

Georges Cuvier

Charles Robert Darwin

Hugo Marie DeVries

Henri Dutrochet

Paul Ehrlich

Adolf Engler

Walter Flemming

Rosalind Elsie Franklin

Galen

Ernst Heinrich Haekel

William Harvey

Jacob Henle

Hippocrates

Dorothy M.C. Hodgkin

Robert Hooke

Joseph Dalton Hooker

Freidrich W.H.A. Humboldt

James Hutton

Thomas Jefferson

Edward Jenner

Har Gobind Khorana

Henrich Hermann Koch

Jean Baptiste Lamarck

Anton van Leeuwenhoek

Carolus Linnaeus

Joseph Lister

Charles Lyell

Gregor Mendel

Stanley Lloyd Miller

Hugo von Mohl

Thomas Hunt Morgan

Fritz Müller

Hermann Joseph Muller

Louis Pasteur

Auguste Antoine & Jacques Piccard

Plato

John Ray

Ernst August Freidrich Ruska

Matthias Jakob Schleiden

Theodor Schwann

Lazzaro Spallanzini

Eduard Adolf Strasburger

Theophrastus

Harold Clayton Urey

Alfred Russel Wallace

Johannes E.B. Warming

James Dewey Watson

Alfred Lothar Wegener

August F.L. Weismann

ACTIVITIES AND NEEDS OF LIVING THINGS

TEACHER'S CLASSWORK AGENDA AND CONTENT NOTES

Classwork Agenda for the Week

1. Students will list the basic activities performed by all living things.
2. Students will list the basic needs common to all living things.
3. Students will explain how plants trap energy from the sun in a process called photosynthesis.
4. Students will explain how plants and animals release trapped solar energy during a process called respiration.

Content Notes for Lecture and Discussion

The systematic study of living things was first conducted by the Ancient Greeks. Other civilizations (e.g., Chinese, Babylonian, Egyptian) approached the study of Nature from a variety of perspectives; but, it was the Greeks who developed the first formative ideas of biology upon which the pillars of the modern discipline rest. The Greek physician **Alcmeaon** (c. 500 B.C.) performed animal dissections directed at discovering the "sensory channels" leading to the brain. **Hippocrates** (b. 460 B.C.; d. 377 B.C.) emphasized the study of "body humours" he thought essential to the maintenance of good health. Hippocrates is often called the founder of medicine for promoting cleanliness and moderation in eating and drinking habits. His *Hippocratic Oath* embodies the modern medical ethic to "do no harm" in the search for a cure. And—as in other sciences—**Aristotle** (b. 384 B.C.; d. 322 B.C.) lent his wisdom to the study of biology. Aristotle's study of sea creatures in their natural habitats convinced him that the structure of each animal organ was a manifestation of the organ's function. His functional approach to anatomy was nothing less than a study of animal adaptations. Since Aristotle believed that nature let nothing go to waste, he inquired about the purpose of life and the point of its seemingly infinite variety. Following Aristotle, the ideas of the Greek physician **Galen** (b. 129; d. 200)—who adopted the "humourology" of Hippocrates—dominated Western medicine for over 1,500 years.

Despite the ancients' interest in the nature of living things, it was not until the early 19th century that "life" as a concept began to take form in the discourse of natural philosophers. Among the growing number of scientists involved in the new field of biology, the idea began to emerge that all living things (e.g., plants and animals)—despite their great variety—were animated by the same dynamic forces. The qualities of the forces that animated organisms, however, became a matter of serious debate. Two schools of thought dominated the debate: the Vitalists and the Mechanists. The father of paleontology, French comparative anatomist **Georges Cuvier** (b. 1769; d. 1832), was a leading "vitalist." The Vitalists held that life could not be explained by the forces of physics and chemistry and was, in fact, a force in opposition to those strict mechanistic forces. The vitalist French physician **Marie François Xavier Bichat** (b. 1771; d. 1802) defined life as the "sum total of functions that resist death." For many, the phenomenon of life could only be completely explained by resorting to metaphysical forces. The Mechanists—on the other hand—believed that life forces would inevitably be reduced to the physico-chemistry of living things: processes activated by known physical causes such as heat or electricity. The Italian biologist **Lazzaro Spallanzini** (b. 1729; d. 1799) discovered that dessicated rotifers (e.g., a minute, multicellular, wheel-like aquatic animals of the phylum Rotifera) could be reanimated by the addition of water. Botanists were well aware that the seeds of plants could lie dormant for years until they

LS1 Content Notes *(cont'd)*

also "sprang to life." The French naturalist **Jean Baptiste Lamarck** (b. 1744; d. 1829) was a leading mechanist. Lamarck is most well-known for his **theory of evolution by acquired characteristics** which was overturned by **Charles Robert Darwin's** (b. 1809; d. 1882) **theory of evolution by means of natural selection.** The mechanist view became firmly entrenched with the discovery of the "cell" as the basic unit of all living things by German theorists **Mathias Jakob Schleiden** (b. 1804; d. 1881) and **Theodor Schwann** (b. 1810; d. 1882). Analysis of cells led to the study of biochemistry and the elucidation of the processes and functions governed by many cell organelles. The field of molecular biology culminated in the 1950s with the discovery of the structure of the gene by American **James Watson** (b. 1928) and Englishman chemist **Francis Crick** (b. 1916). To this day, biologists cannot agree on a single simple definition of life but content themselves with the study of the activities performed by living things.

In Lesson #1, students will list the basic activities performed by all living things.

In Lesson #2, students will list the basic needs common to all living things.

In Lesson #3, students will explain how plants trap energy from the sun in a process called photosynthesis.

In Lesson #4, students will explain how plants and animals release trapped solar energy during a process called respiration.

ANSWERS TO THE HOMEWORK PROBLEMS

Students' charts will vary but should include some of the following information:

Comparisons: photosynthesis and respiration involve the same basic chemical substances (e.g., carbon dioxide, water, sugar, and oxygen)

Contrasts: *photosynthesis* requires chlorophyll, uses carbon dioxide and water to produce sugar and oxygen, requires a source of light to input energy

respiration requires adenosine triphosphate, uses sugar and oxygen to produce carbon dioxide and water, releases energy in the form of heat

Students should explain that plants produce oxygen which is required by all living things to conduct respiration.

ANSWERS TO THE END-OF-THE-WEEK REVIEW QUIZ

1. Mars	6. true	basic activities: move, sense and respond, grow, repair injuries
2. organism	7. true	exchange nutrients/gases, excrete wastes, reproduce
3. true	8. true	
4. energy	9. autotrophs	basic needs (in addition to energy): water, oxygen/carbon
5. true	10. heterotrophs	dioxide, correct temperature range

PHOTOSYNTHESIS

$$carbon\ dioxide + water \xrightarrow{\ chlorophyll\ } sugar + oxygen$$

RESPIRATION

$$sugar + oxygen \xrightarrow{\ adenosine\ triphosphate\ } carbon\ dioxide + water$$

2

LS1 FACT SHEET

ACTIVITIES AND NEEDS OF LIVING THINGS

CLASSWORK AGENDA FOR THE WEEK

(1)   List the basic activities performed by all living things.
(2)   List the basic needs common to all living things.
(3)   Explain how plants trap energy from the sun in a process called photosynthesis.
(4)   Explain how plants and animals release trapped solar energy during a process called respiration.

In 1976 the unmanned spacecrafts—Voyager 1 and Voyager 2—landed on the planet Mars to search for life. The two spacecraft took pictures, measured the temperature and composition of the air, tested the soil, and sent back millions of bits of information to scientists on earth. Had you been one of the scientists in charge of the Voyager missions what tests would you have wanted the spacecraft to perform? What evidence would convince you there is life on Mars? These are not easy questions because they all ask one basic question: What is life?

Scientists have grappled with this question for hundreds of years. Most of us are aware of things around us that are "alive" and things that are not alive. Compare and contrast a chair to a pet or plant. Is the chair "alive?" If you think the chair is not alive, can you explain why it is not alive? If you think the chair is alive, can you explain why you think it is alive? What are the characteristices of living things that set them apart from things we believe are not alive?

Scientists identify living things—called **organisms**—by the activities they perform. Living things are said to be "animated" or "animate" objects. Nonliving things are called "inanimate" objects. According to scientists, all living things perform the same basic activities. Nonliving things cannot perform all these basic activities although they might perform some of them! For example, a toy robot may move as though it were alive; however, it cannot do all the things every living thing can do.

The most important thing living things do is **organize energy**. Living things organize energy so that it can be used to do work. As a result of their ability to organize energy, living things can (1) **move**, (2) **sense** and **respond** to their environment, (3) **grow**, (4) **repair injuries**, (5) **exchange chemical nutrients and gases** with the environment, (6) **excrete waste**, (7) and **reproduce offspring** that have the same basic structure as their parent.

In order to accomplish these activities, organisms on earth have some very basic needs. They need **energy**, **water**, **oxygen** or **carbon dioxide**, and a specific **temperature range** that will allow certain chemical reactions to occur. Different organisms may require a variety of other chemicals, but all must satisfy the basic requirements listed above. The word **metabolism** refers to all the chemical reactions taking place in an organism. The ability of an organism to keep its metabolic activities in proper balance is called **homeostasis**.

Solar energy from the sun is the primary source of energy used by the vast majority of living things on our planet. Some organisms use the **geothermal energy** found near volcanic vents on the ocean floor to satisfy their energy needs. Some organisms (e.g., plants) have the ability to trap energy from the sun in special chemical molecules. These organisms are called **autotrophs**. Autotrophs store these molecules until the energy is used or passed on to other organisms in the form of "food." All green plants are autotrophs. They trap the energy from the sun by a process called **photosynthesis**. During photosynthesis plants trap the energy from the sun in molecules of **chlorophyll** and use the energy to manufacture sugar and oxygen from water and carbon dioxide gas.

$$\text{carbon dioxide + water} \xrightarrow{\text{chlorophyll}} \text{sugar + oxygen}$$

Organisms that get their energy from autotrophs are called **heterotrophs**. All animals are heterotrophs. Animals eat plants and release the energy stored in plant sugar during a process called **respiration**. During respiration animals transfer the energy from plant sugar to molecules of **adenosine triphosphate** and use the energy to manufacture carbon dioxide and water.

$$\text{sugar + oxygen} \xrightarrow{\text{adenosine triphosphate}} \text{carbon dioxide + water}$$

Photosynthesis and respiration are "complementary" processes. Life as we know it on our planet would be impossible without the special chemical molecules named above.

Homework Directions

Make a chart that compares and contrasts the process of photosynthesis to the process of respiration. Explain why animals could not survive without plants.

Assignment due: _____

_____   _____   ____/____/____
Student's Signature   Parent's Signature   Date

ACTIVITIES AND NEEDS OF LIVING THINGS

Work Date: ____/____/____

LESSON OBJECTIVE

Students will list the basic activities performed by all living things.

Classroom Activities

On Your Mark!

Prepare for this lesson by compiling 40–50 magazine pictures of living things so that each group of students has a selection of organisms from each of the living kingdoms (e.g., bacteria, protists, fungi, plants, and animals). Include one picture of an automobile as well.

Refer students to their Fact Sheet and have them spend a moment reading the first paragraph. Ask them to spend several minutes answering the questions posed in that paragraph, writing their answers in brief sentence form. Had they worked with the scientists in charge of the Voyager missions what tests would they have wanted the spacecraft to perform? What evidence would convince them there is life on Mars? Tell them to brainstorm and write down a definition for the term "life." Explain that scientists have struggled with the definition of "life" for centuries. Use the Teacher's Classwork Agenda and Content Notes to give a brief history of the "vitalist" and "mechanists" views. Point out that scientists still do not have a single simple definition for "life."

Get Set!

Distribute the magazine pictures of organisms making sure that each group of students has a selection of organisms from each of the living kingdoms. Define the term "organism" as any thing that is alive. Have them compare and contrast the individual creatures in their collection and to make a list of "life activities" that can be performed by <u>every</u> organism in their picture collection. They must agree upon a list of activities that every organism in their collection can perform. Give the following example: A worm cannot "run"; so, "running" is not a basic life activity. However a worm can move. Are all the pictured organisms capable of movement? If yes, then "movement" is a basic life activity.

Go!

When students are finished making their list discuss them in open forum. List the activities they have chosen on the board and have them copy your list on Journal Sheet #1. Write the following list on the board and compare their selections with the life activities scientists consider common to all living things. All living things can (1) move, (2) sense and respond, (3) grow, (4) repair injuries, (5) exchange chemical nutrients and gases with the environment, (6) excrete waste, and (7) reproduce. Hold up the picture of the automobile. Ask them to quickly list the "life activities" that the automobile can perform. Considering the advances being made by computer and mechanical engineers, have students consider whether or not future automobiles (e.g., or androids) might have to be considered living things.

Materials

magazine pictures of an automobile and living things

LS1 JOURNAL SHEET #1

ACTIVITIES AND NEEDS OF LIVING THINGS

QUESTIONS MY SPACE PROBE WOULD ASK ON A MISSION TO FIND LIFE ON MARS:

ACTIVITIES THAT EVERY CREATURE IN MY PICTURE COLLECTION CAN PERFORM:

ACTIVITIES COMMON TO ALL LIVING THINGS

LS1 Lesson #2
ACTIVITIES AND NEEDS OF LIVING THINGS

Work Date: ____/____/____

LESSON OBJECTIVE

Students will list the basic needs common to all living things.

Classroom Activities

On Your Mark!

Have students work in groups for several minutes to compile a list on Journal Sheet #2 of no more than ten essential items they would need to have with them to survive a trip to Mars. Their list must include everything they will need to stay alive during the long journey. Explain that the Mars mission currently being planned by NASA will take 8 months. Remind students of the hazards that exist in outer space (e.g., it is a vacuum, etc.).

Get Set!

When they are finished, instruct each group to write their list on the board. Compare lists and discuss which groups seem the best prepared. Explain that **food**, **water**, **oxygen**, and **sufficient protection** against the vacuum of space and the dangers of solar radiation are the most essential items they would need to insure bare survival.

Go!

Point out that there is a limit to the weight of material that can be carried by spacecraft launched from earth; so, scientists expect that much of the food, water, and oxygen aboard the ship will need to be "recycled" for reuse by the crew. Now pose the following problem: Have students imagine that their trip to Mars is successful; but upon returning to earth they are forced off course when encountering an undetected asteroid field. Because of their course change, it will take an extra two months to reach earth. However, they are prepared. The mission specialists—realizing the weight limitations of their craft—put aboard items to help them recycle their limited resources. Explain that living things can survive indefinitely in a closed environment (e.g., a spacecraft) as long as energy from the sun is available and nothing goes to waste! Explain that Earth is a similarily closed environment. Have students discuss and write a paragraph explaining how the food and water resources of our planet are constantly being recycled by living things. In doing so, students will confront the problem of recycling natural waste products and have questions about how nature recycles this waste. Point out that Lessons #3 and #4 will help them to answer many of their questions.

Materials

Journal Sheet #2

Name: _____ Period: _____ Date: ____/____/____

LS1 Journal Sheet #2

ACTIVITIES AND NEEDS OF LIVING THINGS

ITEMS NEEDED ABOARD SHIP TO SURVIVE A TRIP TO MARS:

HOW DOES EARTH RECYCLE ITS RESOURCES?

ACTIVITIES AND NEEDS OF LIVING THINGS

Work Date: ____/____/____

LESSON OBJECTIVE

Students will explain how plants trap energy from the sun in a process called photosynthesis.

Classroom Activities

On Your Mark!

Prepare for this lesson: (1) Tape aluminum foil across one half of a sufficient number of the healthy green leaves of a living plant (e.g., geranium leaves work great) so that each group of students can have one leaf. (2) Place the plant in sunlight, or two feet from a bright 75-watt bulb, for 24–48 hours (e.g., 12 hours light then 12 hours dark). (3) Prepare Lugol's solution by dissolving 10 grams of potassium iodide (e.g., KI) in 100 ml of distilled water then add 5 grams of iodine crystals. Lugol's solution tests for the presence of starch and can be purchased pre-prepared from any laboratory supply house.

Begin discussion by pointing out that all living things **organize energy** to perform the basic life activities discussed in Lesson #1. Ask: Where do living things get their energy? Answer: Animals obtain their energy from food (e.g., plants and other animals). Plants obtain their energy from the sun. Classify any organism that obtains its energy from other organisms as a **heterotroph**. Classify organisms that obtain their food from the sun as **autotrophs**. Animals are heterotrophs. Plants are autotrophs.

Get Set!

Explain that green plants have a remarkable molecule called **chlorophyll** that traps and stores energy from the sun inside the **chemical bonds** that hold the atoms of the molecule together. Plants use this energy to manufacture **sugar** and **starch** from **water** and **carbon dioxide**. Refer students to the diagram of a sugar molecule on Journal Sheet #3. Explain that starch is a linked chain of sugar molecules. Point out that oxygen helps release energy trapped in sugar during a process called **respiration**. Plants and animals

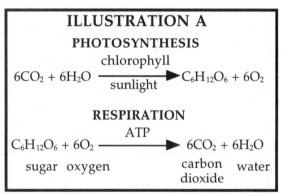

ILLUSTRATION A

PHOTOSYNTHESIS

$$6CO_2 + 6H_2O \xrightarrow[\text{sunlight}]{\text{chlorophyll}} C_6H_{12}O_6 + 6O_2$$

RESPIRATION

$$C_6H_{12}O_6 + 6O_2 \xrightarrow{\text{ATP}} 6CO_2 + 6H_2O$$

sugar oxygen   carbon   water
                                                 dioxide

have a remarkable chemical molecule called **adenosine triphosphate** (e.g., **ATP**) that speeds up the release of energy during this process. Respiration also results in the production of water and carbon dioxide. Write the chemical equations in Illustration A on the board and have students copy them on Journal Sheet #3. The recycling of "energy-rich food" makes life on earth possible. Point out that other animal wastes are used as fertilizer to help plants grow. Plants use many nutrients in fertilizer to build their body parts.

Go!

Give students ample time to perform the experiment described in Figure A on Journal Sheet #3. Explain that plants join sugar molecules together to form starch molecules. Both these energy-rich molecules are called **carbohydrates**. Point out that the element iodine present in Lugol's solution can be used to identify starch present in plant or animal tissue.

Materials

hot plates, 150 ml beakers, 500 ml beakers, water, Lugol's solution (see above), healthy green leafy plant, aluminum foil, tape, sunlight or 75-watt bulb, ethyl alcohol, medicine droppers, safetywear (e.g., heat-resistant gloves, goggles)

LS1 JOURNAL SHEET #3

ACTIVITIES AND NEEDS OF LIVING THINGS

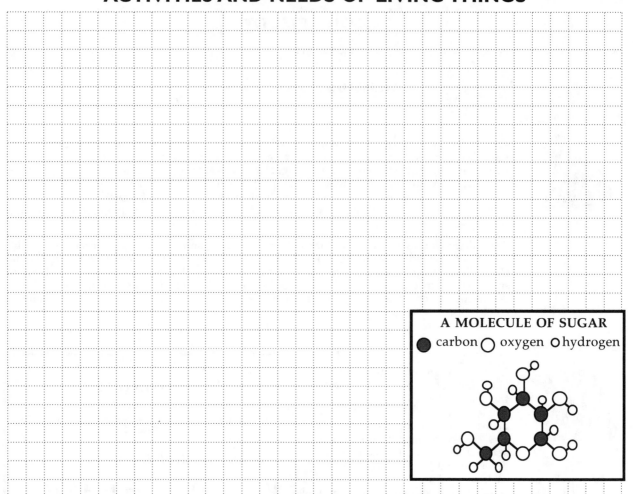

A MOLECULE OF SUGAR
● carbon ○ oxygen ○ hydrogen

FIGURE A

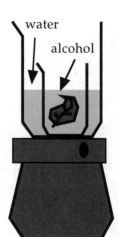

Directions: (1) Carefully remove the aluminum foil from the leaf given to you by your instructor and place the leaf in the large beaker of boiling water on the instructors lab table. The teacher will let the leaves boil for 5 minutes to help soften them (e.g., break down cell walls). (2) While you are waiting for the leaves to soften pour 250 ml water into a large 500 beaker and place the beaker on a hot plate on medium-high setting. (3) Pour 100 ml of ethyl alcohol into a 150 ml beaker and place the smaller beaker into the larger beaker on the hot plate. (4) Place the boiled leaf given to you by your instructor into the 150 beaker of alcohol and wait 5-10 minutes for the leaf to lose its green color. (5) Use tongs to remove the wet leaf from the alcohol and turn off the hot plate. (6) Rinse the leaf and place it in a petri dish. (7) Pour a small amount of the iodine solution over the leaf and allow it to soak for 3-5 minutes. (8) Remove and rinse the leaf again. (9) Hold it up to the light and examine the blackish areas of starch remaining in the leaf. How did the aluminum foil taped over the leaf affect the leaf's ability to produce starch?

water

alcohol

GENERAL SAFETY PRECAUTIONS

Wear goggles, heat-resistant gloves, and an apron. BOILING WATER AND ALCOHOL CAN CAUSE SERIOUS INJURY. Be sure you are familiar with the proper way to use the hot plate. Discard materials and clean up as instructed by your teacher only after the apparatus has cooled.

ACTIVITIES AND NEEDS OF LIVING THINGS

Work Date: ____/____/____

LESSON OBJECTIVE

Students will explain how plants and animals release trapped solar energy during a process called respiration.

Classroom Activities

On Your Mark!

Explain that heterotrophs rely on the energy-rich starch and sugar stored in plants. Hold up a soda cracker and ask students to tell you how the cracker was made. Lead students to the conclusion that the cracker is a plant product rich in sugar and starch. Test a piece of cracker with Lugol's solution to demonstrate the presence of starch in the cracker. Write the chemical equations for **photosynthesis** and **respiration** appearing on page 9—Illustration A—on the board and have students refer to their notes on Journal Sheet #3. Point out that respiration is the reverse of photosynthesis. Explain that molecules of **adenosine triphosphate** (e.g., **ATP**) help to break apart sugar molecules and transfer the released energy to the chemical bonds that hold the ATP molecule together. Explain that respiration requires **oxygen** (e.g., a product of photosynthesis). Point out that the energy of the cracker can also be released by burning in air which is 21% oxygen.

Get Set!

Introduce the concept of the **calorie** and define one calorie as the amount of energy needed to raise the temperature of one gram of pure water one degree Celsius. Raising the temperature of 100 grams (i.e., 100 ml) of water one degree Celsius would require 100 calories of energy. Point out that one **Food Calorie** is equal to 1,000 calories as measured using a thermometer or calorimeter. Have students read the ingredients label on a soda cracker box paying particular attention to the **calories per serving information**. Example: "Calories per serving = 140; serving size = 10 crackers." Have students calculate the number of Food Calories in one cracker. In the example above this is equal to 14 Food Calories (or 14,000 calories) per cracker. Burning one cracker—and using <u>all</u> of the released energy to heat the water in a soda can—would warm 100 ml of water about 140 degrees Celsius. This is quite a lot of heat! However, in the set-up shown in Figure B on Journal Sheet #4 most of the heat from the burning cracker will escape into the atmosphere. In a real **calorimeter** all of the energy is captured so the rise in temperature caused by the total burning of an energy-rich food can be measured with accuracy.

Go!

Give students ample time to perform the activity described in Figure B on Journal Sheet #4. Ask: Do you think the water vapor and carbon dioxide gas released in the burning of the cracker will ever be used again by organisms on the planet? Answer: Yes. Plants can absorb the free water vapor and carbon dioxide and—using chlorophyll and sunlight—produce more sugar for future ingestion by animals.

Materials

Lugol's solution, ring stands and clamps, ring clamps, thermometers, dissecting needles, soda cans, water, soda crackers in box

LS1 JOURNAL SHEET #4

ACTIVITIES AND NEEDS OF LIVING THINGS

FIGURE B

Directions: (1) Pour 100 ml of water from a beaker into a soda can. (2) Secure the soda can with two ring clamps as shown. (3) Lower a thermometer into the can just below the surface of the water. (4) Skewer a soda cracker at the end of a dissecting needle and secure the needle with a clamp as shown. (5) Record the temperature of the thermometer. (6) Light a match to the soda cracker until the cracker burns on its own. (7) Record the temperature reading when the cracker is completely burned. (8) Since one calorie is the amount of energy needed to raise the temperature of water one degree Celsius, the number of calories in the cracker is equal to the rise in temperature caused by the burning cracker x100 (i.e., the volume of water in the can).

GENERAL SAFETY PRECAUTIONS

Wear goggles to protect your skin and eyes when working with a flame. Do not touch any part of the equipment without heat-resistant gloves or tongs. Clean up when the apparatus is cool.

rings

dissecting needle

LS1 REVIEW QUIZ

Directions: Keep your eyes on your own work.
Read all directions and questions carefully.
THINK BEFORE YOU ANSWER!
Watch your spelling, be neat, and do the best you can.

CLASSWORK   (~40): _____
HOMEWORK   (~20): _____
CURRENT EVENT   (~10): _____
TEST   (~30): _____

TOTAL   (~100): _____
(A ≥ 90, B ≥ 80, C ≥ 70, D ≥ 60, F < 60)

LETTER GRADE: _____

TEACHER'S COMMENTS: _____
_____

ACTIVITIES AND NEEDS OF LIVING THINGS

TRUE–FALSE FILL-IN: If the statement is true, write the word TRUE. If the statement is false, change the underlined word to make the statement true. *10 points*

_____ 1. In 1976, unmanned spacecraft landed on the moon to search for life.

_____ 2. Scientists call a living thing a(n) organ.

_____ 3. All living things perform the same basic activities.

_____ 4. The most important thing living things do is organize time.

_____ 5. The word metabolism refers to all the chemical reactions taking place in an organism.

_____ 6. The ability of an organism to keep its metabolic activities in proper balance is called homeostasis.

_____ 7. Solar energy is the primary source of energy used by the vast majority of living things on our planet.

_____ 8. Some organisms use the geothermal energy found near volcanic vents on the ocean floor to satisfy their energy needs.

_____ 9. Organisms that trap energy from the sun in special chemical molecules are called heterotrophs.

_____ 10. Organisms that must eat other organsims to get their energy are called autotrophs.

LS1 Review Quiz *(cont'd)*

List the seven basic activities performed by all living things. *7 points*

_____ _____ _____ _____

_____ _____ _____

List the three basic needs required by all living things on earth in addition to their requirement for energy. *3 points*

_____ _____ _____

Fill in the blanks with the names of the correct chemical substances involved in the processes of photosynthesis and respiration. *10 points*

PHOTOSYNTHESIS

_____

_____ + _____ ⟶ _____ + _____

RESPIRATION

_____

_____ + _____ ⟶ _____ + _____

LS2 CLASSIFICATION OF LIVING THINGS

TEACHER'S CLASSWORK AGENDA AND CONTENT NOTES

Classwork Agenda for the Week

1. Students will classify objects according to structure.
2. Students will classify objects according to function.
3. Students will use a binomial classification system to name objects classified according to structure and function.
4. Students will contrast the major characteristics of the world's five living kingdoms.

Content Notes for Lecture and Discussion

The Greek philosopher **Plato** (b. 427 B.C.; d. 347 B.C.) suggested that all forms of matter—alive or dead—were manifestations of "ideal" metaphysical forms which he called "archetypes." What man observed through the senses were merely "shadows" cast by the light of metaphysical reality. The classification of living things, therefore, involved the selection of appropriate archetypes that suited the "less than perfect" organisms that existed in nature. **Aristotle** (b. 384 B.C.; d. 322 B.C.) followed the "idealist" teachings of **Plato** in proposing archetypes upon which to base the classification of living things. Although the archetypes themselves were sometimes difficult to conceive (e.g., being of metaphysical nature) organisms could be grouped together by comparing them to an accepted archetype. Aristotle used the term *eidos* to describe living things that were similiar in terms of their "organic" qualities. To Aristotle the term "organic" referred to an entire system having animate properties that transcended their individual parts. Birds come in a variety of shapes and sizes but are all easily recognizable as birds for their overall qualities. He used the term *genos* to group organisms with the same "higher order archetypical" qualities. So, bats and bumble bees—both being able to fly—were grouped together for their ability to fly: "flying" being a "higher order" Platonic ideal. *Genos* and *eidos* became the **genus** and **species** categories used by later biologists.

With the Age of Exploration in the 15th and 16th centuries, the discovery of increasing numbers of plant and animal species taxed the Aristotelean method of classification to its demise. The English naturalist **John Ray** (b. 1627; d. 1705) managed to continue the work of Aristotle and set forth the defining characteristic of a species by stating that members of a common species "cannot arise from the seed of other species." The Swedish botanist **Carolus Linnaeus** (b. 1707; d. 1778) created the modern binomial classification system and established the modern convention of **binomial nomenclature** using the classifications of genus and species. However, Linnaeus identified organisms largely according to their structural similarities (e.g., bone structure) and expanded the Aristotelean system to include groups above the level of genus and species. In Linnaeus's system of classification similar genera are grouped into **families**, families into **orders**, orders into **classes**, classes into **phyla**, and phyla into **kingdoms**.

Throughout the 18th and 19th centuries biologists continued to identify organisms discovered by seafaring explorers. The sheer volume of information prompted them to try and make sense of the incredible variety of organisms that went unmentioned in the Book of Genesis, according to which no new species had been created or become extinct since Creation. Further analysis of the relationships between groups of organisms led to the **theory of evolution by acquired characteristics** proposed by the French naturalist **Jean Baptiste Lamarck** (b. 1744; d. 1829) and the more successful **theory of evolution by means of natural selection** deduced by **Charles Robert Darwin** (b. 1809; d. 1882).

LS2 Content Notes (cont'd)

In Lesson #1, students will classify objects according to structure.

In Lesson #2, students will classify objects according to function.

In Lesson #3, students will use a binomial classification system to name objects classified according to structure and function.

In Lesson #4, students will contrast the major characteristics of the world's five living kingdoms.

ANSWERS TO THE HOMEWORK PROBLEMS

Student classification systems will vary but should exhibit the student's ability to compare and contrast objects according to the relevant characteristics of objects within their chosen categories.

ANSWERS TO THE END-OF-THE-WEEK REVIEW QUIZ

1. D
2. B
3. A
4. B
5. E

6. A
7. C
8. A
9. D
10. C

Students may present alternative arrangements to the one presented here. Accept any logical classification that students can defend (e.g., all girls at Desk 5 and all boys at Desk 6, etc.).

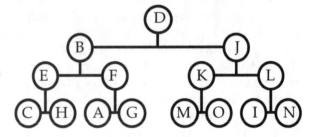

LS2 FACT SHEET

CLASSIFICATION OF LIVING THINGS

CLASSWORK AGENDA FOR THE WEEK

(1) Classify objects according to structure.
(2) Classify objects according to function.
(3) Use a binomial classification system to name objects classified according to structure and function.
(4) Contrast the major characteristics of the world's five living kingdoms.

Learning would be extremely difficult without a plan. The first plan created by early scientists to help them learn about the world was a **system of classification**. Before they could ever hope to study the diversity of living things on this planet they needed to group the long list of familiar organisms in an orderly fashion. In order to do that, early scientists lumped living things together by their familiar characteristics such as size, shape, and behavior.

The science of classification is called **taxonomy**. A good classification system is meaningful and easily understood. It helps to organize things in a logical way and simplifies the communication of ideas between people. The Greek philosopher **Aristotle** (b. 384 B.C.; d. 322 B.C.) invented one of the first systems of classification: a system used for more than 2,000 years. Aristotle classified organisms by the functions of their organs. In Aristotle's system, a bat and a bumble bee were put in the same group as "creatures of the air" because they can fly. But Aristotle's system became more and more disorganized as more and more organisms were discovered and added to it.

Biologists of the 17th and 18th centuries began to realize that the organs of different living things could perform the same function even though they had a different structure. The wings of a bat are built very differently than the wings of a bumble bee; yet both structures enable each creature to fly. Different structures that perform the same function in two different organisms are called **analogous structures**. Biologists also realized that similar structures (e.g., with the same type and arrangement of tissues and bones) could perform completely different functions. The arm of a bat has almost the same number and arrangement of bones as the arm of a man; but—due to the variation in the size and shape of the bat's bones—it can fly while a man cannot. Structures similar in form that perform different functions are called **homologous structures**. A whale's pectoral fin is—like a bat's wing—homologous to a man's arm.

In the 18th century, a Swedish **botanist** (a scientist who studies plants) named **Carolus Linnaeus** (b. 1707; d. 1778) began to classify living things according to their structure. Linnaeus's system used **binomial nomenclature** which means "to give two names." Binomial nomenclature is the system we use today.

Today organisms are grouped into five major categories called **kingdoms**: **monerans** (viruses and bacteria), **protists** (unicellular organisms), **fungi**, **plants**, and **animals.** Each of the five kingdoms is divided into smaller groups. **Kingdoms** are divided into *phyla*; **phyla** are divided into *classes*; **classes** are divided into *orders*; **orders** are separated into *families*; and the member of each **family** is given two names, a **genus** and a **species** name. Refer to the "formal names" of each of the common organisms listed below according to the binomial system of classification.

	HUMAN	DOG	FROG	DAISY
Kingdom	animal	animal	animal	plant
Phyla	vertebrate	vertebrate	vertebrate	tracheophyte
Class	mammal	mammal	amphibian	angiosperm
Order	primate	carnivore	salientia	campanulalae
Family	hominid	canine	ranidae	compositae
Genus	homo	canis	rana	chrysanthemum
Species	sapiens	familiaris	pipiens	leucanthemum

Notice that humans, dogs, and frogs belong to the same kingdom and phyla. Humans and dogs belong to the same kingdom, phyla, *and* class.

Today, organisms can also be classified according to the structure of their **genes**. Genes are made of large chemical molecules of **deoxyribose nucleic acid**: **DNA**. Plants and animals with similar DNA have very similar structures. This is because DNA determines the types of **proteins** that an organism's cells make to give it the structures that comprise its tissues and organs. A chimpanzee and a human differ in less than 5% of their genes. This is not suprising since both creatures have very similar structures.

Homework Directions

Organize fifty objects in your bedroom using a logical system of classification containing no less than five (5) categories. Create a table or diagram to illustrate your system. Make sure you clearly describe the characteristics of each category in your system.

Assignment due: _____

_____   _____   ___/___/___
Student's Signature   Parent's Signature   Date

CLASSIFICATION OF LIVING THINGS

Work Date: ____/____/____

LESSON OBJECTIVE

Students will classify objects according to structure.

Classroom Activities

On Your Mark!

Prepare for this lesson by compiling 50–100 mazagine pictures of animate and inanimate objects so that each group of students has a selection of at least 10 pictures. For the purposes of this lesson, students can also include the everyday objects at hand in the classroom (e.g., desks, chairs, books, cabinets, etc.).

Refer students to their Fact Sheet and have them spend a moment reading the first three paragraphs. Write the terms and phrases "taxonomy", "system of classification", "analogous structure", and "homologous structure" on the board. Have students copy these terms on Journal Sheet #1. Instruct students to write a simple definition of each term or phrase using the Fact Sheet as a reference. Circulate the room as they complete this activity and ask them to further explain the characteristics of a good system of classification mentioned in paragraph #2.

Get Set!

Hold up several pictures and ask students to define the **analogous** and **homologous** structures of objects in the pictures. For example, the wheels of a skateboard and an automobile are analogous structures (e.g., they perform essentially the same function). The wheels of a compact car and a big rig truck are homologous structures (e.g. they have essentially the same mechanical parts). Explain that a system of classification can be based on the comparison and contrasting of structures or the comparison and contrasting of functional parts.

Go!

Have groups of students select five categories they would like to use to classify the objects in the pictures or objects around the classroom according to their structural similarities and differences. They may choose to classify the objects according to their shape (e.g., cabinets and books are rectangular while the globe and lightbulbs are spherical). Or, they may decide to classify the objects according to their material (e.g., objects made of wood, metal, or plastic). They should be able to make a logical argument for including and differentiating objects. Point out that a system of classification is an invention of the human mind and says little or nothing about the "intrinsic" qualities of the objects themselves. To say that a plastic pen belongs in the same groups as a plastic identification card says little about either object.

Materials

magazine pictures, classroom objects

Name: _____ Period: _____ Date: ____/____/____

LS2 JOURNAL SHEET #1

CLASSIFICATION OF LIVING THINGS

OBJECTS CATEGORIZED ACCORDING TO STRUCTURE				

<u>Directions</u>: In the first row indicate the major structural characteristic of each object in that column. Save the last column to make comments about two or three objects that have homologous structures.

CLASSIFICATION OF LIVING THINGS

Work Date: _____/_____/_____

LESSON OBJECTIVE

Students will classify objects according to function.

Classroom Activities

On Your Mark!

Use the same pictures and classroom objects used in Lesson #1 making sure that each group of students has a selection of at least 10 pictures. Review the accomplishments of Lesson #1, by asking students to explain some of their classifications to the class. Have them describe some of the homologies they found in different objects. Define the term "function" as the work achieved by—or purpose of—a machine, machine part, or organ. For example, the work or purpose of a pencil is to leave lines on paper. The work or purpose of heart muscle is to pump blood around an animal's body.

Get Set!

Review the term "analogous structure." Explain that analogous structures are any structures that perform the same function in different organisms. Point out that the wing of a bat and the wing of a bumble bee are analogous structures but not homologous structures. Display a picture of a bat or bird wing (if available) and compare the structure to that of an insect's wing (e.g., bumble bee, mosquito, house fly, etc.). Point out the dissimilarities in the structures of these two types of wings. Emphasize that despite their contrasting structures both organs enable the creatures to fly.

Go!

Have groups of students select five categories they would like to use to classify the objects in the pictures or objects around the classroom according to their functional similarities and differences. They may choose to classify the objects according to the work they perform or the purpose they serve (e.g., the flourescent lights and the bulb in the overhead projector both give off light; the magazines and textbook provide us with information). They should be able to make a logical argument for including and differentiating objects. Emphasize, as in Lesson #1, that a system of classification is an invention of the human mind and says little or nothing about the "intrinsic" qualities of the objects themselves.

Materials

magazine pictures, classroom objects

LS2 Journal Sheet #2

CLASSIFICATION OF LIVING THINGS

OBJECTS CATEGORIZED ACCORDING TO FUNCTION					

Directions: In the first row indicate the major functional characteristic of each object in that column. Save the last column to make comments about two or three objects that have analogous structures.

CLASSIFICATION OF LIVING THINGS

Work Date: ____/____/____

LESSON OBJECTIVE

Students will use a binomial classification system to name objects classified according to structure and function.

Classroom Activities

On Your Mark!

Use the information in the Teacher's Classwork Agenda and Content Notes to introduce students to the work of **John Ray** (b. 1627; d. 1705) and **Carolus Linnaeus** (b 1707; d. 1778). Explain that these early biologists used Latin (e.g., the language of the Roman Empire) to name the creatures they classified. Latin was chosen as the language of science to make communication between scientists of different nationalities easier. All scientists educated during the 15th, 16th, 17th, 18th, and 19th centuries were required to learn Latin as part of their education.

Get Set!

Although students can use imaginary names to identify the objects they classified in Lesson #1 or Lesson #2 the use of a foreign language dictionary (e.g., preferably one of a Romance Language such as Spanish or French which are derived from Latin) will prove more interesting. Instruct students to find names for the object classified in two of the columns used in Lesson #1 or Lesson #2. The first name—which we will call the **genus**—should describe all of the objects in that column <u>and at the same time</u> differentiates those objects from items in the other column. The second name—which we will call the **species**—should describe the qualities of each individual object in that column, differentiating from all of the other items in that particular column. For example: If students classified objects as either wood or plastic, then every object in the "wood" category could belong to the genus "maderus" (e.g., the Spanish word for wood is madera) and every object in the "plastic" category could belong to the genus "plasticus" (e.g., the Spanish word for plastic is plástico). A wooden chair in the genus maderus could be named maderus sillus (e.g., the Spanish word for chair is silla) and a plastic chair in the genus plasticus could be named plasticus sillus. Large and small chairs in the genus madera might be distinguished as maderus silluspequenus (a.k.a., wooden small chair) and maderas silluslargas (a.k.a., wooden large chair). Point out that this naming method first introduced by the Swedish biologist Carolus Linnaeus is called **binomial nomenclature**.

Go!

Give students ample time to name each object in 2 of the columns used in Lesson #1 or Lesson #2. Emphasize again that a system of classification is an invention of the human mind and says little or nothing about the "intrinsic" qualities of the objects themselves. Re-classifying an organism requires that it be given a new name to coincide with its new category. Biologists of the 18th and 19th centuries were constantly re-classifying organisms as new information about them became available.

Materials

Romance language or Latin (if available) dictionaries, Journal Sheets #1 and #2

LS2 JOURNAL SHEET #3

CLASSIFICATION OF LIVING THINGS

USING BINOMIAL NOMENCLATURE TO NAME OBJECTS			
object	genus species	object	genus species

Directions: Give each object in each category picked from Lesson #1 or Lesson #2 a name that describes that category and another name that distinguishes it from the other objects in that category.

CLASSIFICATION OF LIVING THINGS

Work Date: ____/____/____

LESSON OBJECTIVE

Students will contrast the major characteristics of the world's five living kingdoms.

Classroom Activities

On Your Mark!

Introduce the **binomial classification system** developed by **Carolus Linnaeus** (b. 1707; d. 1778). Draw Illustration A on the board and have students copy it onto Journal Sheet #4.

Explain that there are five biological Kingdoms (K) and that each kingdom is divided into many Phyla. The singular term for "phyla" is "phylum." Each phylum is divided into many Classes. Each class is divided into many Orders. Each order is divided into many Families. Each family is divided into many Genera. And, each genus is divided into many Species and even subspecies. The term "species" ends with an "s" in both singular and plural forms. The five kingdoms used by biologists to classify all living things are the **monerans, protists, fungi, plants,** and **animals.**

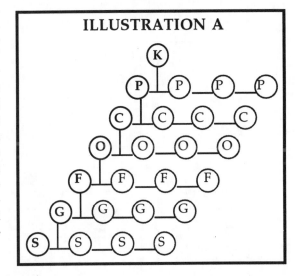

ILLUSTRATION A

Get Set!

Have students record your lecture notes as you identify each of the five kingdoms by its distinguishing characteristics. (1) Monerans include viruses and bacteria. Viruses are strands of genetic material protected by a protective "coat." Bacteria are single-celled organisms that do not contain a nucleus. Point out that a cell nucleus has a protective membrane that separates stored genetic material (e.g., DNA) from the cell. (2) Protists are single-celled organisms that have a cell nucleus (e.g., paramecium and ameba). (3) Fungi (e.g., mushrooms, yeasts, and molds) are colonies of cells that live and thrive on decaying matter. (4) Plants are multicellular organisms that produce their own food by photosynthesis. (5) Animals are multicellular organisms that must ingest plants to live and survive.

Go!

Give students ample to time to write a brief description of a situation in which they personally came in contact with a member of each of the five kingdoms. Remembering a situation in which they came in contact with a plant or animal will, of course, be easy. Tell them to be specific about those situations in which they heard about a fungus, mold, virus, bacteria, etc. Have them explain what they learned about these organisms.

Materials

Journal Sheet #4

Name: _____ Period:_____ Date: ____/____/____

LS2 JOURNAL SHEET #4

CLASSIFICATION OF LIVING THINGS

LS2 REVIEW QUIZ

Directions: Keep your eyes on your own work.
Read all directions and questions carefully.
THINK BEFORE YOU ANSWER!
Watch your spelling, be neat, and do the best you can.

TEACHER'S COMMENTS: _____
_____

CLASSIFICATION OF LIVING THINGS

MULTIPLE CHOICE: Choose the letter of the word or phrase that best answers or completes the question or sentence. *20 points*

_____ 1. Which of the following IS NOT a good characteristic of a good classification system?

  (A) it is organized   (D) it is long list of things
  (B) it is meaningful   (E) it is easily understood
  (C) it show relationships

_____ 2. The science of classification is called _____ .

  (A) taxidermy   (D) taxation
  (B) taxonomy   (E) tax deduction
  (C) taxicab

_____ 3. Who was the first person to invent a usable classification system?

  (A) Aristotle   (D) Einstein
  (B) Linnaeus   (E) Bohr
  (C) Mendeleev

_____ 4. Who invented the modern classification system used today by biologists?

  (A) Aristotle   (D) Einstein
  (B) Linnaeus   (E) Bohr
  (C) Mendeleev

_____ 5. In the modern system of classification organisms are grouped according to their _____ .

  (A) color   (D) size
  (B) strength   (E) structure
  (C) shape

_____ 6. Which two names are used to distinguish one organism from another.

    (A) genus and species   (D) kingdom and phylum
    (B) class and order   (E) family and genus
    (C) order and family

_____ 7. Which shows the correct order of categories of the modern classification system used by biologists?

    (A) kingdom, phylum, genus, species, order, family, class
    (B) kingdom, class, order, phylum, family, genus, species
    (C) kingdom, phylum, class, order, family, genus, species
    (D) kingdom, family, class, order, phylum, species, genus
    (E) kingdom, phylum, class, order, family, species, genus

_____ 8. Which IS NOT one of the five major categories of living organisms?

    (A) bacteria   (D) protists
    (B) plants   (E) animals
    (C) fungi

_____ 9. What is the scientific name for a dog?

    (A) homo sapiens   (D) canis familiaris
    (B) rana pipiens   (E) chrysanthemum leucanthemum
    (C) canis lupus

_____ 10. Biological classification has improved with our increased understanding of _____ .

    (A) how organisms mate   (D) how cells divide
    (B) how animals eat   (E) how cells become cancerous
    (C) how chromosomes work

PROBLEM

Put a capital letter in each circle to show how this list of things can best be classified. *10 points*

(A) Aaron	(I) Phillip		
(B) Desk 5	(J) Desk 6		
(C) Alice	(K) Girls		
(D) Room A	(L) Boys		
(E) Girls	(M) Lisa		
(F) Boys	(N) Andrew		
(G) Juan	(O) Margo		
(H) Angela			

DESCENT AND CHANGE IN LIVING THINGS

TEACHER'S CLASSWORK AGENDA AND CONTENT NOTES

Classwork Agenda for the Week

1. Students will compare and contrast the variety of organisms in the environment.

2. Students will explain why species tend to overpopulate.

3. Students will examine the adaptations of a variety of organisms in the environment.

4. Students will explain how mutation and natural selection result in the evolution of structure in living things.

Content Notes for Lecture and Discussion

The notions of "organic mutability" and the "adaptive radiation of species" did not emerge as viable scientific ideas until the middle of the 18th century. The more popular view of the first half of that century was the view held by the Catholic Church which regarded species as fixed groups of organisms whose form had not changed since the Creation depicted in The Bible: an event that biblical scholars estimated to have occurred six thousand years earlier. Geologists of the century contributed their views on the expanse of geological time by basing their estimations of the earth's age on observable phenomena such as erosion and deposition rates in the soil. They proposed that "change" was a predominating feature of earth history. The Scottish geologist **James Hutton** (b. 1726; d. 1797), known as the "father of geology," suggested that the earth was incredibly old. Hutton proposed that the land undergoes continual transformation by much the same processes as those which occurred in times past. His compatriot, geologist **Charles Lyell** (b. 1797; d. 1875), deduced the age of the earth to be approximately 240,000,000 years old and gave a description of the earth's geological history. Modern techniques using radioactive dating have allowed contemporary geologists to estimate the age of our planet at about 4.5 billion years. The work of these innovative 18th century scientists greatly influenced the work of biologists in their search to explain the origin and diversity of life on the planet.

The first widely accepted theory proposed to explain the then hypothetical "transmutation" of species was suggested by the French naturalist **Jean Baptiste Lamarck** (b. 1744; d. 1829). According to his **theory of acquired characteristics**, organisms acquired adaptive traits during their lifetime which they passed to their offspring. In this manner, complex organisms evolved from simpler ones. Lamarck's most famous illustration of the theory was the evolution of a giraffe's long neck. He suggested that as the short-necked ancestors of modern giraffes reached higher and higher into the trees to find richer vegetation their necks became longer; a trait which was inherited by their offspring. Lamarkian evolution has since been discredited for lack of evidence that traits acquired during a lifespan (e.g., strong muscles acquired from exercise) can be genetically transmitted to offspring. A man who loses an arm in an industrial accident does not pass on this trait to his son or daughter.

From 1831 to 1836, the English naturalist **Charles Robert Darwin** (b. 1809; d. 1882) made his famous voyage aboard the *HMS Beagle*. On the trip, Darwin compiled volumes of information in which he described the enormous variety of plant and animal life off the west coast of South America. He was particularly intrigued by the comparative and contrasting physical characteristics of reptiles and birds inhabiting distant islands. Darwin explained the similarities and differences among the species by proposing that they had all evolved from a common ancestor after acquiring those traits which best adapted them for life on the islands they inhabited. It was not until 1838, however, that Darwin came up with a mechanism to explain the cause of variations between the groups. He suggested that the struggle for survival—resulting from competition for limited resources within large populations of individuals—caused the elimination of those individuals least adapted for the struggle. After 20 years of further research—and after a meeting with the Welch naturalist **Alfred Russel Wallace** (b. 1823; d. 1913) who had come to the same conclusion based on his own voluminous study—Darwin published *The Origin of the Species by Means of Natural Selection.* Darwin likened "natural selection" to the "selective breeding" (e.g., artificial selection) of plants and animals that had been employed by farmers for centuries to create the most desirable domesticated vegetable grains and animal strains. However, Darwin could not explain the mechanism underlying the cause of individual differences that allowed one member of a species to become better adapted to its environment. Ironically, the work of Darwin's unknown contemporary, the Austrian monk **Gregor Mendel** (b. 1822; d. 1884), had already elucidated the laws of inheritance which serve as the foundation of modern genetics. The relevance of Mendel's work went unrecognized until 1900.

In support of Darwin's **theory of evolution by means of natural selection**, the German biologist **August Friedrich Leopold Weismann** (b. 1834; d. 1914) proposed that every organism contains an hereditary substance which he called "germ plasm" within the confines of living cells. According to Weismann, germ plasm did not change with mere alterations to the body. Treatment of living cells with X-rays by American geneticists **Thomas Hunt Morgan** (b. 1866; d. 1945) and **Hermann Joseph Muller** (b. 1890; d. 1967), however, resulted in **mutations** of the physical structure of cells. Experimenting with X-rays, Morgan and Muller were able to alter the morphological structure of the organs of fruit flies (e.g., *Drosophila*). The gene was later located on the **chromosomes** (e.g., "colored bodies") residing in the nuclei of cells. In 1953, the American biologist **James Watson** (b. 1928) and his English associate **Francis Crick** (b. 1916) elucidated the structure of the macromolecule that comprises the gene: **deoxyribonucleic acid—DNA.**

In Lesson #1, students will compare and contrast the variety of organisms in the environment.

In Lesson #2, students will explain why species tend to overpopulate.

In Lesson #3, students will examine the adaptations of a variety of organisms in the environment.

In Lesson #4, students will explain how mutation and natural selection result in the evolution of structure in living things.

ANSWERS TO THE HOMEWORK PROBLEMS

Students can create a "ladder of evolution" displaying a linear transition of the imaginary creatures from the simple to the complex (e.g., I, G, C, A, and D, etc.). Or, they may devise a tree with logical branches. They should, however, derive logical transitions from one creature to the next and may also display creatures with no descendant (e.g., C). In reviewing the homework with the class, discuss the possible placements suggested by different students and explain that the "tree of life" is continually undergoing change by paleontologists. One of the most popular recent changes made in the "tree of evolution" is the assignment of birds to a "branch" of an extinct dinosaur family. Today, the structure of proteins and the orderly arrangement of nucleic acids in DNA molecules is used to map the phylogeny of species.

ANSWERS TO THE END-OF-THE-WEEK REVIEW QUIZ

1. Most
2. true
3. no
4. 4.5 billion
5. have

6. Charles Darwin
7. Natural
8. change
9. true
10. true

11. mutation
12. true
13. true, or a few

PROBLEM

The following letters should be circled: A, C, D, F. Items B, E, and G, are untrue: although monkeys and humans are evolved from a common ancestor. Darwin did not make the observation described in H.

DIAGRAM

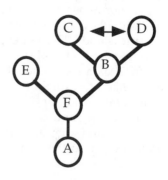

LS3 Fact Sheet

DESCENT AND CHANGE IN LIVING THINGS

CLASSWORK AGENDA FOR THE WEEK

(1) Compare and contrast the variety of organisms in the environment.
(2) Explain why species tend to overpopulate.
(3) Examine the adaptations of a variety of organisms in the environment.
(4) Explain how mutation and natural selection result in the evolution of structure in living things.

Scientists have known for some time that many **species** alive during past ages are no longer alive today. The dinosaurs, for example, perished sixty million years ago but left **fossil** evidence of their existence. Biologists also know that many species, like our own, did not exist long ago. They have no evidence that human beings existed on earth prior to five million years ago. However, **radioactive dating** techniques show the world to be about 4.5 billion years old.

Fossils are an important piece of evidence in the study of our planet's history. Studying the **geologic history** of the world provides evidence that our planet's climate and surface features have changed over the eons. That history can be divided into **eons, eras,** and **periods** during which different kinds of plants and animals inhabited the earth.

In the first half of the 18th century, an English naturalist named **Charles Robert Darwin** (b. 1809; d. 1882) made a voyage to the **Galápagos Islands** off the coast of South America. On his travels aboard the *HMS Beagle*, he gathered information about the variety of plants and animals that inhabited the region. In 1859, Darwin published a book entitled *The Origin of the Species by Means of Natural Selection* in which he explained how those living things might have become so diverse. Today, Darwin's **theory of evolution by means of natural selection** has become the cornerstone of modern biology and medicine.

The term **evolution** means "change." In biology, evolution has a more specific meaning. Evolution refers to the changes that take place in the **hereditary features** of a population of organisms from one generation to the next. For centuries, farmers have chosen those animals and plants best suited to their needs. Plants and animals (e.g., grains, fruits, vegetables, cattle, horses, dogs, etc.) were "selected for breeding" to produce offspring with the same desired traits. The scientists of Darwin's time did not know how hereditary change takes place. But today, biologists understand many of the mechanisms that lead to heredity changes. These changes are called *mutations.*

A **mutation** is a change in the biological molecules that carry hereditary information. Hereditary information (e.g., genes) is found in microscopic structures called chromosomes which are located in living cells. **Chromosomes** are made of a chemical molecule called deoxyribonucleic acid: **DNA.** The DNA molecule instructs a living cell to produce proteins that give a particular organism its own unique physical structure. Changes in the structure of a DNA molecule can, therefore, alter the physical appearance of an organism. Changes in the DNA molecule can occur for a variety of reasons such as exposure to radiation, toxic chemicals, and so on. Changes in chromosomes result in a new **hereditary trait** that can be passed from **parent** to **offspring.** Although most new traits arising from mutations are harmful to offspring and may result in their death, some mutations give an offspring an advantage over other organisms in the struggle for survival.

The four observations that follow can be made by anyone. Darwin used these observations to explain how "nature selects" those organisms that will survive and those that will become **extinct.** These observations serve as the basis for Darwin's theory of evolution by means of natural selection.

LS3 Fact Sheet *(cont'd)*

(1) There are individual differences among the members of a species.
(2) Species overreproduce.
(3) There is limited food and space available to living things.
(4) During competition for limited food and space, organisms least adapted to survive become extinct. Those better adapted survive to reproduce and pass their advantageous traits to their offspring.

Homework Directions

Directions: (1) Examine the imaginary creatures shown below. (2) Draw a "family tree" that shows how the creatures might have evolved from a common ancestor.

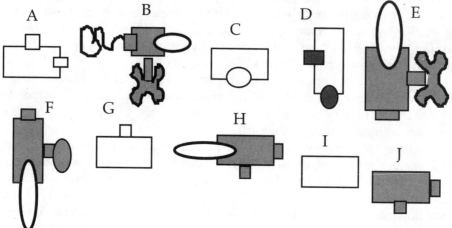

Assignment due: _____

DESCENT AND CHANGE IN LIVING THINGS

Work Date: _____/_____/_____

LESSON OBJECTIVE

Students will compare and contrast the variety of organisms in the environment.

Classroom Activities

On Your Mark!

Prepare for this lesson by compiling pictures of dogs, cats, horses, and flowers so that each group of students has a selection of at least 5 pictures in each category. Pictures should show the common and distinctive characteristics that group the organisms together and at the same time set them apart.

Begin with a discussion of the sport of basketball. Ask students to estimate the height of the average basketball player. Today, the average height of a professional basketball player is between 6 feet-three inches and 6 feet-nine inches. Less than thirty years ago, the height of the average basketball player was between 5 feet-nine inches and 6 feet-three inches. The average height of a professional basketball player has increased. Ask students to explain his phenomenon. Of course, the most successful basketball players are still the best "ball handlers." But a taller player with good ball-handling skills has the advantage over shorter players with the same degree of skill due to the placement of the basket. Point out that the sport of basketball (e.g., the court environment) "selects" for taller players. Point out that the "evolution" of the sport in favor of taller players could never have occured if all human beings matured to the same height. The fact that there is "variation among individuals" within a population makes "selection" possible. The word "selection" implies "choice." Ask students to discuss the factors that have caused a similar evolution in the sport of football.

Get Set!

Distribute the pictures prepared before the start of class and discuss the concept of **artifical selection**. Explain that artificial selection refers to the selective breeding of individuals within a population that have desired characteristics different from those of individuals <u>within the same population</u>. A farmer may choose to "inbreed" plants to make crops more resistant to disease or more attractive in appearance. Selective breeding in animals has given rise to hundreds of breeds of dogs and cats as well as other domesticated farm animals (e.g., horses and cattle). Ask students to study the pictures then list the characteristics they believe plant and animal breeders selected as worthy of reproduction in future generations.

Go!

Give students ample time to perform the activity described in Figure A on Journal Sheet #1. As you circulate around the room, make sure that students correctly identify the individuals having the most obvious common feature as members of the same group despite their individual differences.

Materials

old magazines, newspapers, scissors

LS3 JOURNAL SHEET #1

DESCENT AND CHANGE IN LIVING THINGS

SPECIES 1	SPECIES 2	SPECIES 3	SPECIES 4	SPECIES 5	SPECIES 6

FIGURE A

<u>Directions</u>: Select from the "creatures" shown below to group different individuals together as members of the same "species." Put letter answers in the spaces above and use one word to describe the distinguishing characteristic that identifies every individual as a member of that species.

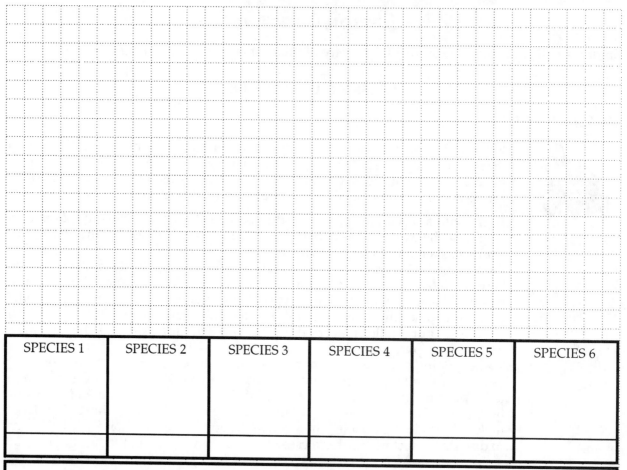

LS3 Lesson #2

DESCENT AND CHANGE IN LIVING THINGS

Work Date: _____/_____/_____

LESSON OBJECTIVE

Students will explain why species tend to overpopulate.

Classroom Activities

On Your Mark!

Have students cut into an apple or orange and count the number of seeds. Ask: "What does each new seed represent?" Answer: A new apple tree that will produce thousands of new apples in the course of one lifetime. Ask: "Why does each apple have so many seeds and each tree so many apples if only a single apple with a single seed contains enough hereditary material to make a new individual?" Answer: Because most of the apples and seeds get eaten by animals before they can produce another tree which might also be destroyed before it can produce more fruit with seeds. Explain that—like apples and oranges—the individuals of all species tend to overpopulate to insure the perpetuation of their species in the face of harsh environmental challenges.

Get Set!

Introduce students to the English **economist** (e.g., a person who studies economics: the study of wealth and product goods) **Thomas Robert Malthus** (b. 1766; d. 1834). In 1798, Malthus published an article arguing for population control. In the article, Malthus argued that the "geometric growth" of the European population would soon exceed the food supply which was growing at a slower rate. **Charles Darwin** (b. 1809; d. 1882)— having read Malthus's many works—based much of the **theory of evolution by means of natural selection** on the idea that organisms tended to overpopulate: a state of affairs that would lead to a "struggle for survival" and the selection of those individuals best adapted to meet the challenge of limited environmental resources. Use the information in the Teacher's Classwork Agenda and Content Notes to give students a brief lecture on the tenets of the modern theory of evolution. Have students copy the four observable principles of the theory listed on their Fact Sheet.

Go!

Give students ample time to perform the quick activity described in Figure B on Journal Sheet #2. Briefly discuss the meaning of this "geometric progression." If every individual member of a species produced just two offspring—and there were no environmental hazards to endanger their survival—the population of the species would be in the millions after only 15 generations.

Have students play the game described in Figure C on Journal Sheet #2. Give each group a single bowl filled with macaroni and each student in the group one of the following items: a straw, a teaspoon, a pair of toothpicks, or a forcep. At the end of the game, discuss the "selective advantages" exhibited by each person in the group and ask students to predict who is more likely to survive and who is more likely to perish—leading to the extinction of their species—over the "long-haul struggle for survival."

Materials

apples/oranges, macaroni, bowls, straws, teaspoons, toothpicks, forceps

LS3 Journal Sheet #2

DESCENT AND CHANGE IN LIVING THINGS

1. _____
2. _____
3. _____
4. _____
5. _____
6. _____
7. _____
8. _____
9. _____
10. _____
11. _____
12. _____
13. _____
14. _____
15. _____
16. _____
17. _____
18. _____
19. _____
20. _____
21. _____
22. _____
23. _____
24. _____
25. _____
26. _____
27. _____
28. _____
29. _____
30. _____

Directions: (1) Imagine that a seemingly honest salesman offers you the following contract. If you will agree to invest 1 penny today, 2 pennies tomorrow, 4 pennies the following day and so on—doubling your investment every day for 30 days—he will pay you $1 million at the end of the month. (2) Decide whether or not you would agree to this deal. (3) Use your calculator to find the amount of money you need to pay the salesman every day for the next 30 days. (4) Did you make a good decision? Explain.

Directions: (1) Fill one bowl with macaroni for the group and place it at the center of the table. (2) Place your paper cup in front of you. (3) Your instructor has given you one of the following items: a straw, a spoon, a pair of toothpicks, or forceps. (4) When your instructor says "GO!" you may use that instrument and no other tool—especially your fingers or hands—to transfer as many macaronies from the bowl into the paper cup in front of you. DO NOT INTERFERE WITH THE EFFORT OF OTHERS!

DESCENT AND CHANGE IN LIVING THINGS

Work Date: _____/_____/_____

LESSON OBJECTIVE

Students will examine the adaptations of a variety of organisms in the environment.

Classroom Activities

On Your Mark!

Begin discussion by asking students how a cat's claws enable it to catch and eat mice. Define an **adaptation** as any feature of an organism that allows it to compete, survive, and reproduce more effectively in its particular environment. If a model of a human skull is available, display the lower jaw of the skull and discuss how human teeth are adapted to eat both meat and plants. The front incisors are used for snipping and cutting; the pointed canines are used for piercing and grasping; the multipointed bicuspids are used for holding and crunching; the back molars are used for grinding. Explain that a horse has teeth that all look like our molars. Ask students to describe the type of food that a horse is adapted to eat. Have students make a list of several animals they have encountered and write a sentence about one particular adaptation the animal uses to survive (e.g., the slimy body of a worm, the web of a spider).

Get Set!

Discuss **Darwin**'s (b. 1809; d. 1882) voyage to the **Galápagos Islands** off the coast of Ecuador on the west coast of South America between 1831 and 1836. Explain his fascination with the variety of life encountered there. Of particular interest to him were the different species of finches he found scattered on different distant islands. Although very similar in overall appearance, each species of finch had evolved a beak adapted for a particular type of diet.

Go!

Give students ample time to perform the activity described in Figure D on Journal Sheet #3. Circulate around the room to make sure that students have a logical explanation for their summary of each bird's particular adaptation.

Materials

Journal Sheet #3

LS3 JOURNAL SHEET #3

DESCENT AND CHANGE IN LIVING THINGS

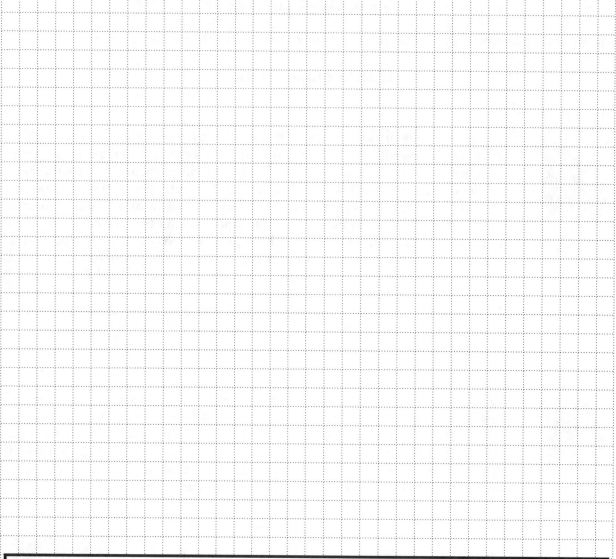

FIGURE D

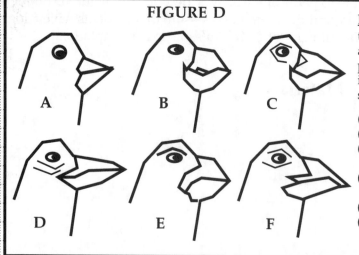

A

B

C

D

E

F

Directions: (1) Discuss with your group the characteristics of each bird's beak and how its shape adapts the bird to its particular eating habits. (2) Summarize your conclusions in one or two sentences.

(A) warblerlike finch eats flies
(B) insect-eating finch eats large insects
(C) cactus-eating finch eats soft cactus seeds
(D) woodpeckerlike finch eats insects from holes drilled in wood
(E) plant-eating finch eats leaves
(F) ground finch eats nuts and seeds off the ground

DESCENT AND CHANGE IN LIVING THINGS

Work Date: _____/_____/_____

LESSON OBJECTIVE

Students will explain how mutation and natural selection result in the evolution of structure in living things.

Classroom Activities

On Your Mark!

Prepare for the lesson by compiling pictures of human arms, dog front legs, and whale pectoral fins.

Review the results of the activity conducted in Figure C on Journal Sheet #2 and ask students to explain how the limited resources of their environment (e.g., the bowl of macaroni) could force the extinction of one or more of the individuals who competed for those resources. Refer to the discussion of artificial selection conducted in Lesson #1 and point out that nature performs a similar type of "selective breeding." In nature's case, the pressures of the harsh environment do the selecting.

Get Set!

Introduce the concept of **genetic mutations** using the information in the last two paragraphs of the Teacher's Classwork Agenda and Content Notes. Define a **mutation** as any alteration the genetic material (e.g., DNA) that carries instructions for the proteins that give an organism its form and organ function. Explain that mutations are the "raw materials" of evolution, giving rise to the infinite variety of characteristics exhibited by individual organisms.

Go!

Distribute the pictures of human arms, dog legs, and whale fins and give students ample time to complete the activity described in Figure E on Journal Sheet #4. Circulate around the room to make sure that students have identified the proper bones and given a logical explanation of how the limbs of each animal were mutated and selected by nature to give each animal an adaptive advantage in its particular environment.

Materials

pictures of human arms, dog front legs, and whale pectoral fins, Journal Sheet #4

LS3 JOURNAL SHEET #4

DESCENT AND CHANGE IN LIVING THINGS

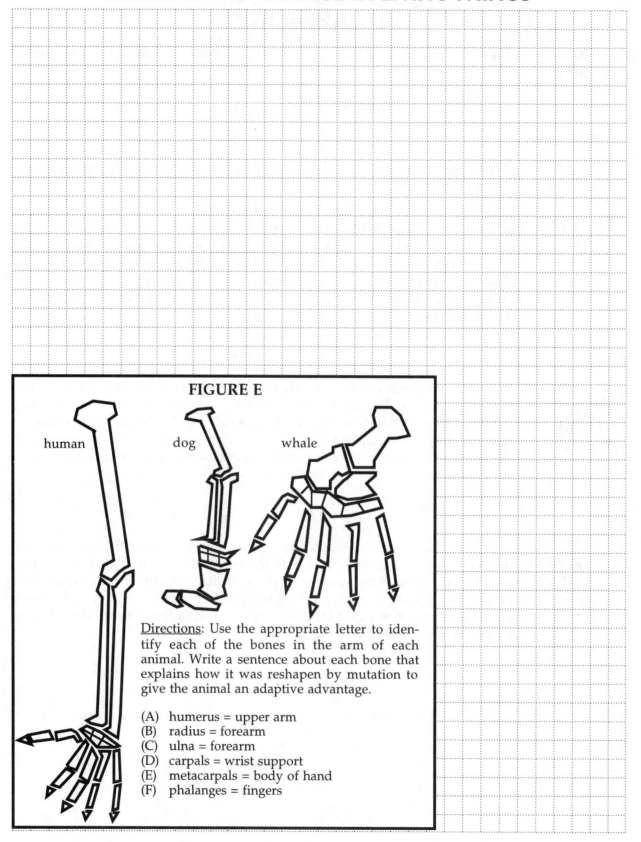

FIGURE E

human   dog   whale

Directions: Use the appropriate letter to identify each of the bones in the arm of each
animal. Write a sentence about each bone that
explains how it was reshapen by mutation to
give the animal an adaptive advantage.

(A) humerus = upper arm
(B) radius = forearm
(C) ulna = forearm
(D) carpals = wrist support
(E) metacarpals = body of hand
(F) phalanges = fingers

LS3 REVIEW QUIZ

Directions: Keep your eyes on your own work.
Read all directions and questions carefully.
THINK BEFORE YOU ANSWER!
Watch your spelling, be neat, and do the best you can.

CLASSWORK   (~40): _____
HOMEWORK   (~20): _____
CURRENT EVENT   (~10): _____
TEST   (~30): _____

TOTAL   (~100): _____
(A ≥ 90, B ≥ 80, C ≥ 70, D ≥ 60, F < 60)

LETTER GRADE: _____

TEACHER'S COMMENTS: _____
_____

DESCENT AND CHANGE IN LIVING THINGS

TRUE–FALSE FILL-IN: If the statement is true, write the word TRUE. If the statement is false, change the underlined word to make the statement true. *13 points*

_____ 1. <u>A few</u> species alive during past ages are no longer alive today.

_____ 2. The dinosaurs perished about <u>sixty million</u> years ago.

_____ 3. Biologists have <u>some</u> evidence that human beings existed on earth more than ten million years ago.

_____ 4. Radioactive dating techniques show the world to be about <u>4.5 million</u> years old.

_____ 5. Studying the geologic history of the world provides evidence that our planet's climate and surface features <u>have not</u> changed.

_____ 6. In 1859, <u>Albert Einstein</u> published a book entitled *The Origin of the Species by Means of Natural Selection* that explains how living organisms may become so diverse.

_____ 7. The Theory of Evolution by Means of <u>Artificial</u> Selection has become the cornerstone of modern biology.

_____ 8. The term evolution means <u>"advance."</u>

_____ 9. To a biologist, evolution refers to changes in <u>hereditary</u> features.

_____ 10. The scientists of Darwin's time <u>did not</u> know how hereditary change takes place.

_____ 11. A(n) <u>adaptation</u> is a change in a cell's chromosomes.

_____ 12. <u>Most</u> new traits arising from mutations are harmful to offspring and may result in their death.

_____ 13. <u>Some</u> mutations can give an offspring an advantage over other organisms in the struggle for survival.

PROBLEM

Circle the letters next to those observations that Charles Darwin made to arrive at his Theory of Evolution by Means of Natural Selection. You will earn plus 3 points for every correct observation circled but lose 3 points for every incorrect observation circled.

(A)   Species overreproduce.

(B)   Monkeys are the ancestors of human beings.

(C)   There are individual differences among the members of a species.

(D)   There is limited food and space available to living organisms.

(E)   Offspring look exactly like their parents in every way.

(F)   Organisms that can best adapt to changes in the environment survive to reproduce and pass on their traits.

(G)   Every animal leaves a fossil remain after it dies.

(H)   The earth is several billion years old.

DIAGRAM

Use capital letters to fill in the blank circles on the family tree to show where each organism most probably belongs. *5 points*

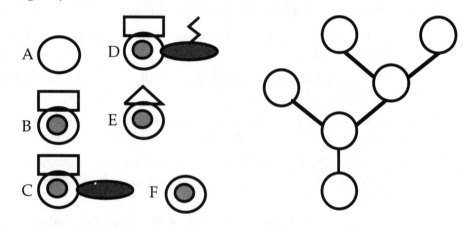

Student's Signature   Parent's Signature   Date

THE HISTORY OF LIFE

TEACHER'S CLASSWORK AGENDA AND CONTENT NOTES

Classwork Agenda for the Week

1. Students will identify the organic molecules found in all organisms.
2. Students will examine the role of extinction in the evolution of life on earth.
3. Students will list and identify the predominant organisms of the precambrian and paleozoic eras.
4. Students will list and identify the predominant organisms of the mesozoic and cenozoic eras.

Content Notes for Lecture and Discussion

The idea that species of plants and animals have evolved to flourish then cease to exist was not fully accepted by biologists until the latter part of the 19th century. Earlier 17th and 18th century biologists—among them the 3rd President of the United States and amateur scientist **Thomas Jefferson** (b. 1743; d. 1826)—suggested that creatures such as the giant sloth, *Megalonyx jeffersoni*, still roamed the unexplored regions of the western territories of North America. The idea of extinction contradicted the biblical doctrine that God expressed loving concern for all his creations and would not let them perish at the whim of nature. The fossilized bones of other creatures were also believed to represent the remains of existing animals that would one day be found alive in the farthest unexplored corners of the globe. However, the French comparative anatomist and "father of paleontology" **Georges Cuvier** (b. 1769; d. 1832) established the fact of extinction in his 1812 publication *Research on the Fossil Bones of Quadrupeds*. In that and later publications, Cuvier reviewed the disposition and absence of fossils in a variety of sequenced rock strata, most notably the sequence at Monmartre, Paris. The fossilized specimens of early sea creatures present in the Monmartre Sequence date back to the early Devonian Period of the Paleozoic Era. Following **Charles Robert Darwin**'s (b. 1809; d. 1882) publication of *The Origin of the Species by Means of Natural Selection* in 1859, the history of life on earth has been studied as a history of **extinction** and **adaptive radiation**. Cuvier believed that extinctions were largely catastrophic, resulting in the wholesale destruction of species on a global scale. Darwin viewed extinction as a more gradual process.

The 1950s experiments of American chemists **Stanley Lloyd Miller** (b. 1930) and **Harold Clayton Urey** (b. 1893; d. 1981) suggested a mechanism by which the organic building blocks of life—**carbohydrates, fats, proteins**, and **nucleic acids**—might have first formed; and, modern radioactive dating techniques allow paleontologists to make accurate estimations of the age of the fossilized remains of successive generations of living kindgoms found scattered across the world's changing continents. Still, the history of life on earth is replete with gaps in the fossil record: a logical consequence of the special circumstances required to create a mineralized remnant of organic tissue (e.g., a fossil). Today, the forces giving rise to the gradual or sudden extinction of species on both small and large scales include climatic changes associated with recurrent Ice Ages, continental drift resulting in the transition of biomes, any number of biotic catastrophes resulting from disease, and—of course—the bombardment of earth by meteors from outer space.

Paleontologists and geologists divide earth history into two major **eons**: the **Cryptozoic Eon** and the **Phanerozoic Eon**. The former spans the time from earth's formation to about 590 million years ago. The Cryptozoic Eon is divided into the **Hadean, Archean**, and **Proterozoic Era**: also collectively referred to as the **Precambrian Era**. The Hadean Era includes the first 100 million years of earth's existence when the planet was still hot and covered with poisonous gases. The molecules necessary for the formation of life were probably manufactured during the Archean Era that lasted to about 2.5 billion years ago. During the Proterozoic Era small bacteria and other single-celled organisms began to form colonies and multicellular creatures. The appearance of numerous fossils at the start of the **Phanerozoic Eon** indicate that life began to flourish at the start of this period. The Phanerozoic Eon is divided into the **Paleozoic Era**, the **Mesozoic Era**, and the **Cenozoic Era**. The **Paleozoic Era** is characterized by the radiation of invertebrates (e.g., mollusks and insects) and the first sea-dwelling and land-dwelling vertebrates (e.g., fishes and amphibians). The Mesozoic Era is identified with the success of the reptiles: particularily those of the dinosaur family. The mass extinction of the dinosaurs was followed by the explosion of mammalian communities (e.g., carnivores, cetaceans, primates, etc.).

In Lesson #1, students will identify the organic molecules found in all organisms.

In Lesson #2, students will examine the role of extinction in the evolution of life on earth.

In Lesson #3, students will list and identify the predominant organisms of the precambrian and paleozoic eras.

In Lesson #4, students will list and identify the predominant organisms of the mesozoic and cenozoic eras.

ANSWERS TO THE HOMEWORK PROBLEMS

Student essays will vary in content but should include the logical conclusion that the melting of the polar ice caps will cause a rise in sea level and a decrease in available land surface area. Accept any logical sequence of ideas proposed by students.

ANSWERS TO THE END-OF-THE-WEEK REVIEW QUIZ

1. D	6. PC	11. P	16. P
2. E	7. M	12. C	17. P
3. A	8. PC	13. C	18. P
4. D	9. P	14. P	19. C
5. E	10. P	15. P	20. C

LS4 Fact Sheet

THE HISTORY OF LIFE

CLASSWORK AGENDA FOR THE WEEK

(1) Identify the organic molecules found in all organisms.
(2) Explain the role of extinction in the evolution of life on earth.
(3) List and identify the predominant organisms of the precambrian and paleozoic eras.
(4) List and identify the predominant organisms of the mesozoic and cenozoic eras.

In the 1950s, American chemists **Stanley Lloyd Miller** (b. 1930) and **Harold Clayton Urey** (b. 1893; d. 1981) did a series of experiments to show how molecules common to all living things— **carbohydrates**, **fats**, **proteins**, and **nucleic acids**—might have formed on the ancient planet earth. Four billion years ago, planet earth was not as it is appears today. The planet's crust was covered with molten lava spewed from erupting volcanoes spotting the landscape. The atmosphere was filled with poisonous gases: **carbon dioxide** (CO_2), **ammonia** (NH_3), and **methane** (CH_4). There was little free **oxygen** (O_2). Most of that element was combined with hydrogen to form **water** (H_2O) or bound to metals to form **metal oxides**. Then, about 4 billion years ago, things changed. The electrical energy from atmospheric lightning sparked these molecules to combine, producing the raw materials needed to form living things. Using a device similar to the one illustrated in Figure I, Miller and Urey demonstrated that the large molecules that make up all living things can be made from carbon dioxide, ammonia, methane, and water. Carbohydrates, fats, proteins, and nucleic acids can all be "synthesized" from the simpler molecules that existed on primitive earth. The first **cells**—the basic units comprising all living things—are believed to have been formed more than 3.4 billion years ago.

Since the formation of the first cells, living things have changed in form. The processes of **mutation** and **natural selection** have resulted in the adaptation of some organisms to their environment and the extinction of others less adapted for survival. More species have become extinct during the history of earth than are alive on the planet today. Extinction has played a major role in the evolution of life on our planet. And, there have been more than a dozen **mass extinctions** that have claimed the lives of the majority of the species living on the planet when the extinction occurred. The dinosaurs who perished about 65 million years ago were the victims of a mass extinction. Nevertheless, a mass extinction can result in a **population explosion** for the species that survive it. Following a mass extinction, surviving species might enjoy freedom from predators and a changing environment. The mammals that survived the mass extinction that killed the dinosaurs flourished to become the planet's most successful biological family. The evolution of new species from a common ancestor—resulting from lack of competition or the migration to new environments—is called **adaptive radiation**. Mass extinctions can occur for a number of reasons. They can be the result of (1) changes in climate, (2) continental drift, (3) disease, or (4) meteor impacts.

The fossilized remains of early **multicellular organisms** (e.g., algae and fungi) appear in rocks more than 2 billion years old during the **Precambrian Era**. The first land plants (e.g., mosses and ferns)

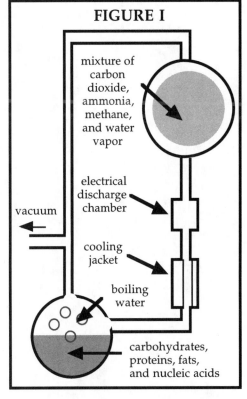

FIGURE I

mixture of carbon dioxide, ammonia, methane, and water vapor

electrical discharge chamber

vacuum

cooling jacket

boiling water

carbohydrates, proteins, fats, and nucleic acids

LS4 Fact Sheet (cont'd)

and animal-like sea creatures (e.g., invertebrate trilobites and brachiopods) appeared about 500 million years ago. Since then, the history of the earth can be divided into three more stages: the **Paleozoic Era** (e.g., **Age of the Fishes**), the **Mesozoic Era** (e.g., **Age of the Reptiles**), and the **Cenozoic Era** (e.g., the **Age of the Mammals**).

Homework Directions

Scientists are concerned that earth's climate has begun to change. There is evidence that the global climate is warming which could result in the melting of the ice caps at the North and South Poles. In an essay of no more than 200 words, explain how a change of this kind could drastically affect the future of existing species on this planet.

Assignment due: _____

_____   _____   ____/____/____
Student's Signature   Parent's Signature   Date

THE HISTORY OF LIFE

Work Date: ____/____/____

LESSON OBJECTIVE

Students will identify the organic molecules found in all organisms.

Classroom Activities

On Your Mark!

Prepare for this lesson by constructing "ball and stick" models of carbon dioxide, methane, ammonia, and water. Use toothpicks and different colors of clay if a molecular model kit is unavailable.

Begin with a discussion of the primitive earth. Point out that earth was most likely formed from a cloud of dust and gas drawn together by the forces of gravity. During the first few billion years following the planet's formation, its crust was cracked with volcanoes that spewed out poisonous gases such as carbon dioxide, methane, ammonia, and acids like sulfuric and phosphoric acids. Refer students to the experiments performed by **Stanley Lloyd Miller** (b. 1930) and **Harold Clayton Urey** (b. 1893; d. 1981) described on the student Fact Sheet. Discuss the experiments which demonstrated that the complex molecules which serve as the building blocks of life—fats, carbohydrates, proteins, and nucleic acids—can all be formed from simpler molecules.

Get Set!

Distribute molecular model kits, if available, or different colors of clay and toothpicks. Assist students in building the simpler molecules (e.g., carbon dioxide, methane, ammonia, and water). Tell students to refer to the fat molecule pictured in Figure A on Journal Sheet #1. Assist them in building one section (e.g., the "chainlike" fatty acid section) of the fat molecule in order to help them recognize the section's similarity with other sections of the more complex fat assembly.

Go!

Give students ample time to perform the activity described in Figure A on Journal Sheet #1, allowing them to build the more complex sections of each molecule, supplies permitting.

Materials

molecular model kits or several colors of clay and toothpicks, Journal Sheet #1

LS4 JOURNAL SHEET #I

THE HISTORY OF LIFE

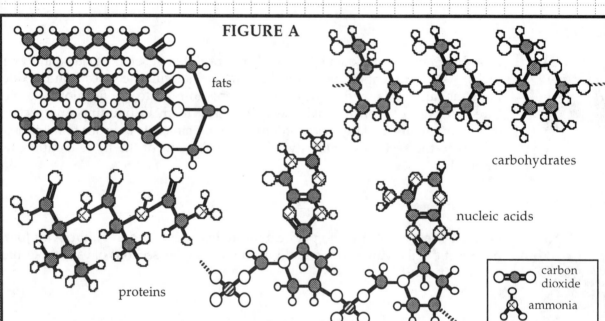

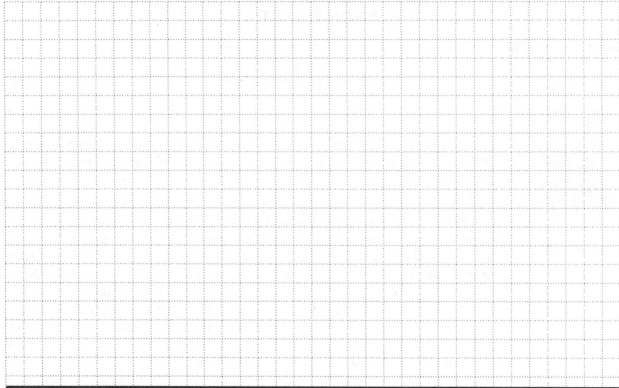

FIGURE A

fats

carbohydrates

nucleic acids

proteins

carbon dioxide

ammonia

water

methane

phosphate

Directions: Refer to the atoms and simple molecules in the legends shown below. Note that all of the complex molecules above have the same atoms. After studying the complex molecules, see if you can find arrangements of groups of atoms that repeat to make up the larger molecule. Circle these repeating groups to show how they link together to form fats, carbohydrates, proteins, and nucleic acids.

○ hydrogen ● carbon
⊗ nitrogen ○ oxygen
◕ phosphorus

THE HISTORY OF LIFE

Work Date: ____/____/____

LESSON OBJECTIVE

Students will examine the role of extinction in the evolution of life on earth.

Classroom Activities

On Your Mark!

Refer students to the illustration of Fossils In Rock Strata shown on Journal Sheet #2. Point out that the layers of rock are similar to the strata sequence that paleontologist **Georges Cuvier** (b. 1769; d. 1832) used to establish the fact of extinction. Use the information in the Teacher's Classwork Agenda and Content Notes to discuss the 17th, 18th, 19th, and 20th century views of extinction. Refer students to their Fact Sheet and review the meaning of mutation and natural selection. Discuss the causes of extinction (e.g., climatic change, continental drift, etc.).

Get Set!

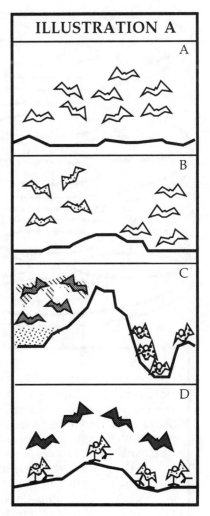

ILLUSTRATION A

Draw Illustration A on the board. Use the illustration to show how two species can evolve from a common ancestor as a result of isolation (e.g., separation, variation by mutation, and environmental pressure). In "A" one species of birds enjoys life on the plain. In "B" isolation and variation resulting from mountain building and mutation begins. In "C" a mountain range separates the divergent species which undergo further variation. In "D" erosion and weathering "flatten" the mountains, allowing the descendants of the common ancestor to once again inhabit the same habitat but not breed as a single species. Point out that this process spans tens of millions of years.

Go!

Give students ample time to perform the activity described in Figure B on Journal Sheet #2. Circulate around the room to make sure that they keep their drawings as simple as the illustration shown here.

(e.g., sample drawing)

If time permits at the end of the lesson, open discussion about the popular notion that the extinction of the dinosaurs was caused by a impact meteor.

Materials

coins

LS4 JOURNAL SHEET #2

THE HISTORY OF LIFE

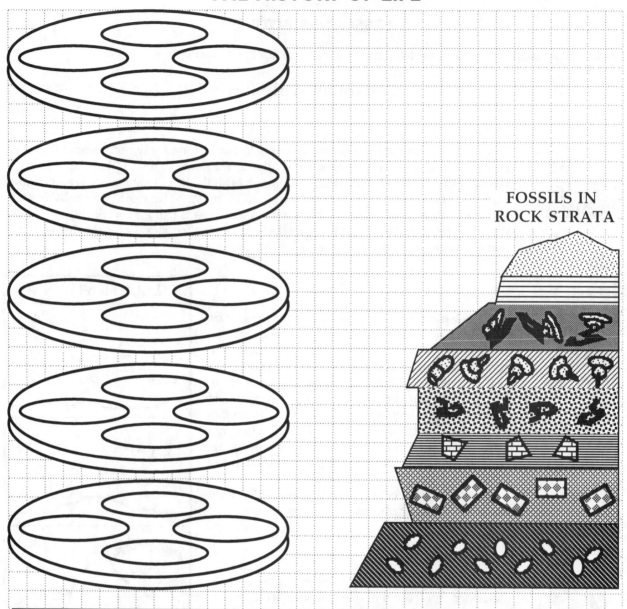

FOSSILS IN
ROCK STRATA

FIGURE B

Directions: (1) In the bottom plate, make a simple drawing (e.g., a geometric shape) of four identical creatures: one in each oval. (2) Add a single mutation (e.g., straight lines, dots, open circles) to each drawing so that you can tell the different "species" apart. (3) Choose two of the species to be "heads" and two to be "tails," before flipping a coin to see which species become extinct as a result of natural selection pressures. Choose one of the remaining two species to be "heads" and the other to be "tails" and flip again so that only one species remains. (4) Redraw four identical offspring of the surviving creature in the ovals on the next plate. (5) Add a different mutation (e.g., limbs, eyes, etc.) to each member of the group to create four new species. (6) Repeat steps #3, #4, and #5 until you reach the final top plate. (7) Write a short paragraph to explain how mutation, natural selection (e.g., the coin flipping), and extinction combined to give rise to the species on the upper plate. Compare your outcome to the outcome of your neighbors. If life exists on other planets, consider how likely it is that their intelligent descendants will look like us?

THE HISTORY OF LIFE

Work Date: ____/____/____

LESSON OBJECTIVE

Students will list and identify the predominant organisms of the precambrian and paleozoic eras.

Classroom Activities

On Your Mark!

Prepare for this lesson by obtaining 10–20 reference/text books from the school or local library that depict ancient life forms corresponding to those listed in Table A. If possible, make a transparency of Table A that you can display and use as an additional reference.

Display the references to give students an idea of the variety of creatures that have existed on our planet since the first single-celled lifeforms began to form more than 3.6 billion years ago until the end of the Paleozoic Era.

TABLE A			
	Beginning Years Ago (in millions)	Dominant Plant Life	Dominant Animal Life
PALEOZOIC ERA			
Permian	280	conifers	modern insects, small reptiles
Pennsylvanian	320	cycads, conifers	amphibians, first reptiles
Mississippian	345	club mosses, cycads	ancient sharks, sea lillies
Devonian	405	first conifer forests	first amphibians, lungfish
Silurian	425	algae, first land plants	wingless insects, first fishes
Ordovician	500	marine algae	coral, trilobites, mollusks
Cambrian	600	marine algae	trilobites, brachiopods
PRECAMBRIAN ERA	4,500	algae, fungi	protists, worms, invertebrates

Get Set!

Refer students to the scaled "geological time chart/rock strata" diagram on Journal Sheet #3. The diagram could correspond to the wall of the Grand Canyon whose layers of strata are clearly visible to any observer. The oldest rocks at the bottom of the Grand Canyon date to the start of the Cambrian Period of the Paleozoic Era. Explain that the Precambrian Era spanned time from the formation of the planet about 4.5 billion years ago to the start of the Paleozoic Era about 600 million years ago.

Go!

Have students share the references you provide in finding the names and illustrations of organisms that existed at the end of the Precambrian Era and during the Paleozoic Era. Have them list/draw these organisms on Journal Sheet #3 using arrows to indicate when each organism flourished.

Materials

library references, Journal Sheet #3

LS4 JOURNAL SHEET #3
THE HISTORY OF LIFE

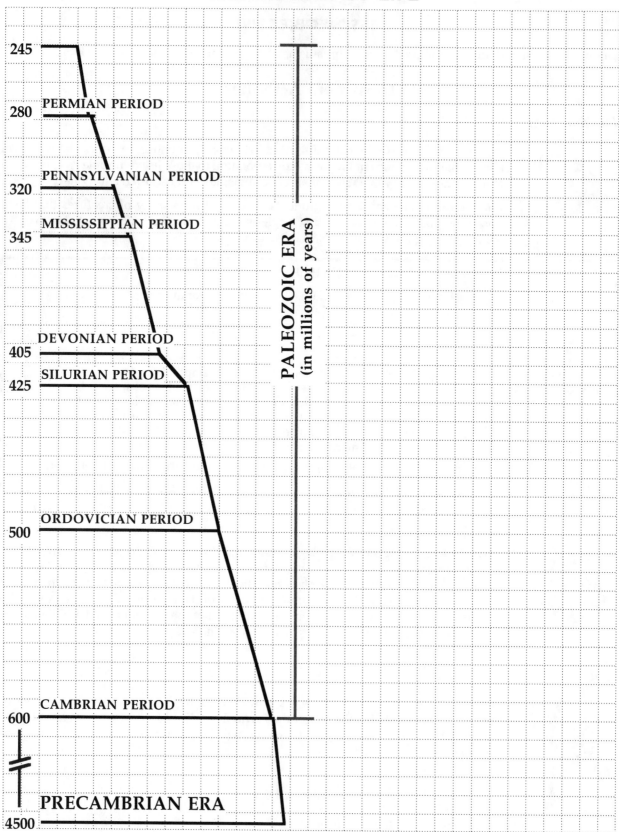

245

280 PERMIAN PERIOD

320 PENNSYLVANIAN PERIOD

345 MISSISSIPPIAN PERIOD

405 DEVONIAN PERIOD

425 SILURIAN PERIOD

500 ORDOVICIAN PERIOD

PALEOZOIC ERA
(in millions of years)

600 CAMBRIAN PERIOD

PRECAMBRIAN ERA
4500

THE HISTORY OF LIFE

Work Date: ____/____/____

LESSON OBJECTIVE

Students will list and identify the predominant organisms of the mesozoic and cenozoic eras.

Classroom Activities

On Your Mark!

Prepare for this lesson by obtaining 10–20 reference/text books from the school or local library that depict ancient life forms corresponding to those listed in Table B. If possible, make a transparency of Table B that you can display and use as an additional reference.

Display the references to give students an idea of the variety of creatures that existed on our planet in the last 245 million years.

TABLE B

	Beginning Years Ago (in millions)	Dominant Plant Life	Dominant Animal Life
CENOZOIC ERA			
Neogene	25	nonwoody herbs	wooly mammoths, saber-tooths, primates
Paleogene	65	grasslands, flowers	rise of placental and hoofed mammals
MESOZOIC ERA			
Cretaceous	145	first protected seeds	dinosaurs, first birds, small mammals
Jurassic	210	cycads and conifers	large dinosaurs, pouched mammals
Triassic	245	ferns and conifers	first dinosaurs, flying dinosaurs, egg-laying mammals

Get Set!

Refer students to the scaled "geological time chart/rock strata" diagram on Journal Sheet #4. Have students compare Journal Sheet #3 to Journal Sheet #4 to get an idea of the scale of the geological time involved. Each division on the Journal Sheets represents a period of 10 million years.

Go!

Have students share the references you provide and continue to find the names and illustrations of organisms that existed during the Mesozoic and Cenozoic Eras. Have them list/draw these organisms on Journal Sheet #4 using arrows to indicate when each organism flourished.

Materials

library references, Journal Sheet #4

LS4 JOURNAL SHEET #4

THE HISTORY OF LIFE

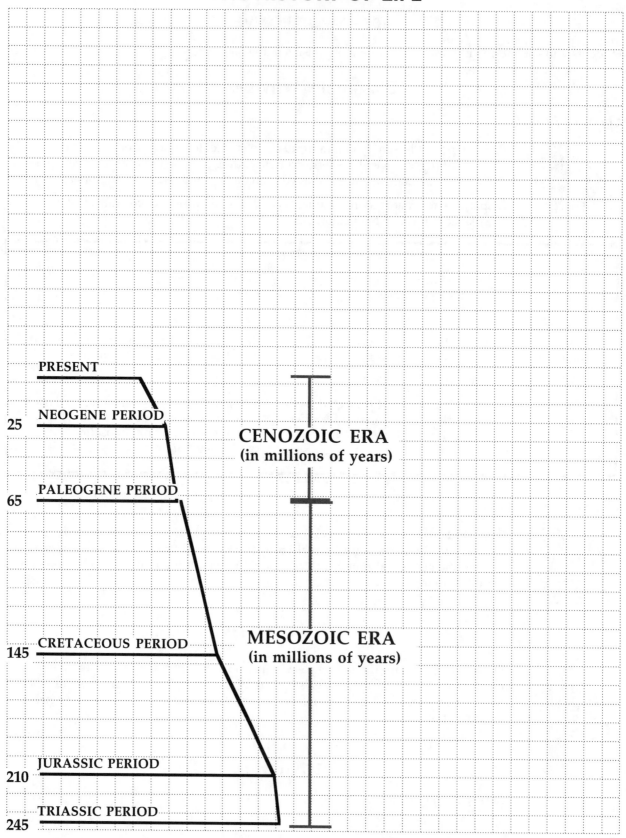

PRESENT

25   NEOGENE PERIOD

CENOZOIC ERA
(in millions of years)

65   PALEOGENE PERIOD

145   CRETACEOUS PERIOD

MESOZOIC ERA
(in millions of years)

210   JURASSIC PERIOD

245   TRIASSIC PERIOD

LS4 REVIEW QUIZ

Directions: Keep your eyes on your own work.
Read all directions and questions carefully.
THINK BEFORE YOU ANSWER!
Watch your spelling, be neat, and do the best you can.

CLASSWORK   (~40): _____
HOMEWORK   (~20): _____
CURRENT EVENT   (~10): _____
TEST   (~30): _____

TOTAL   (~100): _____
(A ≥ 90, B ≥ 80, C ≥ 70, D ≥ 60, F < 60)

LETTER GRADE: _____

TEACHER'S COMMENTS: _____
_____

THE HISTORY OF LIFE

MULTIPLE CHOICE: Choose the letter of the word or phrase that best answers or completes the question or sentence. *15 points*

_____ 1. Which of the following WAS NOT an abundant vapor found in the earth's primitive atmosphere?

    (A) carbon dioxide   (D) oxygen
    (B) ammonia   (E) water
    (C) methane

_____ 2. Which of the following WAS NOT a product of the Miller-Urey experiment?

    (A) carbohydrates   (D) nucleic acids
    (B) fats   (E) water
    (C) proteins

_____ 3. The first cells appear in the fossil record about _____ years ago.

    (A) 3 billion   (D) 3 thousand
    (B) 3 million   (E) 3 hundred
    (C) 3 hundred thousand

_____ 4. Which of the following might lead to adaptive radiation?

    (A) change in climate   (D) A, B, and C
    (B) continental drift   (E) neither A nor B nor C
    (C) meteor impact

_____ 5. The mass extinction of the dinosaurs was followed by a population explosion of _____ .

    (A) trilobites   (D) birds
    (B) fish   (E) mammals
    (C) plants

MATCHING: Next to each group of organisms write the letter or letters of the era in which it flourished by adaptive radiation. Use the letters "PC" for the Precambrian Era, the letter "P" for the Paleozoic Era, the letter "M" for the Mesozoic Era, and the letter "C" for the Cenozoic Era. *15 points*

_____ 6. green algae

_____ 7. dinosaurs

_____ 8. mushrooms

_____ 9. ferns

_____ 10. bony fishes

_____ 11. trilobites

_____ 12. primates

_____ 13. tree shrews

_____ 14. sharks

_____ 15. salamanders

_____ 16. insects

_____ 17. mosses

_____ 18. mollusks

_____ 19. flowering plants

_____ 20. humans

_____   _____   ____/____/____
Student's Signature   Parent's Signature   Date

LEVELS OF ORGANIZATION IN LIVING THINGS

TEACHER'S CLASSWORK AGENDA AND CONTENT NOTES

Classwork Agenda for the Week

1. Students will learn how to use a microscope.
2. Students will identify different types of cells under a microscope.
3. Students will identify different types of tissues under a microscope.
4. Students will list familiar organs and organ systems.

Content Notes for Lecture and Discussion

Scientific revolutions are as frequently the result of advancing technology as they are the product of changing ideas. The **science of optics** which made its first great strides in the 15th and 16th centuries resulted in revolutions in the sciences of astronomy and biology. The word "optics" comes from the Greek word for "eye." Instruments that allow scientists to make closer more detailed observations inevitably result in the accumulation of new and enlightening ideas. The early Romans were among the first to document the observation that a glass sphere filled with water had a magnifying effect on nearby objects. Better techniques for the production and shaping of glass, developed since the 13th century, have resulted in the manufacture of more plentiful and powerful lenses. The Dutch inventor **Anton van Leeuwenhoek** (b. 1632; d. 1723) is credited with the invention of the **microscope**, having been the first to extensively document the small creatures he observed using the tool. He called the microscopic organisms "animalicules". Observations over the next two centuries culminated in **the cell theory** proposed by German biologists **Theodor Schwann** (b. 1810; d. 1882) and **Matthias Jakob Schleiden** (b. 1804; d. 1881). In his publication entitled *Microscopical Investigations*, Schwann wrote, "One may include under the name of cell theory in the wider sense, the exposition of the statement that there exists a general principle of construction for all organic products, and that this principle of construction is cell formation."

Further advances in the art and science of microscopy led to the observation that similar kinds of cells form **tissues** which specialize and combine to form **organs**. **Organ systems** allow large multicellular plants and animals to accomplish the tasks necessary for life.

There are hundreds of different types of plant and animal cells. For the most part all cells have many characteristics and structures in common (cf. LS6 and LS7 for an in-depth description of *The Living Cell*). However, there are two most notable differences between plant and animal cells. The first is the existence of a hard **cell wall** that protects the cells of plants but is absent in animal cells. Plants also contain additional **organelles** (e.g., tiny cell organs) called **chloroplasts** that contain **chlorophyll**. The chlorophyll molecule is responsible for the phenomenon of **photosynthesis**.

In animals, cells form four basic types of tissues: **epithelial** tissue, **connective** tissue, **muscle** tissue, and **nerve** tissue. Epithelial tissues serve as the coverings and linings of body organs (e.g., skin). Connective tissues give an animal its overall structure and cohesiveness (e.g., ligaments and bone). The cells of muscle tissues have the unique capacity to contract as the result of chemical interactions between the remarkable proteins actin and myosin. The cells of nerve tissue have distinctively structured cell membranes that maintain a delicate "ionic differential" between the internal and external environment of the cell. By controlling the balance between these "differentially charged" environments, nerve cells can conduct "electrochemcial messages" from one part of an animal's body to another.

LS5 Content Notes *(cont'd)*

In Lesson #1, students will learn how to use a microscope.
In Lesson #2, students will identify different types of cells under a microscope.
In Lesson #3, students will identify different types of tissues under a microscope.
In Lesson #4, students will list familiar organs and organ systems.

ANSWERS TO THE HOMEWORK PROBLEMS

Heart—pumps blood through arteries and veins as part of the circulatory system; lung—permits the exchange of gases with the environment as part of the respiratory system; eye—collects, focusses, and transforms light energy to nerve signals as part of the nervous system; tongue—manipulates food in the mouth as part of the digestive system and is an organ of taste and speech as part of the nervous system; tooth—assists in the mechanical digestion of food as part of the digestive system and gives structure to the face as part of the skeletal system; liver—manufactures a variety of products used in the chemical digestion of food as part of the digestive system; apple—protects seeds as part of an apple tree's reproductive system; leaf—exchanges gases with the atmosphere as part of a plant's shoot system; stem—gives support and structure to a plant and permits the transport of nutrients up and down the plant as part of the plant's shoot system; root—absorbs water from the soil as part of the plants root system.

ANSWERS TO THE END-OF-THE-WEEK REVIEW QUIZ

1. microscope	6. cell	A. eyepiece	F. stage
2. true	7. cell	B. fine focus	G. diaphragm
3. microscope	8. sometimes	C. objective	H. coarse focus
4. true	9. tissue	D. arm	I. light/mirror
5. true	10. organ	E. stage clip	J. base

11. lowest power
12. coarse focus
13. raise the objective before changing or focussing it
14. do not run; hold it at the center of the body with two hands
15. keep both eyes open

LS5 FACT SHEET

LEVELS OF ORGANIZATION IN LIVING THINGS

CLASSWORK AGENDA FOR THE WEEK

(1) Learn how to use a microscope.
(2) Identify different types of cells under a microscope.
(3) Identify different types of tissues under a microscope.
(4) List familiar organs and organ systems.

Biologists have always wanted to understand how living things are put together. As a result, the dissection of living things has played a major role in biology since ancient times. The first recorded dissection was made by the Greek physician **Alcmaeon** (c. 500 B.C.) around 500 B.C. In 1267, the English philosopher-scientist **Roger Bacon** (b. 1214; d. 1294) constructed a hand-held glass lens which he used to take a closer look at his experiments. In 1665, the English scientist-inventor **Robert Hooke** (b. 1635; d. 1703) designed the prototype of the modern **light microscope** and used it to examine thin slices of cork. What he observed was a section of cork made up of tiny little compartments he called "cella" meaning "a small room." In 1683, the Dutch inventor **Anton van Leeuwenhoek** (b. 1632; d. 1723) constructed a powerful hand-held microscope with lenses able to magnify objects more than 300 times.

Leeuwenhoek published drawings of microscopic creatures he called "animalicules." Today, these tiny organisms are called **protozoa** (e.g., ameba, paramecium) and can be found swimming around in pond water. With the invention of more powerful microscopes, biologists noticed that all living things were made of tiny compartments or **cells**. In 1839, the German biologists **Theodor Schwann** (b. 1810; d. 1882) and **Matthias Jakob Schleiden** (b. 1804; d. 1881) proposed the cell theory. The **cell theory** states that while there are many different kinds of cells, all living things are made of cells filled with a colorless jellylike substance called **protoplasm**.

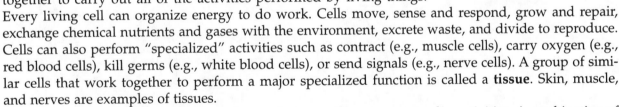

A SECTION OF CORK

Perhaps the most amazing fact of biology is that cells work together to carry out all of the activities performed by living things. Every living cell can organize energy to do work. Cells move, sense and respond, grow and repair, exchange chemical nutrients and gases with the environment, excrete waste, and divide to reproduce. Cells can also perform "specialized" activities such as contract (e.g., muscle cells), carry oxygen (e.g., red blood cells), kill germs (e.g., white blood cells), or send signals (e.g., nerve cells). A group of similar cells that work together to perform a major specialized function is called a **tissue**. Skin, muscle, and nerves are examples of tissues.

Tissues of different types can work together to perform more complex activities. A combination of tissues that work together to perform a specific set of activities is called an **organ**. The **heart** is an organ that pumps blood around an animal's body. The **stomach** is an organ that breaks up food.

Organs work together to allow large organisms to complete all of the activities they need to perform in order to survive. Organs are arranged in **organ systems**. The circulatory system—made up of the heart, arteries, and veins—distributes blood to the individual cells of an animal's body. The respiratory system—made up of the lungs and diaphragm—allows an animal to breath (e.g., exchange poisonous carbon dioxide for fresh oxygen).

Homework Directions

Directions: Write a sentence describing the function of each of the following organs, mentioning the organ system to which it belongs: heart, lung, eye, tongue, tooth, liver, apple, leaf, stem, root.

Assignment due: _____

_____   _____   ___/___/___
Student's Signature   Parent's Signature   Date

LEVELS OF ORGANIZATION IN LIVING THINGS

Work Date: ____/____/____

LESSON OBJECTIVE

Students will learn how to use a microscope.

Classroom Activities

On Your Mark!

Begin with a simple demonstration. (1) Place a straw in a glass or beaker of water and point out how the straw appears to bend. (2) Explain that light waves bend or "refract" as they pass from one medium (e.g., the water) into another medium (e.g., the glass, then air). (3) Give an eyedropper with water to each student. (4) Instruct students to place a droplet of water on any letter of their Fact Sheet. (5) Ask them to report their observations of the letter's image. They will report that the letter under the droplet becomes magnified. Explain that the "bending" of light waves reflecting off the surface of the Fact Sheet as the light from the letter passes across the curved surfaces of the water droplet into the air makes the image of the letter appear larger than the actual object.

Continue with a brief lecture and discussion about the history of the **science of optics** and its impact on the science of biology resulting from the invention of the microscope by **Anton van Leeuwenhoek** (b. 1632; d. 1723). Use the information in the student Fact Sheet and Teacher's Classwork Agenda and Content Notes.

Get Set!

Display a microscope and identify its parts shown on Journal Sheet #1. Have students copy the names of each part and describe its function as you lecture: (1) The **base** and **support arm** support the body of the microscope. Students should walk slowly when carrying the microscope to their observation station, holding the scope with two hands—one grasping the arm with the other under the base—close to the center of their body. (2) Instruct them to use the **coarse focus knob** to raise the **objective lenses** (or lower the stage) so that the lenses are out of the way. (3) After securing a prepared slide on the **stage** under the **stage clips** they can (4) use the **light** or **mirror** to send light up through the hole in the stage. (5) Viewing the stage and slide **from the side**, student should use the coarse focus knob again to bring the **lowest power objective** as close to the slide as possible <u>without touching it</u>. (6) Viewing the object through the **eyepiece**, they can then **focus away from the slide** until the object comes into focus. This procedure prevents the objective lens from smashing into the slide. (7) Students can adjust the **diaphragm** to control the intensity of light passing through their slide. (8) They can use the **fine focus knob** to add clarity to the image. Instruct students to repeat steps #5 through #8 when changing objectives to a higher or lower power.

Go!

Give students ample time to complete the activity described in Figure A on Journal Sheet #1.

Materials

microscopes, microscope slides, microscope coverslips, eyedroppers, water, newspaper, beakers, straws

LS5 JOURNAL SHEET #1

LEVELS OF ORGANIZATION IN LIVING THINGS

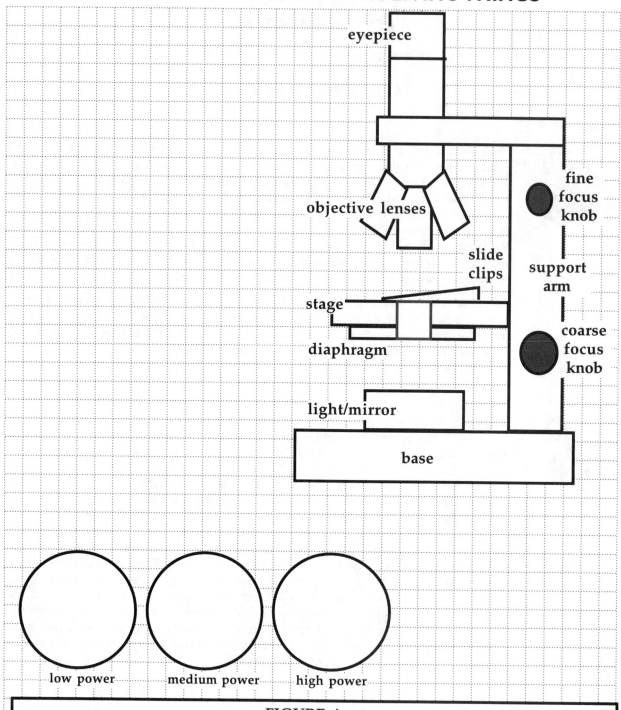

FIGURE A

Directions: (1) Cut out a small piece of newsprint about a quarter of a centimeter square. (2) Place the newsprint on a glass microscope slide. (3) Place a drop of water using an eyedropper on the newsprint. (4) Cover the droplet and newsprint with a plastic coverslip. (5) Use a microscope to help you draw three views of the newsprint in the circles above.

LEVELS OF ORGANIZATION IN LIVING THINGS

Work Date: _____/_____/_____

LESSON OBJECTIVE

Students will identify different types of cells under a microscope.

Classroom Activities

On Your Mark!

Draw Illustration A on the board. Explain the cell theory as proposed by **Theodor Schwann** (b. 1810; d. 1882) and **Matthias Jakob Schleiden** (b. 1804; d. 1881) using the information in the Teacher's Classwork Agenda and Content Notes. Define the following terms and have students copy your definitions on Journal Sheet #2. A **cell** is the basic unit of all living things. A **tissue** is a group of similar cells that perform a like function. An **organ** is a combination of different types of tissues that can perform one or more functions. An **organ system** is a combination of associated organs that allows a large organism to complete one or more of life's basic survival activities.

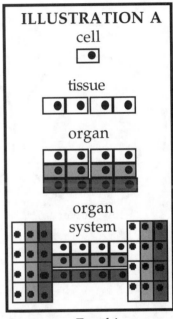

ILLUSTRATION A

cell

tissue

organ

organ system

Get Set!

Explain that most cells and tissues are practically transparent and therefore difficult to view under a microscope. For this reason, scientists "stain" cells with a variety of colored dyes to make them visible. The art and science of staining cells and tissues is called **histology**, a term derived from the Greek word for "tissue."

Go!

Give students ample time to complete the activities described in Figure B on Journal Sheet #2. Also use pre-prepared slides of varying types of cells if available. Slide kits are available through most laboratory supply houses.

Materials

microscopes, microscope slides, microscope coverslips, eyedroppers, water, forceps, methylene blue or Lugol's iodine solution (see LS1, Lesson #3, for a description of the preparation of Lugol's solution), cotton swabs, fresh onion

Name: _____ Period:_____ Date: ___/___/___

LS5 JOURNAL SHEET #2
LEVELS OF ORGANIZATION IN LIVING THINGS

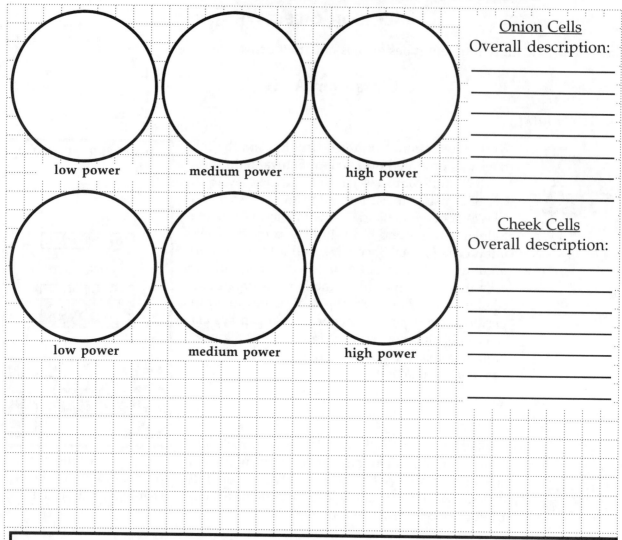

Onion Cells
Overall description:
_____
_____
_____
_____
_____
_____
_____

low power   medium power   high power

Cheek Cells
Overall description:
_____
_____
_____
_____
_____
_____
_____

low power   medium power   high power

FIGURE B

<u>Directions for viewing a slice of onion skin</u>: (1) Slice a raw onion and cut the onion rings into 5 millimeter sections. (2) With forceps or a fingernail gently tear away the inner membrane and flatten it onto a microscope slide. (3) Place a droplet of water on the thin section. (4) Cover the droplet of stain and onion section with a coverslip. (5) Observe the specimen under the microscope. Note that the onion skin is practically transparent. (6) Remove the slide from the microscope. (7) Gently slide the coverslip away from the onion skin and repeat steps #1 through #5. But this time use a drop of the methylene blue or Lugol's iodine solution provided by your instructor to "stain" the specimen. (8) Draw your observations in the circles above.

<u>Directions for viewing dead cheek cells</u>: (1) Gently scrape the lining of your cheek with the flat side of a toothpick. (2) Smear the dead cheek cells onto a microscope slide. (3) Stain the specimen with a drop of methylene blue or Lugol's iodine solution provided by your instructor. (4) Draw your observations in the circles above.

GENERAL HEALTH PRECAUTIONS

Do not touch another student's specimens. Rinse and dry all microscope slides thoroughly and discard specimens, toothpicks, and coverslips. Your instructor will sterilize any equipment to be reused.

LEVELS OF ORGANIZATION IN LIVING THINGS

Work Date: _____/_____/_____

LESSON OBJECTIVE

Students will identify different types of tissues under a microscope.

Classroom Activities

On Your Mark!

Review the definitions of cells, tissues, organs, and organ systems introduced in Lesson #2.

Get Set!

Give students a moment to brainstorm the variety of different tissues they have in their own bodies (e.g., skin tissue, bone tissue, muscle tissue, etc.). Have students discuss and record the major function(s) of each type of tissue.

Go!

Give students ample time to complete the activities described in Figure C on Journal Sheet #3. Also use pre-prepared slides of varying types of tissues if available. Slide kits are available through most laboratory supply houses.

Materials

microscopes, microscope slides, microscope coverslips, eyedroppers, water, forceps, methylene blue or Lugol's iodine solution (see LS1, Lesson #3, for a description of the preparation of Lugol's solution), cotton swabs, green leaves, raw beef

LS5 JOURNAL SHEET #3

LEVELS OF ORGANIZATION IN LIVING THINGS

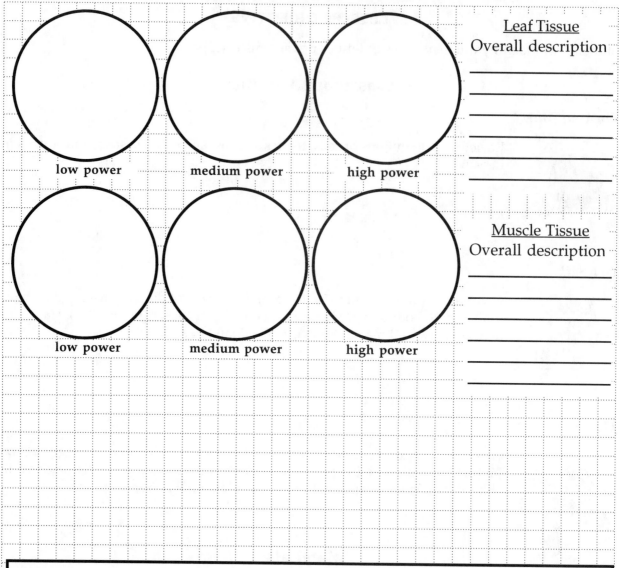

low power   medium power   high power

Leaf Tissue
Overall description
_____
_____
_____
_____

_____
_____

low power   medium power   high power

Muscle Tissue
Overall description
_____
_____
_____
_____
_____
_____

FIGURE C

Directions for viewing a section of leaf tissue: (1) Cut out a small 5 millimeter square section of a leaf and place it on a microscope slide. (2) Use forceps or a dissecting needle to gently tease apart strands of leaf. (3) Place a droplet of methylene blue or Lugol's iodine solution provided by your instructor to "stain" the specimen. (4) Cover the specimen with a coverslip. (5) Observe the specimen under the microscope. (6) Draw your observations in the circles above.

Directions for viewing dead muscle cells: (1) Place several cubic millimeters of raw, lean beef on a microscope slide. (2) Use forceps or a dissecting needle to gently tease apart strands of beef. (3) Place a droplet of methylene blue or Lugol's iodine solution provided by your instructor to "stain" the specimen. (4) Cover the specimen with a coverslip. (5) Observe the specimen under the microscope. (6) Draw your observations in the circles above.

GENERAL HEALTH PRECAUTIONS

Do not touch another student's specimens. Rinse and dry all microscope slides thoroughly and discard specimens, toothpicks, and coverslips. Your instructor will sterilize any equipment to be reused.

LEVELS OF ORGANIZATION IN LIVING THINGS

Work Date: ____/____/____

LESSON OBJECTIVE

Students will list familiar organs and organ systems.

Classroom Activities

On Your Mark!

Prepare for this lesson by compiling 5–10 biology/anatomy texts from the school or local library that contain schematic anatomical drawings of animals from different vertebrate classes (e.g., fish, frogs, lizards, birds, mammals).

Give students a moment to brainstorm the variety of different organs and organ systems they have in their own bodies (e.g., heart and circulatory system, lungs and respiratory system, bones and skeletal system, brain and nervous system, etc.). Have students discuss and record the major function(s) of each organ system with regard to the particular life activities mentioned in their Fact Sheet that each system performs.

Get Set!

Display the library books to show drawings that illustrate the similarities and differences between the anatomical structures of animals in the different vertebrate classes.

Go!

Give students ample time to share the reference material so that they can quickly sketch one of the organ systems (e.g., the digestive system) for each of at least two different vertebrates. Their drawings should show the same basic organs present in each class of animals and the varying arrangements of the organs across the phylum vertebrata.

Materials

library references, Journal Sheet #4

LS5 JOURNAL SHEET #4

LEVELS OF ORGANIZATION IN LIVING THINGS

LS5 REVIEW QUIZ

Directions: Keep your eyes on your own work.
Read all directions and questions carefully.
THINK BEFORE YOU ANSWER!
Watch your spelling, be neat, and do the best you can.

TEACHER'S COMMENTS: _____
_____

LEVELS OF ORGANIZATION IN LIVING THINGS

TRUE–FALSE FILL-IN: If the statement is true, write the word TRUE. If the statement is false, change the underlined word to make the statement true. *10 points*

_____ 1. In 1665, Robert Hooke designed the prototype of the modern light <u>bulb</u>.

_____ 2. Hooke was the first to observe that cork was made up of tiny little compartments he called "<u>cella</u>" meaning "a small room."

_____ 3. In 1683, Anton van Leeuwenhoek constructed a powerful hand-held <u>laser</u> with lenses able to magnify objects more than 300 times.

_____ 4. The first observed microscopic creatures were called "<u>animalicules</u>."

_____ 5. Today, tiny single-celled, microscopic organisms such as ameba and paramecium are called <u>protozoa</u>.

_____ 6. The <u>atomic-molecular</u> theory was first proposed by Schwann and Schleiden.

_____ 7. The <u>atomic-molecular</u> theory states that all living things are made of cells.

_____ 8. Cells <u>always</u> work together.

_____ 9. A group of similar cells that work together to perform a major specialized function is called a(n) <u>organ</u>.

_____ 10. A combination of tissues that work together to perform a specific set of activities is called a(n) <u>cell</u>.

DIAGRAM

Directions: Write the name or each part of the micrsocope next to the appropriate letter. *10 points*

(A) _____

(B) _____

(C) _____

(D) _____

(E) _____

(F) _____

(G) _____

(H) _____

(I) _____

(J) _____

Directions: Answer the following questions in a phrase or two. *10 points*

11. Which objective lens should be used first when putting an object in focus?

    _____

12. Which adjustment knob should be used first when putting an object in focus?

    _____

13. What precautions should be taken to avoid shattering an objective lens when focussing on an object with the coarse focus adjustment knob?

    _____

14. Describe two ways to avoid an accident while carrying a microscope.

    _____

15. How can you avoid straining your eyes when using a microscope for an extended period of time?

    _____

_____   _____   ___/___/___
   Student's Signature   Parent's Signature   Date

THE LIVING CELL: PART I

TEACHER'S CLASSWORK AGENDA AND CONTENT NOTES

Classwork Agenda for the Week

1. Students will compare and contrast the organelles of plant and animal cells.
2. Students will begin gathering information about the structure and function of cell organelles.
3. Students will continue gathering information about the structure and function of cell organelles.
4. Students will develop a cooperative plan for constructing a three-dimensional model of a plant or animal cell.

Content Notes for Lecture and Discussion

For most biologists of the 16th, 17th, and 18th centuries the basic units of plant and animal tissues were fibers or tubules. According to the English scientist **Robert Hooke** (b. 1635; d. 1702)—whose observation of "cella" or "small compartments" in cork had excited biologists to make further use of the microscope—cells were clearly open cavities or "vesicles" fixed within the matrix of living tissue. He was not sure that these "cellular holes" served anything more than a "connective function." Ironically, the French physician and founder of histology **Marie François Xavier Bichat** (b. 1771; d. 1802) made little use of the microscope in his investigation of the effects of disease on plant and animal tissues. Nevertheless, his identification of more than 20 different kinds of tissues—and his proposition that diseases affected some tissues and not others—led to the careful study of tissues by devout microscopists. The reductionist notion of chemists and physicists of the time guided biologists to a "globular theory" of living tissue which suggested that living matter was a composite of proteinaceous globules, 0.003 millimeters in diameter. The French physiologist **Henri Dutrochet** (b. 1776; d. 1847) combined the vesicular and globule theories into a more general theory of living microstructure; but, his ideas were largely abandoned in the face of the enormous diversity of microscopic structures observed in plants and animals. The idea that all organisms could be composed of a common structural unit seemed ludicrous.

The **cell theory** finally proposed by German biologists **Theodor Schwann** (b. 1810; d. 1882) and **Matthias Jakob Schleiden** (b. 1804; d. 1881) in 1839 was based on Schleiden's examination of germinal plant tissues. In 1838, Schleiden announced that plant organs were derived from plant cells: an idea that Schwann expanded to animals the following year. The German botanist **Hugo von Mohl** (b. 1805; d. 1872) coined the term "protoplasm" to describe the fluid material inside cells and was the first to describe the **cell membrane** and **nucleus** as structures common to all cells. Mohl also described the movement of water across the cell membrane and the cell's ability to govern its internal environment by this process of **osmosis**.

The invention of the **electron microscope** in 1933 by the German physicist **Ernst August Friedrich Ruska** (b. 1906; d. 1988) caused a revolution in cellular biology by permitting the detailed examination of the multitude of cellular organelles. The invention was based on the earlier discovery of the French physicist **Louis de Broglie** (b. 1892; d. 1987) that beams of **electrons** moved like light waves with a very small wavelength.

In this and the next unit, an overview of cell structure and cell organelle function will give students the tools they need to construct a three-dimensional model of a plant or animal cell and to grasp the notion that cells are the basic building blocks of all living things.

In Lesson #1, students will compare and contrast the organelles of plant and animal cells.

In Lesson #2, students will begin gathering information about the structure and function of cell organelles.

LS6 Content Notes (cont'd)

In Lesson #3, students will continue gathering information about the structure and function of cell organelles.

In Lesson #4, students will develop a cooperative plan for constructing a three-dimensional model of a plant or animal cell. They will construct their model during the course of the next unit: LS7–*The Living Cell: Part II.*

ANSWERS TO THE HOMEWORK PROBLEMS

Students analogies may vary but should demonstrate an understanding of each organelle's primary function as listed in Table A on their Fact Sheet.

ANSWERS TO THE END-OF-THE-WEEK REVIEW QUIZ

1. all	6. L	11. K	16. C
2. true	7. NP	12. I	17. D
3. plant	8. A	13. B	18. E
4. protoplasm	9. NP	14. F	19. NP
5. can	10. G	15. H	20. J

Students should mention in their essay that plant cells have a cell wall, chloroplasts, plastids, and large water-filled vacuoles that are not present in animal cells. Many animal cells have microvilli or cilia which are generally not present in plant cells.

LS6 FACT SHEET

THE LIVING CELL: PART I

CLASSWORK AGENDA FOR THE WEEK

(1)   Compare and contrast the organelles of plant and animal cells.
(2)   Begin gathering information about the structure and function of cell organelles.
(3)   Continue gathering information about the structure and function of cell organelles.
(4)   Develop a cooperative plan for constructing a three-dimensional model of a plant or animal cell.

The **cell theory** was first proposed in 1839 by German biologists **Theodor Schwann** (b. 1810; d. 1882) and **Matthias Jakob Schleiden** (b. 1804; d. 1881). They suggested that all living things are composed of cells. Since then biologists have tried to get a closer look at the way cells are constructed. When viewing a well-stained animal cell under low power with a simple light microscope, one can clearly see a **cell membrane** that gives the cell its shape. A plant cell is surrounded by a rectangular **cell wall** that surrounds the cell membrane and the rest of the cell. Inside either a plant or animal cell, one can see a small dark structure that biologists call a **nucleus**. The cell appears to be filled with a jellylike substance that biologists call **protoplasm**. The reason the parts of a cell are so hard to see using a light microscope is that the tiny structures that make up the cell are almost as small as the light waves being used to "illuminate" them.

In 1924, the French physicist **Louis de Broglie** (b. 1892; d. 1987) discovered that beams of **electrons** (e.g., the negatively charged subatomic particles that orbit the nuclei of atoms) can move like light waves with a very small wavelength. By 1933, the German physicist **Ernst August Friedrich Ruska** (b. 1906; d. 1988) had built an **electron microscope** able to magnify objects more than 12,000 times. The best light microscopes of that decade had a magnification of only 2,000 times. Since the invention of the electron microscope the incredibly small structures that make up a living cell can easily be photographed and studied. These tiny structures are called **cell organelles**.

Each cell organelle performs a specific function much like the organs of a large plant or animal. Table A lists the many cell organelles present in living cells and summarizes their primary function.

TABLE A

CELL ORGANELLE	PRIMARY FUNCTION	PLANT	ANIMAL
cell wall	hard cellulose wall that protects plant cells	√	
cell membrane	gives cell structure, gateway to environment	√	√
cytoplasm	dissolves chemical nutrients in watery interior	√	√
centrosomes/centrioles	helps the cell to divide	√	√
ribosomes	site of protein synthesis	√	√
mitochondrion	manufactures and stores ATP (e.g., cell fuel)	√	√
nucleus/nucleolus	stores DNA and RNA (e.g., hereditary material)	√	√
endoplasmic reticulum	transport channels may have ribosomes attached	√	√
Golgi bodies	readies proteins for excretion from cell	√	√
lysosomes	breaks down large molecules into usable ones	√	√
peroxisome	neutralizes poisonous substances	√	√
cilia	traps foreign particles or helps the cell to move		√
microvilli	helps the cell to absorb nutrients		√
chloroplasts	stores chlorophyll used in photosynthesis	√	
plastid	stores nutrients in plant cells	√	
vacuole	stores extra water and additional nutrients	√	

Homework Directions

Write a paragraph of at least 150 words that compares a living cell to an automobile factory. In your paragraph, compare at least ten (10) cell organelles to the "working departments" at the automobile plant. For example, the cell nucleus that stores the "blueprints" for manufacturing cell proteins can be compared to the "engineering department" that creates the designs for making the automobiles.

Assignment due: _____

_____   _____   ____/____/____
Student's Signature   Parent's Signature   Date

THE LIVING CELL: PART I

Work Date: _____/_____/_____

LESSON OBJECTIVE

Students will compare and contrast the organelles of plant and animal cells.

Classroom Activities

On Your Mark!

Draw the organelles appearing in Illustration A on the board, identifying each by name. Point out that these structures are called **cell organelles** (e.g., meaning "tiny cell organs") and that each organelle has a specific set of functions which it performs to help the cell stay alive. Refer students to the illustrations of the plant and animal cell appearing on Journal Sheet #1. Ask students to spend a moment studying the organelles present inside each type of cell. Ask them to compare the cells in terms of the organelles common to both cells. Ask them to contrast two kinds of cells by identifying those structures that do not appear in both kinds of cells. They will note that chloroplasts, plastids, a cell wall, and vacuoles, are not present in animal cells. Cilia and microvilli are not present in plant cells.

Get Set!

Briefly discuss the function of each organelle by referring to Table A on the Fact Sheet, drawing analogies between each organelle and the functions performed by the different departments of a factory that produces television sets. For example, the cell nucleus stores the information for the design of specific television parts as does the engineering department of the factory. Each ribosome is a protein assembly line just like the assembly line on the factory floor. The homework assignment this week asks students to draw similar analogies. Allow them to use the same analogies on their homework assignment as a review of the functions of the various cell organelles.

Go!

Give students ample time to complete the activity described in Figure A on Journal Sheet #1. Point out that soap is made of animal fat which comprises the cell membranes of all cells (e.g., phospholipids). They will observe how the soap film "swims around" yet stays intact while allowing the food coloring to pass through onto the paper towel.

ILLUSTRATION A

cell wall

cell membrane

centrosome

Golgi body

endoplasmic reticulum with ribosomes

endoplasmic reticulum without ribosomes

mitochondrion

nucleus

microvilli

lysosome

chloroplast

plastid

peroxisome

vacuole

cilia

Materials

paper cups, bowls, liquid dish soap, glycerol, eyedroppers, food coloring

LS6 JOURNAL SHEET #1

THE LIVING CELL: PART I

ANIMAL CELL   PLANT CELL

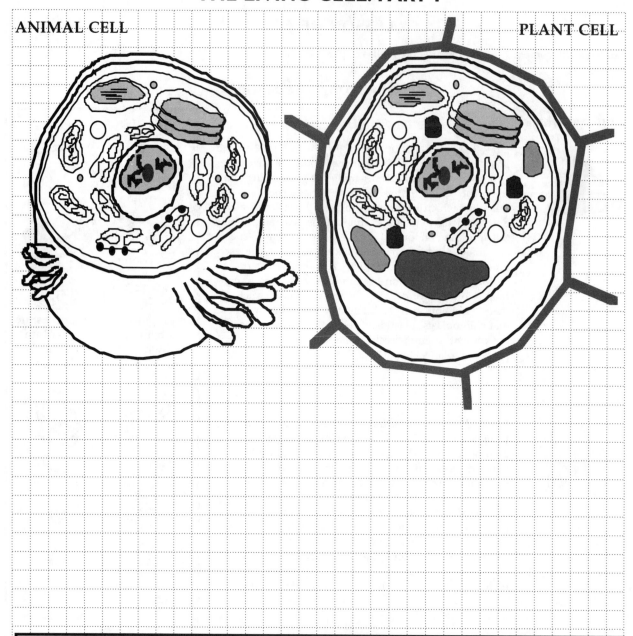

FIGURE A

Directions: (1) Pour about 2 centimeters of liquid dish soap into a small bowl. (2) Add several milliliters of glycerol to the bowl and stir. (3) Cut the top centimeter off the rim of a paper cup to form a ring as shown. (4) Place the ring into the bowl and soak it with soap.

bowl of dish soap   top of cup with soap film

(5) Gently lift the rim out of the soap solution with a soap bubble attached across the ring and place it on a paper towel. (6) Use an eyedropper to gently dip a drop of food coloring onto the soap film. If the soap film bursts, repeat steps #4 through #6. (7) Record your observations. Why do you think a similar kind of "fatty substance" works well as the substance that comprises cell membranes?

THE LIVING CELL: PART I

Work Date: ____/____/____

LESSON OBJECTIVE

Students will begin gathering information about the structure and function of cell organelles.

Classroom Activities

On Your Mark!

Prepare for this lesson by compiling 5–10 biology texts from the school or local library that contain schematic drawings and electron microscopic pictures of cell organelles.

Review the results of the activity performed in Figure A in Lesson #1. Define the term **osmosis** as the movement of water through a semipermeable membrane that separates solutions of different concentrations. Explain that the cell membranes of cells are "semipermeable." That is, the membrane permits the flow of some molecules across it—namely water—and not others.

Get Set!

If thin cellophane or goldbeater's membrane is available through a local laboratory supply house, perform the following demonstration: (1) Hold your finger over the thin opening of a small funnel or thistle tube and fill the funnel halfway with molasses or corn syrup. (2) Cover the funnel or thistle bulb with thin cellophane or goldbeater's membrane and secure the membrane with a rubber band. (3) Invert the funnel and immerse it in water, securing it with a clamp as shown in Illustration B. The level of water in the funnel tube will rise as water passes through the membrane into the funnel. Explain that specialized proteins attached to the cell membrane (e.g., usually present on microvilli) also help to "pull" molecules into the cell by a process called **active transport**.

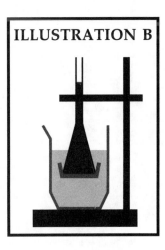

ILLUSTRATION B

Go!

Distribute the references obtained from the school/local library and give students the rest of the session to begin gathering information about the structure and function of cell organelles. Encourgage them to sketch some of the electron microscope drawings they find and inform them that they will be constructing a three-dimensional model of a cell in the next unit: *The Living Cell: Part II.*

Materials

library references, ringstand and clamp, large beaker, funnel or thistle tube, thin cellophane or goldbeater's membrane, water, molasses or corn syrup

LS6 JOURNAL SHEET #2

THE LIVING CELL: PART I

Use this Journal Sheet to sketch and record information about the organelles you find described in the references provided by your instructor. In the next unit—THE LIVING CELL: PART II—you and your groupmates will work together to construct a three-dimensional model of a plant or animal cell.

THE LIVING CELL: PART I

Work Date: ____/____/____

LESSON OBJECTIVE

Students will continue gathering information about the structure and function of cell organelles.

Classroom Activities

On Your Mark!

Prepare for this lesson by compiling 5–10 biology texts from the school or local library that contain schematic drawings and electron microscopic pictures of cell organelles.

Use the following example to give students a perspective on the relative size of an average animal or plant cell as compared to other objects with which they are familiar. Remind them that a chloroplast is a tiny cell organelle present in plant cells. Hold up a meter stick and draw two circles—one tiny circle at 1 millimeter in diameter and the second 100 millimeters (e.g., 10 centimeters) in diameter. The two circles represent the chloroplast and plant cell to scale, respectively. If a chloroplast were 1 millimeter in diameter, then the whole plant cell would be about 10 centimeters in diameter. Using this same scale, a house fly would be 10 meters long and a human being would be more than 1 kilometer tall.

Get Set!

Give students a moment to set up the osmosis experiment described in Figure C on Journal Sheet #3 before allowing them to continue with their organelle research.

Go!

Distribute the references obtained from the school/local library and give students the rest of the session to continue gathering information about the structure and function of cell organelles. Encourage them again to sketch some of the electron microscope drawings they find and remind them that they will be constructing a three-dimensional model of a cell in the next unit: *The Living Cell: Part II.*

Materials

library references, metric ruler, raisins, test tubes, test tube stoppers (or corks), water

Name: ______________________________ Period: ________ Date: ___/___/___

LS6 Journal Sheet #3

THE LIVING CELL: PART I

FIGURE C

Directions: (1) Place several dried raisins into a test tube. (2) Fill the test tube with water and cap it with a stopper or cork. (3) Set the tube in a test tube rack or other secure place overnight. (4) Record your observations the following day. (5) Cut into the raisin to see what has happened on the inside. Is it hollow? Explain your observation.

THE LIVING CELL: PART I

Work Date: ____/____/____

LESSON OBJECTIVE

Students will develop a cooperative plan for constructing a three-dimensional model of a plant or animal cell.

Classroom Activities

On Your Mark!

Give students sufficient time to record their observations of the raisins placed in water in Lesson #3. They will note that the raisins are swollen, having absorbed water by **osmosis**. After cutting into the raisins, they will note that the water caused the entire "fabric" of each raisin to swell. Each plant cell absorbed water so the fruit is now a hollow ball filled with water.

Get Set!

Explain that the construction of their three-dimensional cell will require teamwork. Everyone in the groups needs to take responsibility for the common household materials they will bring to class to help construct the individual organelles that will make up their plant or animal cell. Point out that every student must record on Journal Sheet #4 a complete list of the activities that will be performed by each of the other members of their group. This will insure that they will be able to complete the project in the event that a member of the group becomes ill or is otherwise incapable of completing the assignment.

Go!

Circulate around the classroom to make sure that each student is accepting a reasonable amount of responsibility and that each student has been assigned a fair share of the work. Let students use their imagination in deciding on the materials they will use to complete the project, but dissuade them from purchasing expensive "props" to do the job (e.g., chloroplasts can be represented by green jelly beans).

Materials

scissors or scalpels to cut the raisins

LS6 JOURNAL SHEET #4

THE LIVING CELL: PART I

Use this Journal Sheet to record the specific, agreed upon responsibilities assigned to every member of your group. In the next unit—THE LIVING CELL: PART II—you and your groupmates will work together to construct a three-dimensional model of a plant or animal cell. It is important that every member of your group understands and makes a sincere effort to carry out his or her assignment.

LS6 REVIEW QUIZ

Directions: Keep your eyes on your own work.
Read all directions and questions carefully.
THINK BEFORE YOU ANSWER!
Watch your spelling, be neat, and do the best you can.

CLASSWORK   (~40): _____
HOMEWORK   (~20): _____
CURRENT EVENT   (~10): _____
TEST   (~30): _____

TOTAL   (~100): _____
(A ≥ 90, B ≥ 80, C ≥ 70, D ≥ 60, F < 60)

LETTER GRADE: _____

TEACHER'S COMMENTS: _____
_____

THE LIVING CELL: PART I

TRUE–FALSE FILL-IN: If the statement is true, write the word TRUE. If the statement is false, change the underlined word to make the statement true. *10 points*

_____ 1. <u>Most</u> living things are composed of cells.

_____ 2. The cell nucleus and membrane of a properly stained cheek cell <u>can</u> be seen with a light microscope under low power.

_____ 3. A(n) <u>animal</u> cell is surrounded by a cell wall.

_____ 4. The cell is filled with a jellylike substance called <u>plasma</u>.

_____ 5. The details of most cell organelles <u>cannot</u> be seen with the aid of an electron microscope.

ESSAY: Write a few sentences that explain the main differences between a plant cell and an animal cell. *5 points*

_____

_____

_____

_____

_____

_____

_____

_____

DIAGRAM: Put the letter touching the organelle in the diagram next to its name. If the named organelle is not present, then write "NP" in the blank. *15 points*

_____ 6. cell membrane

_____ 7. cell wall

_____ 8. centrosome

_____ 9. chloroplast

_____ 10. cilia

_____ 11. cytoplasm

_____ 12. endoplasmic reticulum

_____ 13. Golgi body

_____ 14. lysosome

_____ 15. microvilli

_____ 16. mitochondrion

_____ 17. nucleus

_____ 18. peroxisome

_____ 19. plastid

_____ 20. ribosome

_____   _____   ___/___/___
Student's Signature   Parent's Signature   Date

THE LIVING CELL: PART II

TEACHER'S CLASSWORK AGENDA AND CONTENT NOTES

Classwork Agenda for the Week

1. Students will examine the stages of cell division.
2. Students will begin cooperative construction of a three-dimensional model of a plant or animal cell.
3. Students will complete cooperative construction of a three-dimensional model of a plant or animal cell.
4. Students will evaluate the three-dimensional cell models of their classmates.

Content Notes for Lecture and Discussion

A clear understanding of how cells divide to reproduce was not possible until the development of adequate staining techniques and the construction of microscopes able to magnify and resolve images on the order of several thousand times. It was not until the 1860s that biologists could clearly see cells dividing to form "daughter cells" having first accomplished a division of the "parent cells" nuclear material. The German biologist **Walter Flemming** (b. 1843; d. 1905) is best recognized for his accomplishments in this line of study. Flemming is credited for having coined the term "mitosis" and for describing the duplication of the easily stained "threadlike" nuclear structures called **chromosomes** (e.g., meaning "colored bodies"). By 1879, Flemming had accurately described several stages of **mitosis** although the terminology he used has since been changed. Today, cell division is preceded by a period of **interphase** during which chromosomes duplicate. The four phases of mitosis which follow—**prophase**, **metaphase**, **anaphase**, and **telophase**—are marked by a series of events which carry the cell to its final division into two independent cells during **cytokinesis** (e.g., meaning "cells in motion"). Flemming also reported that reproductive cells, gametes like sperm and eggs, divided without reproducing their chromosomes first: a process which he called **meiosis**. This observation was later explained by the German botanist **Eduard Adolf Strasburger** (b. 1844; d. 1912). Strasburger clarified the role of chromosomes in heredity by concluding that fertilization required the joining of "haploid" cells: cells having a single set of chromosomes instead of the usual duplicate set present in diploid cells. Only the joining of **haploid cells** resulted in the formation of **diploid cells** capable of developing into a new organism with the same characteristics as its parent. Strasburger is also credited for having coined the terms "nucleoplasm" (e.g., the region inside the cell nucleus), "cytoplasm" (e.g., the region outside the cell nucleus), and "chloroplast" (e.g., the structure in which photosynthesis takes place).

In Lesson #1, students will examine the stages of cell division.

In Lesson #2, students will begin cooperative construction of a three-dimensional model of a plant or animal cell.

In Lesson #3, students will continue cooperative construction of a three-dimensional model of a plant or animal cell.

In Lesson #4, students will evaluate the three-dimensional cell models of their classmates.

LS7 Content Notes (cont'd)

ANSWERS TO THE HOMEWORK PROBLEMS

Students should provide an accurate accounting of their contributions to the group project of constructing a three-dimensional plant or animal cell. Give their groupmates an opportunity to verify their participation.

ANSWERS TO THE END-OF-THE-WEEK REVIEW QUIZ

1. interphase
2. true
3. DNA
4. chromosomes/DNA
5. true

6. true
7. true
8. anaphase
9. telophase
10. true

Students should mention that meiosis involves the production of reproductive cells by parent cells that do not duplicate their chromosomes before they divide. The process results in haploid cells. Prior to mitosis, however, chromosomes duplicate, then separate, so that daughter cells will be diploid, containing the same number of chromosomes as the parent cell.

(A) telophase—a cleavage furrow "pinches in" the cell membrane to complete cell division resulting in two daughter cells able to complete another cell cycle
(B) interphase—the cell grows and duplicates its chromosomes
(C) prophase—centrioles move to opposite sides of the cell and throw out spindle fibers that attach to chromosomes
(D) metaphase—chromosome pairs line up across the cell's midline and are pulled apart by spindle fibers
(E) anaphase—chromosomes complete their journey to opposite poles of the cell

LS7 FACT SHEET

THE LIVING CELL: PART II

CLASSWORK AGENDA FOR THE WEEK

(1) Examine the stages of cell division.
(2) Begin cooperative construction of a three-dimensional model of a plant or animal cell.
(3) Complete cooperative construction of a three-dimensional model of a plant or animal cell.
(4) Evaluate the three dimensional cell models of their classmates.

Cells grow in size during a period called **interphase**, then divide to reproduce. The process of cell division is called **mitosis**. Although mitosis is a continuous process, biologists divide the event into four main phases: *prophase, metaphase, anaphase,* and *telophase.*

Interphase is the time between cell divisions when a "parent cell" performs its normal range of activities. Also during interphase, **chromosomes** in the nucleus are duplicated. This duplication process insures that the next generation of cells—called "daughter cells"—will contain the correct kind and number of genes as the parent cell. Chromosomes are made of large **deoxyribonucleic acid** (e.g., **DNA**) molecules that carry the "blueprint" or "hereditary instructions" of the cell.

When mitosis begins at **early prophase** tiny organelles called **centrioles** move to opposite sides of the cell. By **late prophase** the centrioles have thrown out long **spindle fibers** that attach like long ropes to matching pairs of chromosomes.

At the start of **metaphase**, the chromosome pairs have lined up across the midline of the cell and the spindle fibers begin to pull the chromosome pairs apart toward opposite sides of the cell.

As the cell works through **anaphase**, the chromosomes become completely separated from one another and take up positions at opposite poles of the cell.

At the start of **telophase**, a **cleavage furrow** begins to form at the cell's "equator" like a string tightening around the middle of a balloon. The cleavage furrow is a "pinching in" of the cell membrane that will eventually "cut" the cell in half. In late telophase, the cleavage furrow contracts toward the center of the cell and **cytokinesis** (e.g., meaning "cells in motion") creates two new, independent cells.

Different kinds of cells divide at different rates. Skin cells, for example, can divide rapidly following an injury such as a cut or scrape. Thousands of new skin cells take the place of the dead ones within a matter of hours or days. Nerve cells may not duplicate at all.

Another kind of cell division is called **meiosis**. Meiosis is similar to mitosis in that both processes result in the production of new cells. However, meiosis only occurs in the **reproductive organs** of a plant or animal. The reproduction of offspring in both plants and animals involves the joining of a "male reproductive cell" and a "female reproductive cell." The process involved is called **pollination** in plants and **fertilization** in animals. To insure that an offspring will have the same number of chromosomes as its parent, reproductive cells can only have half as many chromosomes. Meiosis insures that the specialized cells of reproductive organs have the correct number of chromosomes.

Homework Directions

List and complete the activities assigned to you by your groupmates to make sure that you are pre-pared to assist in class in the construction of a three-dimensional model of a plant or animal cell.

Assignment due: _____

_____   _____   ___/___/___
Student's Signature   Parent's Signature   Date

THE LIVING CELL: PART II

Work Date: ____/____/____

LESSON OBJECTIVE

Students will examine the stages of cell division.

Classroom Activities

On Your Mark!

Draw the illustration appearing on Journal Sheet #1 or make a transparency of the journal sheet to be used on an overhead projector. Have students take notes on Journal Sheet #1 as you describe the events taking place during the process called **mitosis** (e.g., cell division). Emphasize the fact that cells live and reproduce in a continual cycle, the process of mitosis resulting in the production of **daughter cells** having the same genetic characteristics (e.g., and therefore structural and functional characteristics) as the **parent cell**.

Get Set!

Use the information in the Teacher's Classwork Agenda and Content Notes to give students a brief introduction to the scientist who elucidated the cell cycle: German biologist **Walter Flemming** (b. 1843; d. 1905).

During **interphase** the **chromosomes** carrying hereditary information of the **parent cell** are duplicated within the confines of the **nuclear membrane**. In **prophase**, the nuclear membrane begins to dissolve and the tiny cylindrical-shaped **centrioles**—confined during interphase in a structure called a **centrosome**—spread apart and throw out **spindle fibers** that attach to chromosomes. By the end of **metaphase**, the chromosomes are aligned at the midline of the cell. During **anaphase**, the chromosomes split apart and are dragged to opposite poles of the cell. A **cleavage furrow** begins to form around the equator of the cell at the start of **telophase** and begins to pinch the cell in half. The final division and separation into two completely independent **daughter cells** is called **cytokinesis** (e.g., meaning "cells in motion"). Each daughter cell continues the cycle on its own.

Go!

Have students refer to Journal Sheet #4 from Lesson #4, unit LS6: *The Living Cell: Part I.* Have them review their individual responsibilities, reminding them that the construction of their three-dimensional cell will require teamwork and that everyone in the groups needs to take responsibility for the common household materials they will bring to class to help construct the individual organelles that will make up their plant or animal cell. Circulate around the room to make sure that each student clearly understands their personal role in the project and will be ready to start construction in Lesson #2.

Materials

Journal Sheet #1

LS7 Journal Sheet #1

THE LIVING CELL: PART II

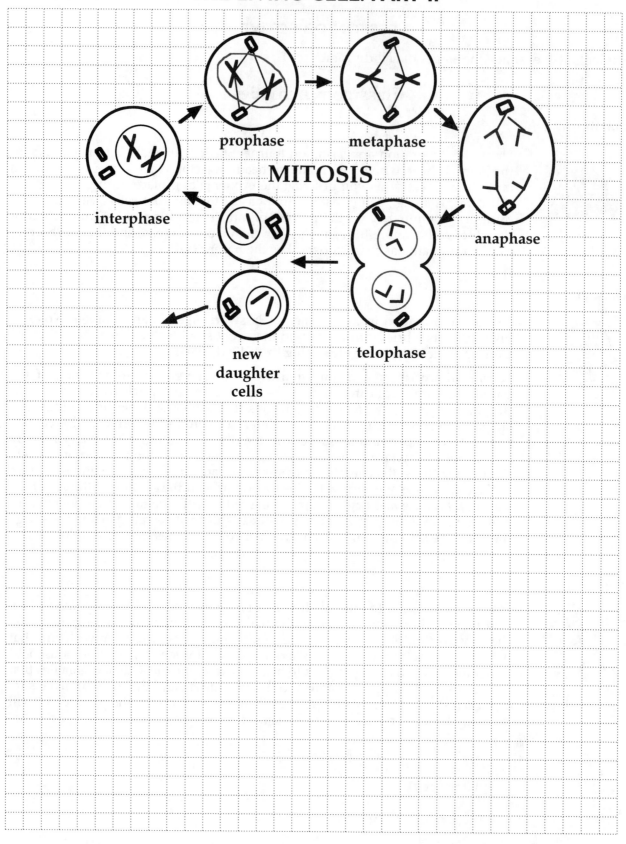

THE LIVING CELL: PART II

Work Date: ____/____/____

LESSON OBJECTIVE

Students will begin cooperative construction of a three-dimensional model of a plant or animal cell.

Classroom Activities

On Your Mark!

Set out standard classroom supplies that will assist students in the construction of their three-dimensional cell.

Get Set!

Remind students of the need for teamwork. Explain that they will have two complete periods to finish the project and to use Journal Sheet #2 to record any "last minute" items or activities they need to perform for homework to make sure that their project will be completed in class tomorrow.

Go!

Give students the remainder of the period to work on the project. Circulate around the room to insure that the effort is cooperative. Give them detailed instructions on where and how to store their materials so that as few materials as possible need leave the classroom.

Materials

standard project supplies (e.g., construction paper, butcher paper, scissors, glue, tape, etc.)

LS7 JOURNAL SHEET #2

THE LIVING CELL: PART II

Use this Journal Sheet to record any "last minute" supplies or activities that you need to perform for homework to insure that your group project will be completed by the end of the class period tomorrow.

THE LIVING CELL: PART II

Work Date: ____/____/____

LESSON OBJECTIVE

Students will complete cooperative construction of a three-dimensional model of a plant or animal cell.

Classroom Activities

On Your Mark!

Set out standard classroom supplies that will assist students in the construction of their three-dimensional cell. Have groups retrieve the materials they stored at the end of the last session.

Get Set!

Remind students of the need for teamwork. Explain that they must finish the project by the end of the period. Tell them to use Journal Sheet #3 to plan a brief oral presentation of their project in Lesson #4. Each student should be assigned a task to be performed during the presentation and description of their work.

Go!

Give students the remainder of the period to complete the project. Circulate around the the room to insure that the effort is cooperative and that each student has been given a fair share of the activities to be performed during the presentation that will be given in Lesson #4. Give them detailed instructions on where and how to store their finished project in preparation for their group presentation.

Materials

standard project supplies (e.g., construction paper, butcher paper, scissors, glue, tape, etc.)

LS7 JOURNAL SHEET #3

THE LIVING CELL: PART II

Use this Journal Sheet to plan a brief oral presentation that your group will give to the class in Lesson #4. Be sure that each member of your group knows what they will say and when they will say it. Write a short script if necessary so that your presentation goes smoothly.

THE LIVING CELL: PART II

Work Date: ____/____/____

LESSON OBJECTIVE

Students will evaluate the three-dimensional cell models of their classmates.

Classroom Activities

On Your Mark!

Display the models around the classroom. Give students a moment to circulate around the classroom to get a close look at the individual projects of other groups. Tell them to **look but not to touch!**

Get Set!

Instruct students to use Journal Sheet #4 to take notes on how they might have used some of the techniques or supplies employed by their classmates in order to make their model even more impressive.

Go!

Divide the class period so that each group has the same amount of time to give a thorough description of their plant or animal cell.

Materials

class projects

LS7 JOURNAL SHEET #4

THE LIVING CELL: PART II

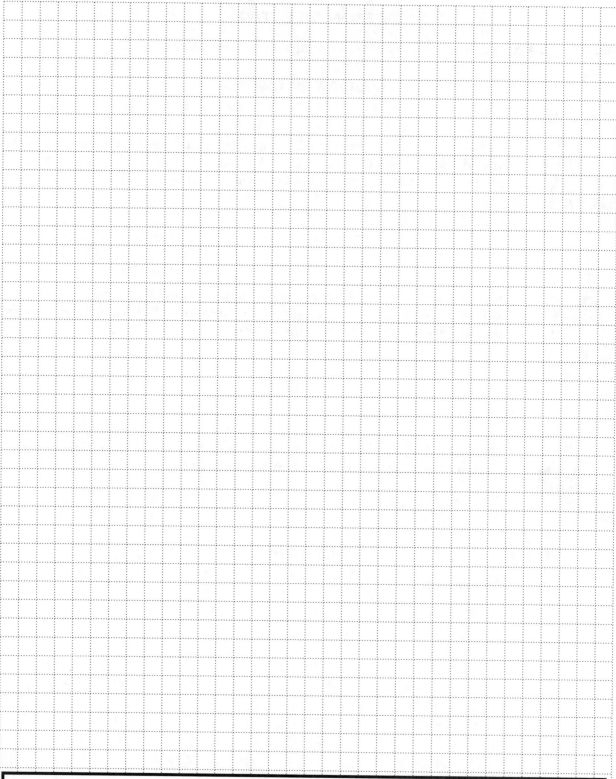

As you listen to the presentations of your classmates, use this Journal Sheet to record the specific supplies or techniques you could have used to make your project even more impressive.

LS7 REVIEW QUIZ

Directions: Keep your eyes on your own work.
Read all directions and questions carefully.
THINK BEFORE YOU ANSWER!
Watch your spelling, be neat, and do the best you can.

CLASSWORK   (~40): _____
HOMEWORK   (~20): _____
CURRENT EVENT   (~10): _____
TEST   (~30): _____

TOTAL   (~100): _____
(A ≥ 90, B ≥ 80, C ≥ 70, D ≥ 60, F < 60)

LETTER GRADE: _____

TEACHER'S COMMENTS: _____

_____

THE LIVING CELL: PART II

TRUE–FALSE FILL-IN: If the statement is true, write the word TRUE. If the statement is false, change the underlined word to make the statement true. *10 points*

_____   1. Cells grow in size during a period called <u>prophase</u>.

_____   2. Chromosomes in the nucleus are duplicated during <u>interphase</u>.

_____   3. Chromosomes are made of a chemical substance whose name can be abbreviated with the letters <u>ATP</u>.

_____   4. Hereditary instructions are carried on <u>ribosomes</u>.

_____   5. In early <u>prophase</u>, centrioles move to the opposite sides of a cell.

_____   6. In late <u>prophase</u>, centrioles throw out spindle fibers that attach to chromosomes.

_____   7. Chromosome pairs line up along the center plane of the cell during <u>metaphase</u>.

_____   8. Chromosomes separate completely and move to opposite poles of the cell during <u>telophase</u>.

_____   9. A cleavage furrow starts to "pinch in" the cell membrane during <u>anaphase</u>.

_____   10. Two completely independent cells are created during <u>cytokinesis</u>.

ESSAY: Write a few sentences that explain the main difference between mitosis and meiosis. *5 points*

_____

_____

_____

DIAGRAM: In the blanks labelled A, B, C, D, and E name the phase of cell division and write a sentence to describe what is happening in the cell during that phase. *15 points*

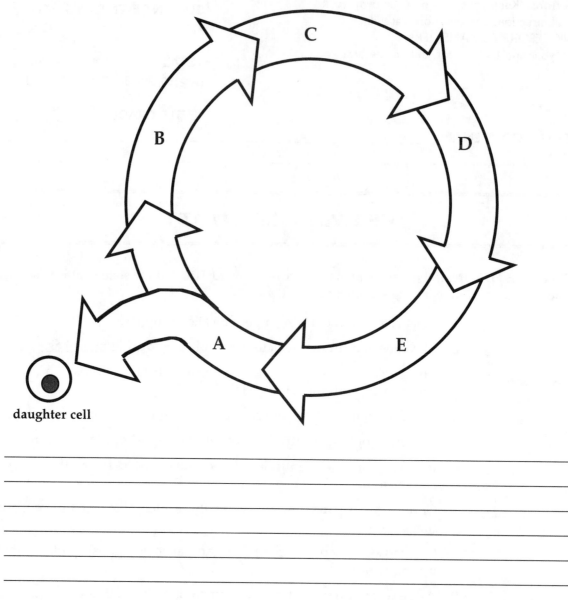

daughter cell

(A) _____

_____

(B) _____

_____

(C) _____

_____

(D) _____

_____

(E) _____

_____

_____   _____   ____/____/____
Student's Signature   Parent's Signature   Date

HEREDITY

TEACHER'S CLASSWORK AGENDA AND CONTENT NOTES

Classwork Agenda for the Week

1. Students will identify common and diverse human traits.
2. Students will explain how Gregor Mendel discovered the concept of the "gene."
3. Students will use a Punnet Square to predict the traits of offspring.
4. Students will show why "sex-linked" genetic diseases are more common in males.

Content Notes for Lecture and Discussion

Ancient people were aware that plants were generated from seeds. The method of reproduction employed by animals was believed to involve the "mingling" of male (e.g., seminal) and female (e.g., menstrual) fluids; but the actual reproductive mechanism used by either plants or animals remained unclear until the refinement of tissue staining and microscopic observation. With the cell theory proposed in 1839 by German biologists **Theodor Schwann** (b. 1810; d. 1882) and **Matthias Jakob Schleiden** (b. 1804; d. 1881), 19th century microscopists were able to clarify the involvement of the cell nucleus in the process of both plant and animal sexual reproduction.

The study of hybridization in plants was a major curiosity of 18th century biologists including **Carolus Linnaeus** (b. 1707; d. 1778) who created the binomial system of classification. Linnaeus believed that only a few members of every genus had been "divinely created" and that the rest were generated by the "crossing" of slightly different strains. According to Linnaeus, hybridization lay at the roots of variation. **Hybridization** experiments continued with fervor until the middle of the 19th century when they were largely abandoned following **Charles Darwin**'s (b. 1809; d. 1882) proposal that natural selection was the primary mechanism responsible for the diversity of species. However, Darwin could not account for the mechanism that gave rise to new variations. Still, the practical uses of hybridization continue to benefit horticulturists and agriculturists even to this day. The Austrian monk **Gregor Mendel** (b. 1822; d. 1884) was responsible for establishing hybridization as a method for determining the mechanisms of heredity rather than as the process underlying organic variation.

In 1865, Mendel published a report entitled *Experiments in Plant Hybridization* in which he established the basic laws of inheritance. The key point of the work was the assertion that reproductive cells carried "factors" that embodied the organic characters of living organisms (e.g., genes). Mendel reported that some strains of common garden pea plants bred true to their characteristics. That is, their offspring exhibited the same characteristics as the parent plant. Mendel noted that other strains, however, gave rise to offspring with variations that were a departure from the parents' traits, although they could be found elsewhere in members of related populations. By careful mathematical analysis of the plant populations he hybridized, Mendel was able to determine the statistical probablility of producing particular traits in any population of offspring by careful analysis of the traits of each parent. He had, in effect, discovered the laws that governed the passing of traits from one generation to the next: the laws of heredity.

Mendel's work was lost until 1900 when it was rediscovered by Dutch botanist **Hugo Marie de Vries** (b. 1848; d. 1935). De Vries also introduced the notion of "mutation" as the mechanism responsible for the origination of entirely new traits. De Vries noted that offspring of the evening primrose exhibited traits that were a marked departure from the traits of their purebred parents; and in his 1901 publication, *The Mutation Theory*, he argued that evolution was due to the process of natural selection acting on these new variations. The English geneticist **William Bateson**

(b. 1861; d. 1926) further popularized Mendel's ideas and was the first to publicly use the term "genetics" to describe the field relating to the heredity and variation of organic traits. It was Bateson who used Mendel's findings to begin the elucidation of the physiology of descent.

In Lesson #1, students will identify common and diverse human traits.

In Lesson #2, students will explain how Gregor Mendel discovered the concept of the "gene."

In Lesson #3, students will use a Punnett Square to predict the traits of offspring.

In Lesson #4, students will show why "sex-linked" genetic diseases are more common in males.

ANSWERS TO THE HOMEWORK PROBLEMS

(1) Populations of "purebred" white mice can be obtained by inbreeding white mice generation after generation after generation.

(2) The genotypes of the parents are as follows: parent #1 is hybrid tall (Tt) and parent #2 is purebred short (tt). So, 50% of parent #1's genes are "tall" genes and 50% are "short" genes. 100% of parent #2's genes are "short" genes. The Punnett Square appears as shown to illustrate the statistical results of a cross between these two parents. 50% of the offspring will be hybrid tall and 50% will be purebred short. Among the first generation of 100 offspring there should be 50 tall plants and 50 short plants.

parent #1

	T	t
t	Tt	tt
t	Tt	tt

parent #2

ANSWERS TO THE END-OF-THE-WEEK REVIEW QUIZ

1. true	6. Mendel	11. hybrid
2. true	7. true	12. purebred
3. trait	8. plants	13. true
4. heredity	9. true	14. true
5. true	10. true	15. true

PROBLEM

male genotype–GGFf; female genotype–ggff

16. The percentage of yellow floozers is zero since the male parent is purebred for a dominant "green" gene.

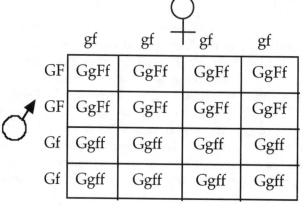

	gf	gf	gf	gf
GF	GgFf	GgFf	GgFf	GgFf
GF	GgFf	GgFf	GgFf	GgFf
Gf	Ggff	Ggff	Ggff	Ggff
Gf	Ggff	Ggff	Ggff	Ggff

LS8 FACT SHEET

HEREDITY

CLASSWORK AGENDA FOR THE WEEK

(1) Identify common and diverse human traits.
(2) Explain how Gregor Mendel discovered the concept of the "gene."
(3) Use a Punnett Square to predict the traits of offspring.
(4) Show why "sex-linked" genetic diseases are more common in males.

If your cat gave birth you would expect it to have kittens. You expect chicks to hatch from chicken eggs and apple trees to grow from apple seeds. You do not expect a rhinoceros to give birth to an ostrich. The **offspring**, or young, of a living thing is expected to resemble its parents. Of course, caterpillars do not resemble their parents—which are moths or butterflies—and tadpoles do not resemble their parents—which are frogs. But eventually these creatures grow to look like their adult parents. **Organisms** that breed and reproduce offspring with "traits" like the parent belong to the same **species**.

A **trait** is any characteristic of an organism that makes it different from other organisms, such as the number of arms or legs an organism has, its skin color, hair color, or its ability to fly. All members of a species have the same **species traits**. Human beings have the largest brains compared to their body size of all members of the mammalian class. A comparatively large brain is a species trait of all human beings. **Species traits** are those traits common to every member of a species. However, individuals within a species can also have **individual traits**. Individual traits result in variation between individuals within a single species.

Heredity refers to the passing of traits from parents to offspring. The study of heredity is called **genetics**. The "father of genetics" was an Austrian monk named **Gregor Mendel** (b. 1822; d. 1884). Mendel discovered the concept of the "gene." A **gene** is a unit of inherited material. For example, eye color is an inherited trait represented by a gene. But eyes can be different colors such as blue, brown, or hazel. These individual traits for eye color are called **alleles**. Today, biologists know that genes and their many alleles are **biochemical** units stored in living cells. The biochemical units of heredity are found on **chromosomes**.

Mendel's research was done mainly on common garden pea plants. He found that certain traits were always passed from parents to their offspring while other traits "skipped" a generation before showing up in a descendant. Traits that are always passed from one generation to the next are called **dominant traits**. Traits that skip generations are called **recessive traits**. An organism that carries both dominant and recessive traits is called a **hybrid**. An organism that carries only dominant or recessive traits for a particular characteristic is **purebred** for that particular trait. The combination of genes present in the cells of an organism is called the organism's **genotype**. The traits "expressed" by genes so that they are visible to anyone who looks at the organism are the organism's **phenotype**.

Mendel discovered three laws known today as **Mendel's Laws**. Mendel's Laws laid the foundation for modern genetics.

MENDEL'S LAWS

(1) Inherited traits can be either dominant or recessive.
(2) Many traits are inherited in pairs.
(3) Hybrids do not breed true.

Homework Directions

Read each question carefully and write a brief answer for each.

    (1) In mice, black hair is dominant over white hair. Biologists prefer to use white mice for their experiments. How can the suppliers of mice be sure to get only white mice from their breeding pairs?

    (2) In peas, tallness (T) is dominant over shortness (t). If one parent is hybrid tall and the other is purebred short, predict the expected genotypes and phenotypes in the first generation of 100 plants. Find your answer using a Punnett Square.

Assignment due: _____

_____   _____   ____/____/____
Student's Signature   Parent's Signature   Date

HEREDITY

Work Date: ____/____/____

LESSON OBJECTIVE

Students will identify common and diverse human traits.

Classroom Activities

On Your Mark!

Begin by asking students to look around the room and prepare a list of common and diverse human traits apparent among their friends in the classroom. Have them spend several minutes listing the "like" traits and "unlike" traits of their classmates (e.g., everyone has hair—a like or common trait; some people have brown hair, others black hair, etc.— an unlike or diverse trait). Explain that traits common to all members of a species are called **species traits**. Traits that distinguish one individual from another within a species are called **individual traits**. A **trait** is any characteristic of an organism that makes it different from other individuals of the same or different species.

Get Set!

Refer students to the activity described in Figure A on Journal Sheet #1. In addition to the two individual traits shown for each species trait displayed, have students add three more species traits each having two individual traits.

Go!

Give students ample time to complete the activity described in Figure A on Journal Sheet #1. When students have completed their drawings have them compare their results to those of their classmates. Have students note the incredible variety apparent between individuals resulting from the possible multiple combinations using only a small selection of traits (e.g., 6 common species traits each having two individual traits). Explain that every human being carries more than 100,000 genes and that there are multiple forms—called alleles—for each gene. Define an **allele** as any one of a number of "forms" of a particular gene (e.g., brown and blue are two of more than eight alleles for eye color).

Materials

colored pens/pencils, coins

LS8 Journal Sheet #1

HEREDITY

FIGURE A

Directions: (1) Add three additional species traits each having two individual traits to the "human face traits" shown. (2) Flip a coin to determine which individual traits your human face will have. Then draw the face according to those specifications.

BROWLINE

| widow's peak | smooth |

CHIN

| chin cleft | no cleft |

EARLOBES

| attached | free |

HEREDITY

Work Date: ____/____/____

LESSON OBJECTIVE

Students will explain how Gregor Mendel discovered the concept of the "gene."

Classroom Activities

On Your Mark!

Begin with an introduction to the study of heredity using the information in the Teacher's Classwork Agenda and Content Notes and the student Fact Sheet. Define the term **heredity** as the passing of traits from one generation to the next. Define **genetics** as the study of how biological traits are passed from parent to offspring.

Get Set!

Explain the diagram entitled "Mendel's Pea Plants" on Journal Sheet #2, making sure that students take notes to make sense of the diagram. Explain how **Gregor Mendel** (b. 1822; d. 1884) started with pure strains of pea plants. Each **purebred** strain was obtained by "inbreeding" parents with identical characteristics. Define a **purebred** strain as organisms having identical alleles for multiple genetic traits. Define **inbreeding** as the mating of closely related (e.g., very similar) individuals within a species. Upon mating plants with different alleles (e.g., tall or short) for a particular trait (e.g., plant height) Mendel found that all individuals of the first generation (F-1) were tall. In the second generation (F-2), however, 25% of the offspring were short. Ask students to explain how the gene for "short" wound up in the "grandchilden" of the original plants. Answer: The gene for "short" must have been "carried but hidden" in the individuals of F-1 and not expressed as a visible trait. An organism that carries different types of alleles for a given trait is a **hybrid**. Alleles that are always expressed are called **dominant** alleles. Alleles that are hidden and, therefore, can skip generations are called **recessive** alleles. Some alleles can also be expressed together. Such alleles are said to be **codominant alleles**. Hazel eyes is an example of "codominance", since more than one eye color is expressed. Define **genotype** as the genetic combination of alleles present in an organism, including those alleles that may or may not be expressed. Define **phenotype** as the traits visibly apparent in an organism.

Review briefly how **mitosis** allows cells to reproduce. Point out that the cells of sexual organs undergo a process called **meiosis** in which the chromosomes are not duplicated before division. Sex cells called **gametes** (e.g., sperm and eggs in animals; pollen and ovules in plants) have only half of each parent's genes. During **fertilization** (e.g., in animals) or **pollination** (e.g., in plants) the alleles for each particular trait are matched in the offspring. However, only the dominant alleles are expressed in the phenotype of the organism. Explain how a Punnett Square can be used to display "gametes" that combine to form new offspring.

Go!

Give students ample time to complete the activity described in Figure B on Journal Sheet #2. The offspring of the first and third plants of the second generation would be 50% purebred tall and 50% hybrid tall. The offspring of the second and fourth plants of the second generation would be 50% hybrid tall and 50% purebred short.

Materials

Journal Sheet #2

LS8 JOURNAL SHEET #2

HEREDITY

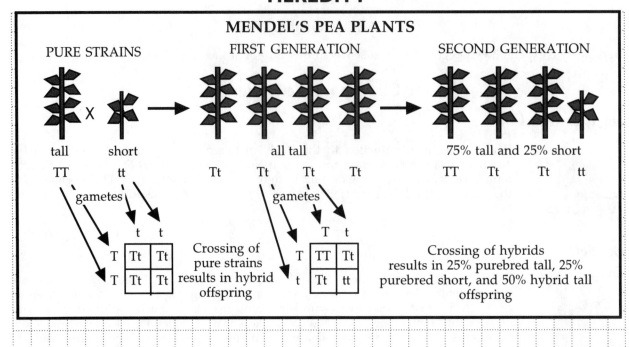

MENDEL'S PEA PLANTS

FIGURE B

<u>Directions</u>: (1) Use a PUNNETT SQUARE to show the genotypes and phenotypes of possible offspring that would result from a crossing of the first and third offspring of the second generation. (2) Use a PUNNETT SQUARE to show the genotypes and phenotypes of possible offspring that would result from a crossing of the second and fourth offspring of the second generation.

HEREDITY

Work Date: _____/_____/_____

LESSON OBJECTIVE

Students will use a Punnett Square to predict the traits of offspring.

Classroom Activities

On Your Mark!

Review the Punnett Squares drawn to predict the possible percentages of offspring generated in Lesson #2. Review the difference between genotype and phenotype.

Get Set!

Refer students to the large Punnett Square on Journal Sheet #3. Assist them in separating the genotypes of both imaginary parents described in Figure C into the eight possible gametes created during meiosis in the sexual organs of either creature. The male's possible gametes will have the following genotypes: EHF, EHF, EHf, EHf, EhF, EhF, Ehf, Ehf. The female's gametes will have the following genotypes: eHf, eHf, eHf, eHf, ehf, ehf, ehf, ehf.

Go!

Give students ample time to complete the activity described in Figure C on Journal Sheet #3. Circulate around the room to make sure that students are combining the male and female genotypes to end up with 6 letters (e.g., the alleles) in each box. A mating of these two creatures will result in 100% of the offspring being hybrid one-eyed like Dad. 25% will be purebred one-horned, 50% hybrid one-horned, 25% purebred two-horned, making 75% of the children one-horned in appearance and 25% two-horned in appearance although neither parent was two-horned. 50% will be hybrid flyers, and 50% purebred walkers like their mother.

Materials

Journal Sheet #3

LS8 JOURNAL SHEET #3

HEREDITY

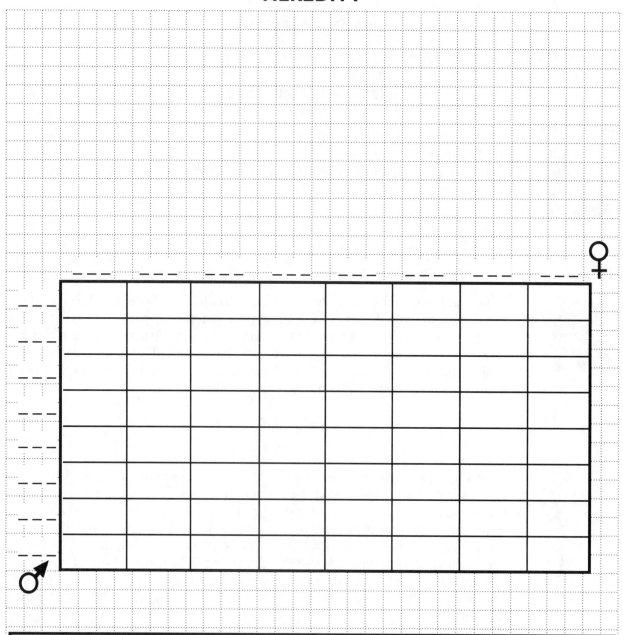

FIGURE C

<u>Directions</u>: (1) Use the PUNNETT SQUARE to show the genotypes and phenotypes of all possible offspring that would result from the mating of a male purebred one-eyed, hybrid one-horned, hybrid flying Andromedan and his mate, a female purebred two-eyed, hybrid one-horned, pure-bred walking Andromedan. In this species of Andromedans the alleles for one-eye, one-horn, and flying are dominant alleles.

one-eyed   one-horned   flyer

two-eyed   two-horned   walker

DAD (EEHhFf)

MOM (eeHhff)

HEREDITY

Work Date: ____/____/____

LESSON OBJECTIVE

Students will show why "sex-linked" genetic diseases are more common in males.

Classroom Activities

On Your Mark!

Refer students to the illustrations on Journal Sheet #4. Explain that gender is determined in humans by the presence of "X" and "Y" chromosomes. A person having two "X" chromosomes will be a female. A person having an "X" and a "Y" chromosome will be a male. Use the Punnett Square shown to indicate why the odds of having a boy or girl is 50:50.

Get Set!

Point out that biologists have determined that the "Y" chromosome carries little else than the genetic instructions for the production of male sexual characteristics, whereas the "X" chromosome carries other genes that determine a variety of other traits. For example, the gene that determines a person's ability to clot blood quickly after an injury is present on the "X" chromosome. When this gene is defective, the ability to clot quickly may not be present in the newborn male of a mother with a defective gene. This would happen because the "Y" chromosome has no "healthy" blood clotting gene to take over the function of a defective "X" chromosome. The male offspring will be hemopheliacs. A female offspring, on the other hand, could inherit a healthy "X" chromosome from her father to counteract the bad gene on the mother's matching "X" chromosome.

Go!

Give students ample time to brainstorm and complete the activity described in Figure D on Journal Sheet #4. They will note the following: (1) Should a female with a defective clotting gene on one of her "X" chromosomes mate with a hemopheliac male, then 50% of the female offspring will be hemopheliacs and 50% of the male offspring will be hemopheliacs. (2) Should a normal female mate with a hemopheliac male, then none of the offspring will be hemopheliacs. (3) All of the offspring of a female hemopheliac and a male hemopheliac will be hemopheliacs. Emphasize that the presence of a healthy "X" chromosome paired with a "Y" chromosome or a defective "X" chromosome will not result in the disease.

Materials

Journal Sheet #4

LS8 JOURNAL SHEET #4

HEREDITY

MALE
CELLS

FEMALE
CELLS

FEMALE
EGGS

MALE
SPERM

FIGURE D

<u>Directions</u>: Use PUNNETT SQUARES to determine the answers to the following questions: (1) What would be the percentage of female and male hemopheliacs among the offspring of a female with a defective clotting gene on one of her "X" chromosomes and a hemopheliac male? (2) What would be the percentage of female and male hemopheliacs among the offspring of a normal female and a hemopheliac male? (3) What would be the percentage of female and male hemopheliacs among the offspring of a female hemopheliac and a male hemopheliac?

LS8 REVIEW QUIZ

Directions: Keep your eyes on your own work.
Read all directions and questions carefully.
THINK BEFORE YOU ANSWER!
Watch your spelling, be neat, and do the best you can.

CLASSWORK   (~40): _____
HOMEWORK   (~20): _____
CURRENT EVENT   (~10): _____
TEST   (~30): _____

TOTAL   (~100): _____
(A ≥ 90, B ≥ 80, C ≥ 70, D ≥ 60, F < 60)

LETTER GRADE: _____

TEACHER'S COMMENTS: _____
_____

HEREDITY

TRUE–FALSE FILL-IN: If the statement is true, write the word TRUE. If the statement is false, change the underlined word to make the statement true. *15 points*

_____   1. The young of living things are called <u>offspring</u>.

_____   2. <u>All</u> members of a species have the same species traits.

_____   3. A <u>gene</u> is any characteristic of an organism that makes it different from other organisms.

_____   4. The passing of traits from one generation of living things to another is called <u>genetics</u>.

_____   5. The study of how biologicial traits are passed from parent to offspring is called <u>genetics</u>.

_____   6. The "father of genetics" was <u>Mendeleev</u>.

_____   7. Genes determine the <u>traits</u> of an organism.

_____   8. The first genetic research was done on <u>humans</u>.

_____   9. Traits that are always expressed when passed from one generation to the next are called <u>dominant</u> traits.

_____   10. Traits that skip generations are called <u>recessive</u> traits.

_____   11. An organism that carries both dominant and recessive genes for a particular trait is called a(n) <u>purebred</u>.

_____   12. An organism that carries only dominant genes for a particular trait is called a(n) <u>hybrid</u>.

_____   13. Hybrids <u>do not</u> breed true.

_____   14. The combination of genes present in the cells of an organism is called the organism's <u>genotype</u>.

_____   15. The traits visible to anyone who looks at an organism are the organism's <u>phenotype</u>.

PROBLEM

Directions: Read and complete the problem as directed. *15 points*

A male and female "flingdinob" met and mated in the wilds of Nova Bologna. The male flingdinob was a pure-bred green, hybrid floozer while his mate was a purebred yellow, purebred snoozer. Flingdinob color traits, like green and yellow, are inherited in pairs. Floozer-snoozer traits are also inherited in pairs. Show the genotypes of the male and female flingdinobs. Use the Punnett Square to show all possible genotypes of their offspring. Answer question #16 in the space provided.

Trait	Code
green	G
yellow	g
floozer	F
snoozer	f

male genotype: ____ ____ ____ ____

female genotype: ____ ____ ____ ____

possible female sex cells

—— —— —— —— —— —— —— ——

possible male
sex cells

— —

— —

— —

— —

16. What percentage of the offspring of these two flingdinobs will be yellow floozers?

_____

INTRODUCTION TO GENETICS

TEACHER'S CLASSWORK AGENDA AND CONTENT NOTES

Classwork Agenda for the Week

1. Students will construct a model of a protein molecule.
2. Students will construct a model of a DNA molecule.
3. Students will use models to show how DNA codes for the production of proteins.
4. Students will use models to show how scientists manufacture recombinant DNA.

Content Notes for Lecture and Discussion

The early decades of the 20th century saw the birth of genetics. The rediscovery of **Gregor Mendel**'s (b. 1822; d. 1884) work in 1900 by Dutch botanist **Hugo Marie de Vries** (b. 1848; d. 1935) and its subsequent popularization by English geneticist **William Bateson** (b. 1861; d. 1926) inspired American geneticists **Thomas Hunt Morgan** (b. 1866; d. 1945) and **Hermann Muller** (b. 1890; d. 1967) to examine the effects of X-rays and chemicals on the chromosomes of the common fruit fly: *Drosophila melongaster*. Their discovery that injury to chromosomes was the direct cause of genetic mutations was the start of the genetic revolution. While many geneticists sought to further understand the role of chromosomes in the mutation process and the transmission of hereditary information, others sought to elucidate the biochemical structure of the chromosome. The pioneering work of English biochemist **Dorothy Mary Crowfoot Hodgkin** (b. 1910; d. 1994) in the field of X-ray crystallography allowed microbiologists to deduce the three-dimensional structure of a variety of organic molecules such as calciferol (e.g., vitamin D_2) and cholesterol. With the assistance of the brilliant biophysicist and X-ray crystallographer **Rosalind Elsie Franklin** (b. 1920; d. 1958), molecular biologists **James Dewey Watson** (b. 1928) and **Francis H.C. Crick** (b. 1916) succeeded in constructing a three-dimensional model of **deoxyribonucleic acid**, abbreviated **DNA**, and received a Nobel Prize in 1962 for their efforts. Since the 1950s the field of genetics has grown to include the science of genetic engineering which has changed the face of medical research.

The genetic code carries chemical instructions for the production of proteins such as **fibrous** (e.g., connective tissue) and **globular** (e.g., hormonal enzymes) **proteins**. While some proteins comprise the structural material of an organism, others regulate body metabolism. The basic unit of the genetic code is called a **codon**. A codon consists of three **nucleotides** arranged in sequence. A nucleotide consists of three smaller molecules: a **phosphate**, a **deoxyribose** or **ribose sugar**, and a **nucleic acid** base [e.g., purines–adenine (A) and guanine (G); pyrimidines–cytosine (C), thymine (T), and uracil (U)]. Both DNA and its "messanger" **RNA** (e.g., **ribonucleic acid**) are constructed in the same fashion; RNA using the nucleic acid uracil in lieu of thymine. A single codon determines which of about 20 **amino acids** (e.g., glycine, alanine, valine, etc.) will be linked to the previous amino acid in the chain of amino acids that comprises every protein. Since there are 4 nucleic acid bases in a DNA molecule which can be arranged in any combination of 3 per codon, there are $4 \times 4 \times 4 = 64$ different codons. That is more than enough to code for the 20 different amino acids found in proteins. Since the 64 codons can be arranged in virtually any order (e.g., AAA, GAC, TAT, AAA, ATT, GCT, etc.), the number of possible proteins is extremely large (e.g., more than the number of atoms in the solar system).

In the nucleus, the information in DNA is "transcribed" to molecules of "messenger" or **mRNA** that make their way out into the cytoplasm to the ribosomes. Molecules of "transfer" or **tRNA** that code differentially for particular amino acids attach to individual amino acids floating free in the cytoplasm. Each tRNA molecule delivers its amino acid shipment to a ribosome. There, the mRNA molecule "translates the code" by assuring the ordered construction of a protein having an appropriately sequenced chain of amino acids.

In Lesson #1, students will construct a model of a protein molecule.

In Lesson #2, students will construct a model of a DNA molecule.

In Lesson #3, students will use models to show how DNA codes for the production of proteins.

In Lesson #4, students will use models to show how scientists manufacture recombinant DNA.

ANSWERS TO THE HOMEWORK PROBLEMS

Students should use the idea that genes carry the instructions for the synthesis of proteins and that proteins give living things their structure as well as assist in the chemical reactions that make life possible. Genetic engineers are extremely careful about insuring that new forms of recombinant DNA are manufactured and controlled under very secure conditions so that risks to the environment can be minimized. The introduction of recombinant DNA into the environment at large could present a biohazard.

ANSWERS TO THE END-OF-THE-WEEK REVIEW QUIZ

1. chromosomes
2. nucleus
3. can
4. DNA, deoxyribonucleic acid
5. DNA, deoxyribonucleic acid

6. proteins
7. amino
8. building blocks
9. mutation
10. true

11. female "X"
12. can
13. true
14. bacteria
15. recombinant

PROBLEM

Any of the following names are acceptable in addition to others to whom students can attribute a reasonable contribution: Mendel, De Vries, Bateson, Morgan, Muller, Watson, Crick, Franklin, etc.

ESSAY

Students should mention that sex-linked genetic diseases are carried on the female "X" chromosome. A male with a sex-linked genetic disorder can marry a female who does not carry a gene for the disorder. Either of her healthy "X" chromosomes will be sufficient to counteract the effects of the male's defective "X" chromosome.

LS9 FACT SHEET

INTRODUCTION TO GENETICS

CLASSWORK AGENDA FOR THE WEEK

(1)   Construct a model of a protein molecule.
(2)   Construct a model of a DNA molecule.
(3)   Use models to show how DNA codes for the production of proteins.
(4)   Use models to show how scientists manufacture recombinant DNA.

Biologists discovered early in the 20th century that the traits of organisms carried by genes are located on the **chromosomes** of living cells. This discovery was largely due to the pioneering work of American geneticists **Thomas Hunt Morgan** (b. 1866; d. 1945) and **Hermann Muller** (b. 1890; d. 1967). Chromosomes appear as dark wormlike structures inside the **nucleus** of a cell. Injury to chromosomes—caused by toxic chemicals or radiation—can result in mutations or even the death of the injured cells. In the early 1950s, the American molecular biologists **James Dewey Watson** (b. 1928) and his English colleague **Francis H. C. Crick** (b. 1916), assisted by the brilliant English X-ray crystallographer **Rosalind Elsie Franklin** (b. 1920; d. 1958), worked out the structure of the large molecule that makes up all chromosomes. The chemical name for that molecule is **deoxyribonucleic acid**: abbreviated **DNA**.

The DNA macromolecule contains the "code of life." DNA gives chemical instructions for the building of **proteins**. DNA is a chain of small molecules called **nucleic acids**. The nucleic acids are arranged in a sequence that tells the cell which proteins to build. Proteins give organisms their structure and assist in the chemical processes that make life possible. While DNA is the "blueprint" of life, proteins are life's "building blocks." Proteins are long chains of smaller molecules called **amino acids**. Amino acids are linked together in chains to form proteins. The nucleic acid "code" on a DNA molecule orders a cell to link up specific amino acids in sequence to form a particular protein.

Nucleic acids, amino acids, DNA, and proteins are made of carbon, hydrogen, oxygen, nitrogen, and phosphorus atoms. Because molecules are chemical substances they can be changed by chemical reactions. Changes in the sequence of instructions stored in a molecule of DNA are called **mutations**. Mutations can improve or impair an organism's ablity to survive. Most mutations impair an organism's ability to survive and can quickly result in its death. Other mutations might give an organism a new structure—or a faster way to perform chemical reactions—that result in an adaptive advantage for that organism. Because chromosomes carry hereditary information, these changes will be passed to the next generation: assuming the organism survives to reproduce. Whether or not a particular mutation produces a competitive advantage for a species depends upon environmental pressures. Natural selection chooses which mutations will be beneficial to a species by causing poorly adapted species to become extinct while allowing those better adapted to survive.

Many substances in our environment can cause mutations. They are called **mutagens**. Radiation such as the ultraviolet radiation of the sun is one cause of mutations. Scientists who study mutations are trying to discover ways to prevent and correct the harmful effects of genetic mutations.

The new science of **genetic engineering** takes advantage of the fact that some organisms have large chromosomes that can be "dissected apart" then "teased back together." By inserting sections of human DNA into the chromosomes of bacteria, scientists can make those bacteria manufacture human proteins. The new DNA constructed for this purpose is called "recombined" or **recombinant DNA**. The science of genetic engineering is changing the way researchers and physicians think about disease and how they might use this revolutionary technique to cure illness and birth defects.

Homework Directions

In a brief essay of no more than 200 words, explain why genetic research should be conducted under controlled conditions. *Be specific* about the risks of genetic engineering. Do not simply voice your opinion. Use the facts you read about in this Fact Sheet to support your ideas!

Assignment due: _____

_____   _____   ___/___/___
     Student's Signature   Parent's Signature   Date

INTRODUCTION TO GENETICS

Work Date: _____/_____/_____

LESSON OBJECTIVE

Students will construct a model of a protein molecule.

Classroom Activities

On Your Mark!

Begin by asking students to list the nutrients they eat as part of their everyday diet (e.g., carbohydrates, vitamins/minerals, fats, proteins, etc.). Ask them to identify the nutrient that is responsible for giving their body its particular shape. Fats are a popular answer and to some extent fats do alter the shape of an otherwise average physique. But point out that proteins are the building blocks of organic structure and also serve to regulate metabolic activity (e.g., enzymes). Give students a moment to read their Fact Sheet then test their recollection of what they learned about proteins. Use the information in the Fact Sheet and the Teacher's Classwork Agenda and Content Notes to clarify any misunderstandings. Define a **protein** as a large molecule (e.g., a **macromolecule**) made of smaller molecules called **amino acids**.

Get Set!

Draw Illustration A on the board and have students copy your drawing on Journal Sheet #1. Point out how the separable amino acids are linked together to form a chain of molecules called a protein. The bonds holding together the amino acids are called **peptide bonds**. The structure of proteins was worked out by the American chemist and biologist **Linus Carl Pauling** (b. 1901; d, 1994). In 1954, Pauling received a Nobel Prize in Chemistry for his efforts.

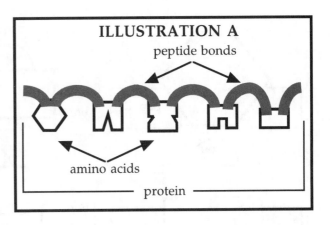

ILLUSTRATION A

peptide bonds

amino acids

protein

Go!

Give students ample time to complete the activity described in Figure A on Journal Sheet #1. Encourage several groups to connect their individual molecules into a long chain before they get to Step #4 and explain that an average protein contains hundreds of amino acids. Assist them in gently twisting the chain in order to tape the "plus" and "minus" tabs together. Explain that a protein obtains its final stable shape by forming weak bonds called "hydrogen bonds." Hydrogen bonds represented by the joined "plus" and "minus" tabs are formed by the attraction between different sides of amino acid molecules having different "electrical charges."

Materials

construction paper, scissors, glue and tape

LS9 Journal Sheet #1

INTRODUCTION TO GENETICS

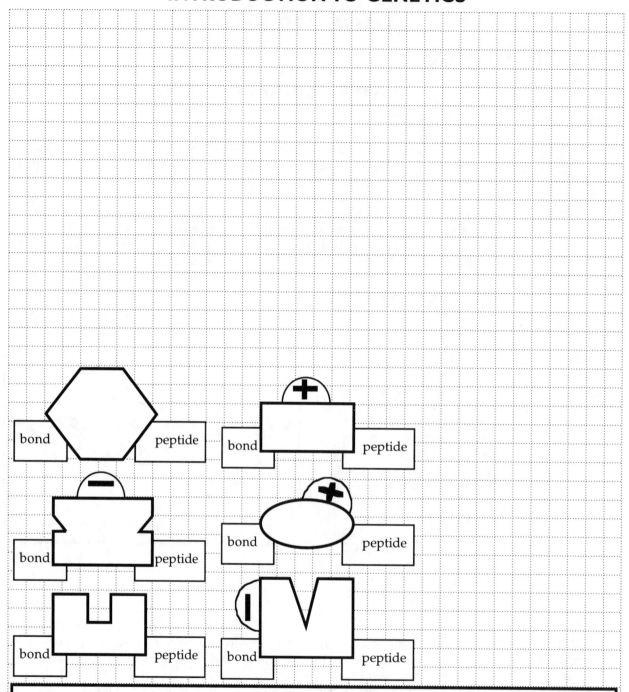

FIGURE A

Directions: (1) Each of the puzzle pieces shown above represents an amino acid molecule that helps to make up a protein molecule. (2) Reproduce 2 pieces of each pattern on a separate sheet of paper making sure to include the "peptide", "bond", "plus" and "minus" sign tabs with the pieces. (3) Cut out the puzzle pieces and tape or glue them together in random sequence by attaching the "peptide" tab of one molecule to the "bond" tab of the next molecule. (4) Gently twist the chain of molecules and use 1-2 centimeter lengths of tape to attach "oppositely charged" tabs. (5) Why do you think proteins come in so many shapes or sizes?

INTRODUCTION TO GENETICS

Work Date: _____/_____/_____

LESSON OBJECTIVE

Students will construct a model of a DNA molecule.

Classroom Activities

On Your Mark!

Use the information in the Fact Sheet and the Teacher's Classwork Agenda and Content Notes to give students a brief introduction to the history of genetics research. If available, use textbook or other photographs to show students a picture of the DNA double helix.

Get Set!

Draw Illustration B on the board and have students copy your drawing on Journal Sheet #2. Point out how the separable **nucleic acids** are linked together against a "backbone" of sugar and phosphate molecules. The sugar in DNA is a "deoxyribose" sugar meaning it contains one less oxygen atom. The sugar in RNA is "ribose" sugar. Nucleic acids pair together on the inside of the molecule as the

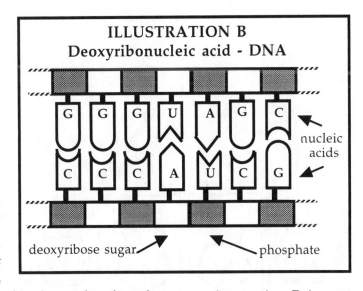

ILLUSTRATION B
Deoxyribonucleic acid - DNA

nucleic acids

deoxyribose sugar   phosphate

result of the same kind of hydrogen bonding that occurs in proteins. Point out that there are two kinds of nucleic acids: **purines** and **pyrimidines**. The nucleic acids **adenine** (A) and **guanine** (G) are purines. The nucleic acids **cytosine** (C) and **thymine** (T) are pyrimidines. RNA uses uracil (U) in the place of thymine.

Go!

Give students ample time to complete the activity described in Figure B on Journal Sheet #2. Encourage several groups to connect their individual molecules into a long chain before they get to Step #5 and explain that an average DNA molecule contains thousands of nucleic acids. Assist them in gently twisting the chain in order to visualize the full three-dimensional structure of the double helix.

Materials

construction paper, scissors, glue and tape

LS9 JOURNAL SHEET #2

INTRODUCTION TO GENETICS

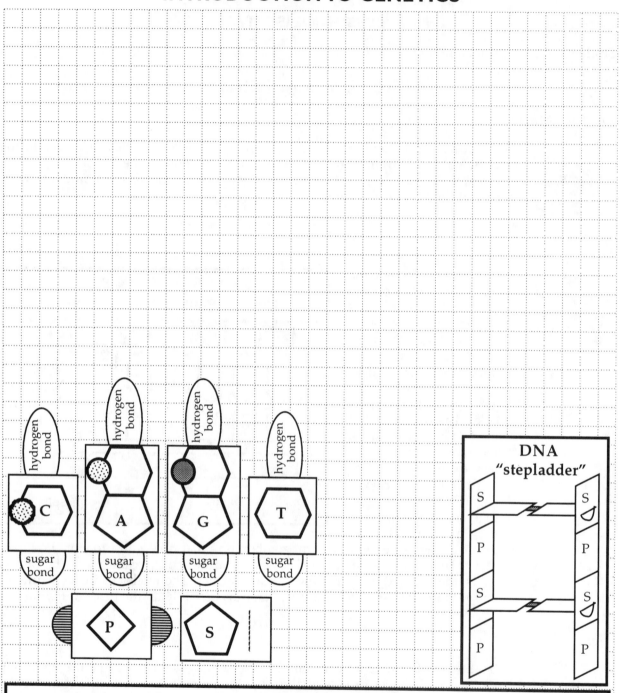

FIGURE B

Directions: (1) Each of the puzzle pieces shown above represents a molecule that helps to make up a DNA macromolecule (e.g., S = sugar base; P = phosphate; A = adenine; G = guanine; C = cytosine; T = thymine). (2) Accurately reproduce 8 sugars, 8 phosphates, and two of each nucleic acid on a separate sheet of paper. (3) Cut out the puzzle pieces and the dotted line on the sugar molecule and glue together a large molecule of DNA as shown in the diagram. (4) Attach your "stepladder" model to those of your groupmates to make a longer chain of DNA. (5) Gently twist the long DNA chain to see how it forms a "double helix".

INTRODUCTION TO GENETICS

Work Date: ____/____/____

LESSON OBJECTIVE

Students will use models to show how DNA codes for the production of proteins.

Classroom Activities

On Your Mark!

Begin by asking students if they have ever used a "code." Discuss the various kinds of codes they may have used to send secret messages to their friends (e.g., letter or number substitution techniques). Point out that Morse Code relies on only two basic symbols: a dot and a dash. The whole alphabet can be created using only dots and dashes as long as the symbols are arranged in a specific sequence. Explain that computers also work on a "binary code" since electronic switches can only be in one of two positions: on or off. Explain that the DNA molecules uses a "triplet code" to send messages to the cell.

Get Set!

Use the information in the Teacher's Classwork Agenda and Content Notes to give a brief lecture on how DNA codes for the production of proteins. Go over the explanation step by step, completing the lecture with the following summary: "Each **codon** containing 3 nucleic acids is the message for a single amino acid. So, a long chain of codons arranged in a particular sequence codes for a particular protein."

Go!

Give students ample time to complete the activity described in Figure C on Journal Sheet #3. Instruct them to copy the symbols as accurately as they can as they draw the puzzle pieces on their poster. Have them work cooperatively to save time. They will note that each amino acid fits into a particular transfer RNA molecule which has a complimentary code to the codons (e.g., CCC–AUC) on the messenger RNA molecule. Point out that the RNA molecule uses the nucleic acid uracil instead of thymine as a match for adenine.

Materials

construction paper or butcher paper, pens/pencils, crayons

LS9 JOURNAL SHEET #3

INTRODUCTION TO GENETICS

AMINO ACIDS

FIGURE C

Directions: Use a large piece of construction or butcher paper to show how the amino acids on the left can be linked together in the proper sequence using the transcribed genetic code present on the section of mRNA. Your poster should show how the tRNA "picks up" amino acids floating around the cell and transfers them to the ribosome where they can be linked by peptide bonds to form a protein.

TRANSFER RNA

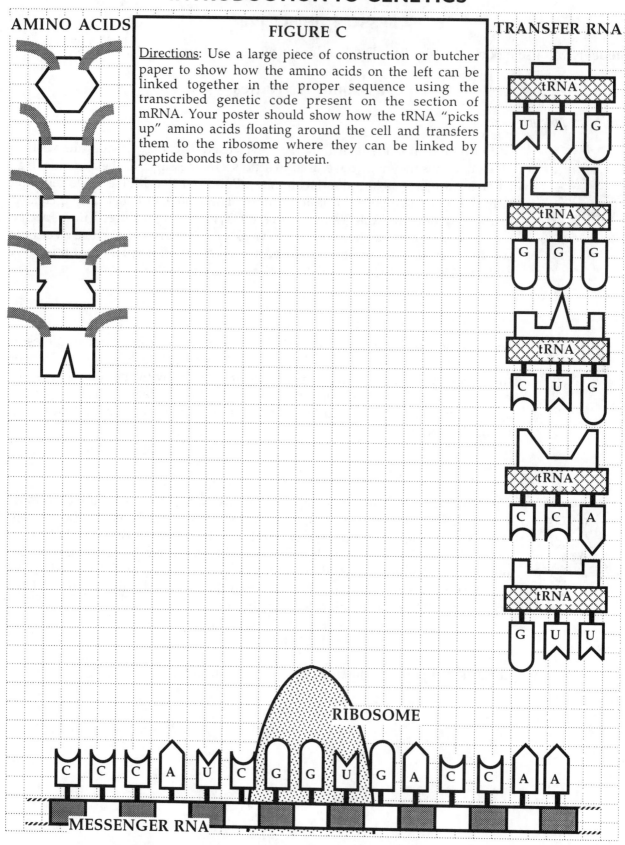

RIBOSOME

MESSENGER RNA

INTRODUCTION TO GENETICS

Work Date: ____/____/____

LESSON OBJECTIVE

Students will use models to show how scientists manufacture recombinant DNA.

Classroom Activities

On Your Mark!

Begin by asking students to report on any recent news they have heard about genetic engineering. Explain that this revolutionary new technique allows pharmaceutical firms to produce drugs such as insulin (e.g., for the treatment of diabetes) much less expensively than only a few years ago. Less than a few decades ago, diabetics used insulin taken from sheep to control their blood-sugar levels. Today they use real human insulin taken from bacteria! Ask: "How did scientists get bacteria to produce human insulin?"

Get Set!

Draw Illustration C on the board and have students copy your drawing on Journal Sheet #4. Explain that genetic engineers first had to locate the site on the human DNA molecule that codes for human insulin. Second, they cut out that specific section from any human cell (e.g., a cheek cell) since every cell in the body has the same 23 chromosomes as every other human cell. Third, they inject the DNA section into a bacteria. One of the convenient things about bacteria is that their DNA forms large rings called **plasmids** that are relatively easy to handle. In addition, bacteria do not have a nucleus to get in the way of the operation and the bacteria multiply quickly. So after several days, millions of bacteria are producing human DNA according to the coded instructions on the human DNA molecule. The last step is to extract and purify the insulin for medical use.

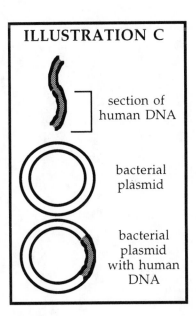

ILLUSTRATION C

section of human DNA

bacterial plasmid

bacterial plasmid with human DNA

Go!

Give students ample time to build a clay model of two bacteria: one with normal bacterial plasmids, a second with a piece of **recombinant DNA**.

Materials

different colors of clay

LS9 JOURNAL SHEET #4

INTRODUCTION TO GENETICS

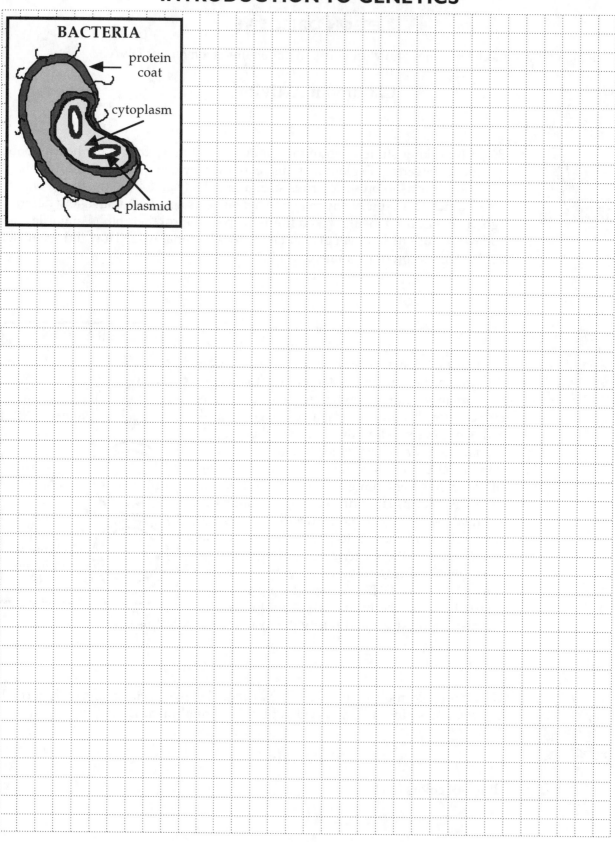

BACTERIA

protein coat

cytoplasm

plasmid

LS9 REVIEW QUIZ

Directions: Keep your eyes on your own work.
Read all directions and questions carefully.
THINK BEFORE YOU ANSWER!
Watch your spelling, be neat, and do the best you can.

CLASSWORK   (~40): _____
HOMEWORK   (~20): _____
CURRENT EVENT   (~10): _____
TEST   (~30): _____

TOTAL   (~100): _____
(A ≥ 90, B ≥ 80, C ≥ 70, D ≥ 60, F < 60)

LETTER GRADE: _____

TEACHER'S COMMENTS: _____
_____

INTRODUCTION TO GENETICS

TRUE–FALSE FILL-IN: If the statement is true, write the word TRUE. If the statement is false, change the underlined word to make the statement true. *15 points*

_____ 1. Genes are located on the <u>mitochondria</u> of living cells.

_____ 2. Chromosomes are found in the <u>membrane</u> of a cell.

_____ 3. Stained chromosomes <u>cannot</u> be seen with a microscope.

_____ 4. Chromosomes are made of a large chemical molecule called <u>phosphate</u>.

_____ 5. <u>Protein</u> contains the "code of life" that controls cellular activity.

_____ 6. DNA gives chemical instructions for the building of <u>amino acids</u>.

_____ 7. Proteins are made of large molecules called <u>nucleic</u> acids.

_____ 8. Proteins are the "<u>code of life</u>" that give organisms their form and function.

_____ 9. A change of instructions stored in a DNA molecule can result in a <u>mutagen</u> that may cause the organism's death.

_____ 10. Because DNA is a chemical molecule it <u>can be</u> changed by chemical reactions.

_____ 11. "Sex-linked" genes are carried on the <u>male "Y"</u> chromosome.

_____ 12. Radiation such as the ultraviolet radiation from the sun <u>cannot</u> cause mutations.

_____ 13. Mutations can <u>sometimes</u> benefit an organism.

_____ 14. Genetic engineers insert human DNA into <u>pea plants</u> to manufacture human protein.

_____ 15. Sections of DNA that have been spliced together by genetic engineers is called <u>reconstituted</u> DNA.

PROBLEM

Directions: Write the last names of four scientists whose research has helped us to understand how genes work. *8 points*

_____ _____ _____ _____ _____

ESSAY: Write several sentences to explain how a male with a sex-linked disease can insure that his children will not have the same sex-linked disease. *7 points*

_____

_____

_____

_____

_____

_____

_____

_____

_____ _____ ___/___/___
Student's Signature   Parent's Signature   Date

MICROORGANISMS

TEACHER'S CLASSWORK AGENDA AND CONTENT NOTES

Classwork Agenda for the Week

1. Students will compose a graphic organizer showing the relationships between different types of microorganisms.
2. Students will contrast the structures and characteristics of viruses and bacteria.
3. Students will compare and draw different species of protozoa.
4. Students will contrast the structures and characteristics of molds and protozoa.

Content Notes for Lecture and Discussion

Early ideas concerning the nature of disease were based largely on the views of the Greek physician **Hippocrates** (b. 460 B.C.; d. 377 B.C.). According to Hippocrates, illness was the result of an "imbalance in the body humours" that could be brought on by a variety of causes including changes in the weather as well as personal and other local conditions. The observation of microbes—including bacteria—made by the Dutch inventor **Anton van Leeuwenhoek** (b. 1632; d. 1723) under the microscope did little to change that view until the middle of the 19th century. The English physician **Edward Jenner** (b. 1749; d. 1823) used the first effective **vaccine** against smallpox in 1796, but he could not explain how the treatment worked. In 1840, the German anatomist and histologist **Jacob Henle** (b. 1809; d. 1885) published a work entitled *Pathological Investigations* in which he argued that living organisms were responsible for diseases in man, animals, and plants. He reasoned that living things alone were capable of reproduction; therefore, progressively morbid infectious diseases must have an organic cause. He suggested that methods of "filtration" be developed to isolate the parasites responsible for ill health. The German bacteriologist **Heinrich Hermann Koch** (b. 1843; d. 1910) fulfilled that dream less than four decades later. Koch and his associates devised techniques for the isolation and culturing of bacteria so that they could be used to replicate diseases under controlled conditions in the laboratory. Among his many discoveries were the causes of tuberculosis and cholera for which he received a Nobel Prize in Physiology or Medicine in 1905. In 1860, the French chemist and microbiologist **Louis Pasteur** (b. 1822; d. 1895) discovered that the fermentation of sugars to produce alcohol was dependent upon the action of microorganisms (e.g., anaerobic bacteria and yeasts) and that the "germs" could be killed by heat. **Pasteurization**—a method of heating the fermenting mixture gently to 50°C—is used today as the primary method of killing yeasts used in the manufacture of beers, wines, and dairy products. Pasteur published his **germ theory** in 1865, inspiring the English surgeon **Joseph Lister** (b. 1827; d. 1912) to perform the first antiseptic operation in 1867. In 1891, the German bacteriologist **Paul Ehrlich** (b. 1854; d. 1915) developed the first techniques in **chemotherapy**: the use of synthetic drugs to kill infectious organisms. In the 1880s, the Dutch bacteriologist **Martinus Willem Beijerinck** (b. 1851; d. 1931) found the causative agent responsible for the mottling and destruction of tobacco leaves which he determined to be several magnitudes smaller than any known bacteria. He called the germ a **virus**, meaning "poison" (e.g., tobacco mosaic virus).

Twentieth century advances in the art and science of electron microscopy have led to the elucidation of structure and function of thousands of microorganisms belonging to the **Kingdom Monerans** (e.g., bacteria) and **Kingdom Protista** (e.g., protozoa). And, since the first genetic engineering experiments performed on the plasmids of the bacterium *Eschericia coli* by American biochemists **Stanley Cohen** (b. 1922) and **Har Gobind Khorana** (b. 1922) in the early 1970s, researchers have concentrated their efforts in exploring the positive role of bacteria in the future of medical research.

LS10 Content Notes *(cont'd)*

In Lesson #1, students will compose a graphic organizer showing the relationships between different types of microorganisms.

In Lesson #2, students will contrast the structures and characteristics of viruses and bacteria.

In Lesson #3, students will compare and draw different species of protozoa.

In Lesson #4, students will contrast the structures and characteristics of molds and protozoa.

ANSWERS TO THE HOMEWORK PROBLEMS

Students essays should reflect the orderly distinctions made in their graphic organizer composed in Lesson #1.

ANSWERS TO THE END-OF-THE-WEEK REVIEW QUIZ

1. viruses	6. true	11. B	16. A
2. true	7. true	12. D	17. B
3. electron	8. Monerans	13. D	18. D
4. vaccines	9. Protista	14. D	19. C
5. true	10. true	15. C	20. E

LS10 Fact Sheet

MICROORGANISMS

CLASSWORK AGENDA FOR THE WEEK

(1) Compose a graphic organizer showing the relationships between different types of microorganisms.
(2) Contrast the structures and characteristics of viruses and bacteria.
(3) Compare and draw different species of protozoa.
(4) Contrast the structures and characteristics of molds and protozoa.

When the Dutch inventor **Anton van Leeuwenhoek** (b. 1632; d. 1723) peered through his newly constructed, hand-held light microscope in 1683 he could not have imagined the world of tiny creatures he was about to discover. His smoothly polished, glass lenses were able to magnify objects more than 300 times; and what Leeuwenhoek saw would revolutionize the science of biology. The inventive lens-maker published his drawings of these **microorganisms** (e.g., meaning "very small living things") and called them "animalicules." Today, these tiny organisms are classified as **protozoa** and can be found swimming around in pond water among decaying leaves. With the invention of the electron microscope at the beginning of the 20th century by the German physicist **Ernst August Friedrich Ruska** (b. 1906; d. 1988) biologists could probe an even smaller realm. Ruska's electron microscopes could magnify objects more than 12,000 times. Modern electron microscopes have since revealed the presence of **viruses** and **bacteria** inhabiting the "submicroscopic" world.

Viruses are tiny **noncellular particles** that can infect living cells. They are **parasites** that use the cell's resources to reproduce themselves while interfering with the healthy activities of the cell. A virus is hardly more than a strand of hereditary material (e.g., RNA) protected by a sugar-protein coat. A virus will invade a **host cell** and take advantage of a cell's "chemical machinery" to carry on life functions that the virus cannot perform on its own. The common cold, chicken pox, rabies, polio, and AIDS are caused by viruses. Weakened or dead viruses can be used to make **vaccines**. A vaccine helps the body to build defenses against invasion by a specific virus. With the advances in our knowledge of how genes work, viruses have been "taught" to kill pests. They have also been used to help scientists to "genetically engineer" the hereditary material of cells.

All **bacteria** belong to the **Kingdom Monera**. **Monerans** are **unicellular organisms** that do not have a nucleus to protect their **chromosomes**. There are four major groups of bacteria: **autotrophs, heterotrophs, parasites**, and **decomposers**. Bacteria may develop a **symbiotic relationship** with their host. This means that both the bacteria and the host *benefit* from the presence of the bacteria. All animals—even humans—have bacteria in their digestive tracts that help them digest certain foods (e.g., dairy products). In a **parasitic relationship** the bacteria uses up too much of the host's resources and the host always suffers and may die.

Protozoa belong to the **Kingdom Protista**. They are microscopic unicellular organisms that have a nucleus. Protozoa also have a number of other specialized cell structures: such as **pseudopod, cilia**, and **flagella**. These structures help the protozoa to move on their own through their environment. Protozoa can live in "sympathy" with other organisms, allowing both creatures to benefit from the relationship. (e.g., symbiotic relationship); or they can be parasites (e.g., parasitic relationship). There is much debate about how to classify protozoa because they come in so many different forms. However, they are generally grouped into two major categories: *animal-like protists* and *plant-like protists*.

Animal-like protists are all heterotrophs. They contain a nucleus and lack a cell wall. Animal-like protists are divided into four groups: *sarcodines, ciliates, zooflagellates*, and *sporozoans*. **Sarcodines** have **pseudopods** (e.g., meaning "false feet"). The most well known sarcodine is the **ameba**. Under the microscope an ameba can be observed changing shape, its cell membrane twisting and turning as the organism goes in search of food. **Ciliates** have cilia (e.g., meaning "small lashes"). The **paramecium** is the most well known ciliate. Under the microscope paramecium can be studied darting around in a drop of pond water, their cilia spinning and twirling like the oars of a Viking ship. **Zooflagellates** have flagella (e.g., meaning "tiny flags"). **Giardia** are zoo-flagellates that use their flagella to attach themselves to the walls of the human digestive tract. Although this can cause illness in a human, giardia helps a termite to digest wood. **Sporozoans** are all **parasites**. One of the deadliest sporozoans is the **plasmodium** which causes **malaria**. Plasmodia live in the saliva of **Anopheles mosquitos**. Before the mosquito bites and draws blood from its victim it injects its saliva into the wound. The host becomes infected with the deadly plasmodium protist. The plasmodia invade the liver and destroy the host's red blood cells. **Plantlike protists** such as *algae* are **autotrophs**. **Algae** use light energy from the sun to make their own food by photosynthesis. **Euglenas, diatoms**, and **dinoflagellates** are three of the many different varieties of plantlike protists. Because they perform photosynthesis, plantlike protists supply about 70% of the earth's atmospheric oxygen.

Slime molds are another group of microorganisms that behave like protozoa in many ways. They can be either *acellular* or *cellular*. **Acellular slime mold** spreads out as a thin sheet of cytoplasm called **plasmodium** containing many nuclei confined by a single membrane. **Cellular slime mold** are independent cells that reproduce by growing small "fruiting bodies." When it is ready to reproduce the fruiting body bursts and expels **spores** containing the hereditary information for the production of new offspring. Because their manner of reproduction is more similar to that of fungi (e.g., mushrooms) than that of protozoa, slime molds are considered members of **Kingdom Fungi**.

Homework Directions

Use the graphic organizer you composed in Lesson #1 to write an essay of no less than 200 words describing the variety and characteristics of microorganisms present in our environment.

Assignment due: _____

_____	_____	____/____/____
Student's Signature	Parent's Signature	Date

MICROORGANISMS

Work Date: _____/_____/_____

LESSON OBJECTIVE

Students will compose a graphic organizer showing the relationships between different types of microorganisms.

Classroom Activities

On Your Mark!

Begin preparing the samples of protozoa, bacteria, and molds to be used in this unit at least one week in advance! Although pre-prepared microscope slides of a number of microorganisms can be obtained from laboratory supply houses, students will more easily recognize the everyday relevance of microorganisms by seeing the habitats they share with us. Preparation of protozoa: Protozoa can be found in lakes or ponds congregating on decaying leaves ladened with ingestible bacteria. Dip a glass jar into the pond and collect some of the mud and decaying leaves to go with the water sample. Add a pinch of raw ground beef to the mixture and seal the jar with a perforated lid. Keep the culture at room temperature in medium light for one week. Preparation of bacteria: Pour 100 ml of milk into a jar and seal it. Spoon a tablespoon of yogurt into a second jar and seal it. Keep both cultures in a warm—but not hot—place for one week. Preparation of mold: Place small slices of bread, orange, and cheese into a ziplock® baggie. Add a teaspoon of water and seal the bag. Keep both cultures in a warm—but not hot—place for one week.

Begin Lesson #1 by displaying the **sealed labelled samples** of "Protozoa", "Bacteria", and "Mold" prepared during the previous week. Explain that most protozoa, bacteria, and molds are not harmful to humans although some can cause serious illness. Use the information in the Teacher's Classwork Agenda and Content Notes to give a brief lecture about the history of discovery that led to the present understanding about the relationship between microorganisms and disease.

Get Set!

Give students the opportunity to read the Fact Sheet before briefly testing their knowledge of what they have read. Explain that simply making a list of the facts they recalled is not the best way to remember those facts. A graphic organizer that groups information from the general to the specific is an easier way to remember scientific principles and the examples that illustrate them.

Go!

Give students ample time to complete the activity described in Figure A on Journal Sheet #1. Circulate around the room to insure that students are creating a logical graphic organizer that breaks down the characteristics of viruses, bacteria, protists, and mold from general classifications to specific examples.

Materials

pre-prepared samples of protozoa, bacteria, and mold

LS10 JOURNAL SHEET #1

MICROORGANISMS

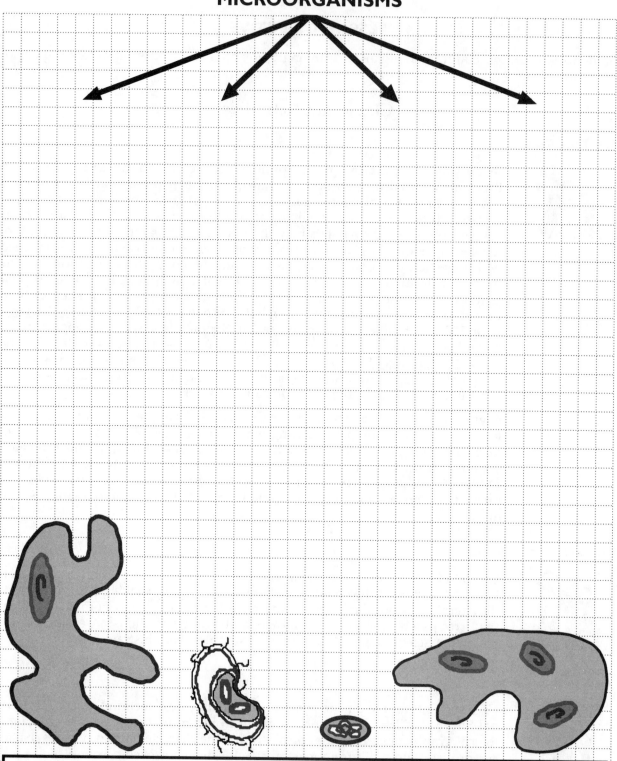

FIGURE A

Directions: (1) Read the FACT SHEET. (2) Start with the arrows to create a graphic organizer that has as many facts as you can gather about each group of microorganisms. (3) Identify the schematic drawings above.

MICROORGANISMS

Work Date: ____/____/____

LESSON OBJECTIVE

Students will contrast the structures and characteristics of viruses and bacteria.

Classroom Activities

On Your Mark!

Begin with a brief description of the structures present in viruses and bacteria as shown in Journal Sheet #2 and have students label the structures of each microorganism. **Viruses** range in size from 10–100 nanometers (e.g., nm = billionths of a meter). Their hereditary material is confined by a membrane or sugar-protein **capsid** casing. The **bacteriophage** has a "stalklike" **tail** and **fiber** "feet" that attach to the membranes of host cells. **Bacteria** range in size from 1–10 micrometers (e.g., μm =

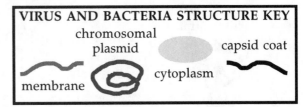

VIRUS AND BACTERIA STRUCTURE KEY
chromosomal
plasmid   capsid coat
cytoplasm
membrane

millionths of a meter). They are, therefore, thousands of times larger than viruses. Point out that the diagrams on Journal Sheet #2 are not to scale! Bacteria are frequently protected by an outer sugar-protein **capsule** that may contain "hairlike" **fimbrae**.

Get Set!

Draw Illustration A on the board and have students copy your drawing on Journal Sheet #2 in order to explain the life cycle of a virus. A **virus** is a **noncellular particle** that has no life of its own. It must invade a host cell to produce new viruses; so, technically a virus is not alive. In "A" the virus attaches to the host cell. In "B" the virus injects its viral chromosome into the host. In "C" the host's chromosomes are impaired or destroyed and the viral gene orders the cell to make new viral parts. In "D" new viruses are constructed. And in "E" the cell bursts allowing the new viruses to spill into the extracellular medium where they are free to attack new hosts. **Bacteria** carry on all of the life activities common to all living things because they contain most of the organelles present in other living cells. They duplicate themselves by mitosis (e.g., asexual reproduction).

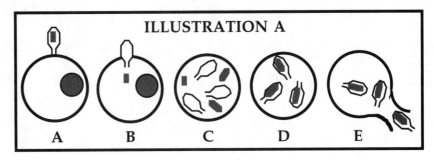

ILLUSTRATION A

A   B   C   D   E

Go!

Give students ample time to solve the problems posed in *How Infectious Diseases Spread* on Journal Sheet #2. If 10 new viruses are produced every 24 hours there will be more than 100,000,000 new viruses at the end of 7 days (e.g., $10 \times 10 \times 10$, etc., *plus* the original "parent" viruses). If 10 new people are infected everyday there will be more than 100,000,000 infected people at the end of one week.

Materials

Journal Sheet #2

LS10 JOURNAL SHEET #2

MICROORGANISMS

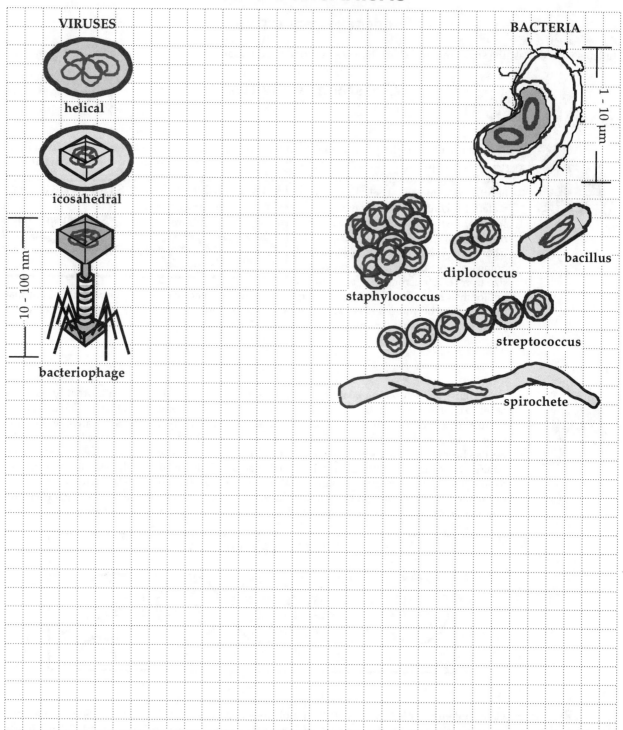

VIRUSES

helical

icosahedral

10 - 100 nm

bacteriophage

BACTERIA

1 - 10 μm

staphylococcus

diplococcus

bacillus

streptococcus

spirochete

HOW INFECTIOUS DISEASES SPREAD

If every virus-infected cell produced 10 new viruses in 24 hours, how many virus infected cells would there be after one week? If a person sneezed only once per day, expelling 10 airborne viruses with each sneeze, and 10 other people inhaled 1 virus each and began sneezing at the same rate, how many people would be infected after one week?

MICROORGANISMS

Work Date: ____/____/____

LESSON OBJECTIVE

Students will compare and draw different species of protozoa.

Classroom Activities

On Your Mark!

Display the jar cultures labelled "Bacteria" and "Protozoa." Begin with a review of the graphic organizers composed by students in Lesson #1. Point out that **protozoa** belonging to **Kingdom Protista** were the first microorganisms to be observed by the Dutch inventor **Anton van Leeuwenhoek** (b. 1632; d. 1723) in the 17th century using a low power (e.g., 200–300x) light microscope. Explain that protozoa range in size from 100μm to 1 mm in size. They are 100 to 1,000 times larger than bacteria and feed on the smaller microorganisms that cause the active decay of dead organic matter (e.g., pond leaves). Under the best lighting some protozoa can even be seen with the naked eye. Explain how you prepared your jar cultures of bacteria and protozoa.

Get Set!

Explain that while most forms of bacteria and protozoa are not harmful to humans, many can cause illness or even death. Instruct all students to wear goggles, plastic surgical (e.g., dissection) gloves, and surgical masks (e.g., double-ply paper towel taped to the face if surgical masks are unavailable) during the preparation of microscope slides. Following the viewing and drawing of the microorganisms instruct students to discard all slides in a **biohazard container** (e.g., sealable plastic or glass container labelled "Biohazard"). Discard the material according to your state and district hazardous materials guidelines.

Go!

Give students ample time to prepare their slides and draw the microorganisms in the spaces provided according to the directions in Figure B on Journal Sheet #3.

Materials

goggles, plastic surgical (e.g., dissection) gloves, surgical masks (e.g., double-ply paper towel taped to face if surgical masks are unavailable), microscope slides and cover slips, water, eyedroppers, tissues, microscopes

LS10 JOURNAL SHEET #3

MICROORGANISMS

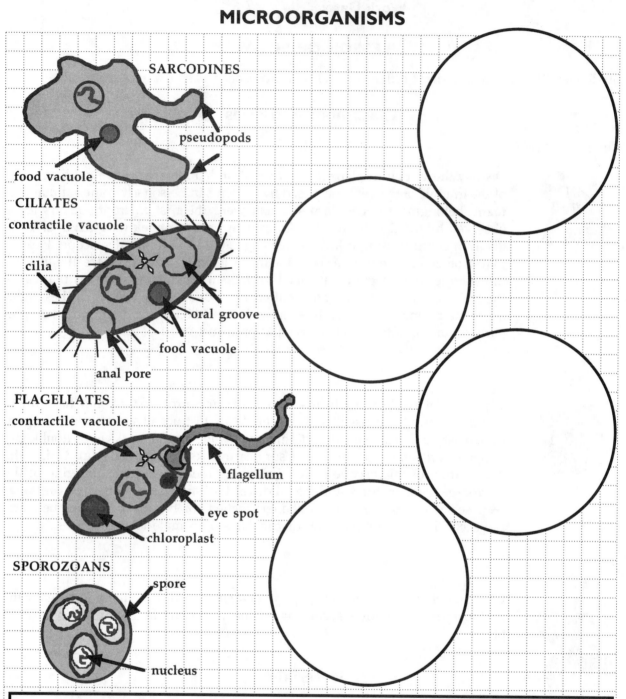

FIGURE B

Directions: (1) Wear goggles, surgical gloves, and a surgical mask during the preparation of your slides. (2) Use an eyedropper to obtain a sample drop from the "PROTOZOA" culture. (3) Place the drop on a microscope slide and gently cover the drop with a cover slip. (4) Place the corner of a tissue into the excess water leaking from the sides of the cover slip. This will draw up any excess water from under the slide and slow down the activity of the protozoa. (5) Observe and draw the sample under the microscope beginning with a low-power objective. (6) Repeat the procedure for the "BACTERIA" sample. Add a drop of water to the droplet of milk or yogurt before covering with the coverslip; then draw off excess water with the tissue.

MICROORGANISMS

Work Date: ____/____/____

LESSON OBJECTIVE

Students will contrast the structures and characteristics of molds and protozoa.

Classroom Activities

On Your Mark!

Display the baggie culture labelled "molds." Begin with a review of the graphic organizers composed by students in Lesson #1. Point out that **molds** can be **acellular** or **cellular**: the former having many nuclei contained within a single cell membrane that can stretch to several square meters in area and the latter reproducing with fruiting bodies. In 1928, the Scottish bacteriologist **Alexander Fleming** (b. 1881; d. 1955) discovered that the mold *penicillium* could kill many different strains of bacteria. Treated preparations of the mold were injected into patients to cure them of a variety of bacterial infections. The new **antibiotic** (e.g., meaning "against life") was named **penicillin**.

Get Set!

Draw Illustration B on the board and have students copy your drawing on Journal Sheet #4 in order to explain the life cycle of a cellular slime mold. Explain that while most

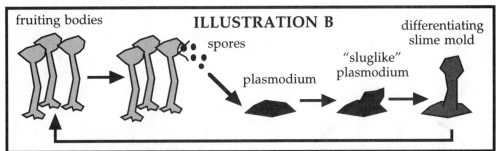

fruiting bodies **ILLUSTRATION B** differentiating slime mold

spores

plasmodium

"sluglike" plasmodium

molds are not harmful to humans many can cause illness or even death. Instruct all students to wear goggles, plastic surgical (e.g., dissection) gloves, and surgical masks (e.g., double-ply paper towel taped to the face if surgical masks are unavailable) during the preparation of microscope slides. Following the viewing and drawing of the microorganisms instruct students to discard all slides in a **biohazard container** (e.g., sealable plastic or glass container labelled "Biohazard"). Discard the material according to your state and district hazardous materials guidelines.

Go!

Give students ample time to prepare their slides and draw the microorganisms in the spaces provided according to the directions in Figure C on Journal Sheet #4. Have them compare their drawings of the slime mold to those of the protozoa drawn in Lesson #3.

Materials

goggles, plastic surgical (e.g., dissection) gloves, surgical masks (e.g., double-ply paper towel taped to face if surgical masks are unavailable), microscope slides and cover slips, water, eyedroppers, tissues, microscopes, dilute solution of methylene blue

LS10 Journal Sheet #4

MICROORGANISMS

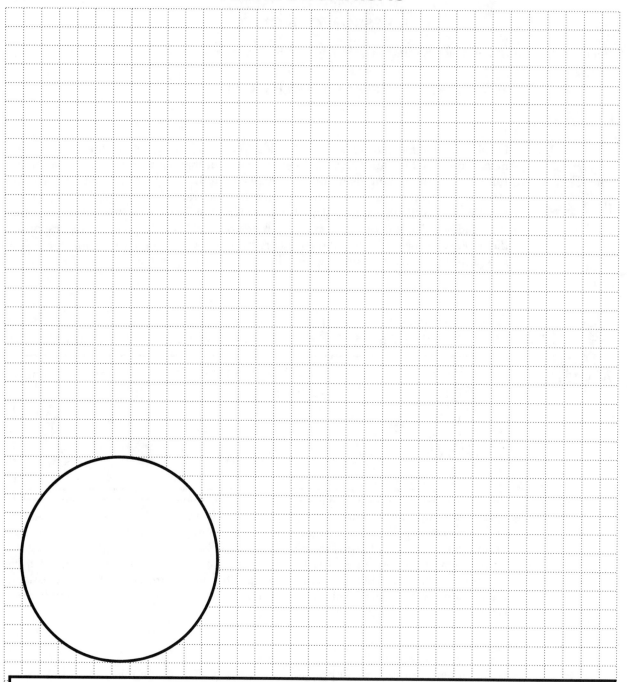

FIGURE C

Directions: (1) Wear goggles, surgical gloves, and a surgical mask during the preparation of your slides. (2) Use an eyedropper to obtain a sample drop from the "MOLD" culture. (3) Place the drop on a microscope slide. (4) Add a drop of dilute methlyene blue stain if available to better view the nuclei of the mold. (5) Gently cover the drop with a cover slip. (6) Place the corner of a tissue into the excess water leaking from the sides of the cover slip. This will draw up any excess water from under the slide. (7) Observe and draw the sample under the microscope beginning with a low-power objective. (8) Compare your drawings to the protozoa observed in Lesson #3.

LS10 Review Quiz

Directions: Keep your eyes on your own work.
Read all directions and questions carefully.
THINK BEFORE YOU ANSWER!
Watch your spelling, be neat, and do the best you can.

TEACHER'S COMMENTS: _____
_____

MICROORGANISMS

TRUE–FALSE FILL-IN: If the statement is true, write the word TRUE. If the statement is false, change the underlined word to make the statement true. *10 points*

_____ 1. <u>Bacteria</u> are tiny noncellular particles that can infect living cells.

_____ 2. <u>Viruses</u> take advantage of a cell's "chemical machinery" to carry on life functions they cannot perform on their own.

_____ 3. The machine used to see what a virus looks like is called a(n) <u>light</u> microscope.

_____ 4. Weakened or dead viruses can be used to make <u>antibiotics</u>.

_____ 5. Most bacteria are <u>harmless</u>.

_____ 6. In a <u>symbiotic</u> relationship both bacteria and host can benefit.

_____ 7. In a <u>parasitic</u> relationship the host always suffers and may die.

_____ 8. Bacteria belong to the Kingdom <u>Protista</u>.

_____ 9. Protozoa belong to the Kingdom <u>Monerans</u>.

_____ 10. Slime molds belong to the Kingdom <u>Protista</u>.

MULTIPLE CHOICE: Choose the letter of the word or phrase that best answers or completes the question or sentence. *10 points*

_____ 11. Which of the following is a characteristic of most protists?

    (A) they cannot move   (D) they have a cell wall
    (B) they have a nucleus   (E) can be seen with the naked eye
    (C) they are multicellular

_____ 12. Which structure helps a protist to get rid of water?

    (A) food vacuole   (D) contractile vacuole
    (B) nucleus   (E) cilium
    (C) flagella

____ 13. Which protist causes malaria?

    (A) zooflagellate   (D) sporozoan
    (B) sarcodine   (E) diatom
    (C) ciliate

____ 14. Which protist is a ciliate?

    (A) diatom   (D) paramecium
    (B) euglena   (E) ameba
    (C) dinoflagellate

____ 15. Which microorganism has many nuclei contained with a single membrane?

    (A) zooflagellate   (D) diatom
    (B) sarcodine   (E) ciliate
    (C) slime mold

LIFE CYCLE OF A VIRUS: Put the letters A, B, C, D, and E in the blanks next to each statement to show the order of events that takes place in the "life cycle" of a virus. *10 points*

16. ____ A virus attaches to the outside of a host cell.

17. ____ The virus injects hereditary material into the cell.

18. ____ The cell bursts open.

19. ____ The cell is forced to manufacture more viruses.

20. ____ New viruses go in search of new host cells.

PLANTS

TEACHER'S CLASSWORK AGENDA AND CONTENT NOTES

Classwork Agenda for the Week

1. Students will compose a graphic organizer showing the relationships among algae, mosses, seedless, and flowering plants.
2. Students will examine the basic characteristics of algae and mosses.
3. Students will examine the roots, stems, and leaves of seedless plants.
4. Students will examine the roots, stems, leaves, and reproductive organs of flowering plants.

Content Notes for Lecture and Discussion

Although the agricultural, medical, and horticultural uses of plants were known to the ancient Mesopotamians, Egyptians, and Chinese the first well-organized and documented study of plants was conducted by the Greek philosopher **Theophrastus** (b. 372 B.C.; d. 287 B.C.) who is regarded as the "father of **botany**." Many of the known characteristics of plants which determine their classification were first introduced by Theophrastus. He classified plants such as cycads and conifers—having little or no protection for their seeds—as **gymnosperms**. He regarded **angiosperms** that guarded their seeds with flowers and fruit as either **monocotyledon** or **dicotyledon**. A **cotyledon** is the "rudimentary leaf" present in the embryo of a seed plant. Theophrastus classified grasses, lillies, and palms as monocotyledons having narrow leaves with parallel veins and a single cotyledon. He classified the great majority of flowering plants as dicotyledons having broad leaves with branching veins and two cotyledons. These classifications are still used today to describe the variety of land plants.

The works of Theophrastus were lost to the Middle Ages but rediscovered during the Renaissance. During the Age of Exploration in the 15th, 16th, and 17th centuries, exotic plants from the Orient and Americas were added to the list of European varieties stimulating the birth of classical taxonomy. **Carolus Linnaeus** (b. 1707; d. 1778)—the originator of the system of binomial classification—believed that even more variety could be introduced into plant species within a particular "divinely created and immutable" genus by interbreeding. His thoughts prompted studies of hybridization that lasted through the latter half of the 19th century. **Charles Darwin**'s (b. 1809; d. 1882) theory of evolution by means of natural selection raised interest in fossilized plants which served on an equal scale with fossilized animals as evidence of Earth's changing geological history.

Plant tissues were among the first to be examined and most easily studied using the revolutionary histological and microscopic techniques of the 17th century. The involvement of the cell nucleus in cell function and reproduction were first elucidated in plants rather than animals by leading botanists of the time. Interest in plant function eventually led to the analysis of chemical cycles in plants: such as the nitrogen and carbon cycles which are so essential to the interplay of events that sustain earth's ecosystem. And since the middle of the 19th century, the study of plants has leaned heavily in favor of plant physiology.

The dependence of animals on plants as simple as seafaring algae is absolute. The ability of plants to capture and store the energy of the sun, and make use of that energy in the production of food and oxygen through the process of photosynthesis, serves as the foundation upon which earth's entire ecosystem is based.

In Lesson #1, students will compose a graphic organizer showing the relationships among algae, mosses, seedless and flowering plants.

In Lesson #2, students will examine the basic characteristics of algae and mosses.

In Lesson #3, students will examine the roots, stems, and leaves of seedless plants.

In Lesson #4, students will examine the roots, stems, leaves, and reproductive organs of flowering plants.

ANSWERS TO THE HOMEWORK PROBLEMS

Students will note in Experiment A how each side of the plant takes up a different color. The vertical arrangement of xylem cells does not cross the vertical midline. Students will note in Experiment B a sweet taste in the celery soaked in sugarwater. Both experiments demonstrate that plants have a vascular system that can transport water and nutrients up the step.

ANSWERS TO THE END-OF-THE-WEEK REVIEW QUIZ

1. true	6. do not have	11. do not have	16. do
2. true	7. true	12. true	17. true
3. photosynthesis	8. true	13. stems	18. true
4. true	9. do	14. leaves	19. tropisms
5. true	10. true	15. true	20. pollination

ESSAY: Angiosperms are flowering plants whose seeds are protected by fruit. Gymnosperms do not have true flowers or fruit to protect their seeds. Gymnosperm seeds are protected by specialized leaves called cones.

ESSAY: Annuals complete their life cycle in one year. Biennials take two years to complete their life cycle. Perennials can live for much longer than two years.

LS11 Fact Sheet

PLANTS

CLASSWORK AGENDA FOR THE WEEK

(1) Compose a graphic organizer showing the relationships among algae, mosses, seedless and flowering plants.
(2) Examine the basic characteristics of algae and mosses.
(3) Examine the roots, stems, and leaves of seedless plants.
(4) Examine the roots, stems, leaves, and reproductive organs of flowering plants.

All **plants** are autotrophs serving as the primary source of food and oxygen for other living things. They are the only organisms that can trap the energy radiated by the sun in molecules of **chlorophyll**. Chlorophyll is contained in important cell organelles called **chloroplasts**. By using solar energy to rearrange the atoms in molecules of carbon dioxide and water, plants produce simple sugar (e.g., glucose) and oxygen. This chemical process is called **photosynthesis** (e.g., meaning "making things with light"). The process of photosynthesis can be represented by the following chemical equation:

$$6CO_2 \quad + \quad 6H_2O \quad \longrightarrow \quad C_6H_{12}O_6 \quad + \quad 6O_2$$

| six molecules of carbon dioxide | six molecules of water | one molecule of glucose | six molecules of oxygen |

Algae belonging to **Kingdom Protista** were the first organisms on the planet to contain chlorophyll; so, many scientists consider algae to be the first plants. Algae—like protozoa—reproduce by **asexual reproduction**. They simply "split in half." Organisms that reproduce "asexually" do not require a mate to complete the process. Algae are **nonvascular** organisms, meaning that they do not have specialized organs to transport water around their body. They do not have roots and stems like land plants and are completely dependent upon a watery environment to survive. **Brown algae**, **red algae**, and **green algae** are the three main groups of algae. Algae are not only the main source of food for sea animals but also provide humans with a variety of foods and other commercial products. Seaweeds can be ground into meal for livestock. **Algin** found in **kelp** (e.g., brown seaweed) is used to make ice cream, puddings, and other food products. Algin is an ingredient in cosmetics, paints, and insecticides.

Mosses were probably the first "chlorophyll-containing" organisms to live on land. Mosses are mutlicellular organisms that have thick protective cells that prevent the organism from losing too much water. However, mosses still need lots of water to survive. They are nonvascular plants like algae and still require a moist environment to sustain life and reproduce.

The first plants to have a **vascular system** for transporting water and nutrients to the different parts of their body were ferns. **Ferns** are **seedless plants** that have roots, stems, and leaves to help them survive on land. **Roots** absorb water from the soil. **Stems** move the water and nutrients up and down the plant. **Leaves** take in carbon dioxide, release oxygen, and catch the rays of the sun. Ferns do, however, require lots of water to spread their reproductive **spores**.

Plants with seeds have the same basic needs as seedless plants but have made additional adaptations to the land. In addition to evolving a sophisticated **vascular system** plants have developed a method of reproducing out of the water. Plants were also the first organisms to begin reproducing "sexually." **Sexual reproduction** involves the exchange of hereditary information between "male" and "female" partners within a species. Plants breed.

The vascular system of a land plant consists of two types of tissue: xylem and phloem. **Xylem** carries water and dissolved materials up from the roots to the leaves. **Phloem** carries food up and down the plant. Stem cells can be rigid or pliable depending upon how much water they have in them. By emptying or filling stem cells with water a plant can cause its stems to bend. Plants bend their stems to direct their leaves toward the sun. Movement in plants are called **tropisms**. Tropisms are controlled by plant hormones that are produced by the cells in response to environmental stimuli.

During sexual reproduction, the male gamete (e.g., reproductive cell) called **pollen**, "pollinates" (e.g., fertilizes) a female gamete inside a structure called an **ovule**. Ovules are protected by **flower petals**. After fertilization an ovule becomes a **seed**. The seeds of many land plants are surrounded by a protective and nutrient-filled organ called a **fruit**. Land plants that produce fruit from flowers are called **angiosperms**. Animals eat the fruit of angiosperms but do not digest the seeds. The seeds are spread by animal excretions. Land plants that do not produce flowers and fruit are called **gymnosperms**. Gymnosperms have **cones** to protect their seeds. Gymnosperms include cycads, ginkgoes, and conifers (e.g., pine trees). Different seed plants complete their life cycle in different amounts of time. **Annuals** complete their cycle in one year or less. **Biennials** take two years to complete their life cycle. **Perennials** live very long lives.

Homework Directions

Perform one of the following experiments to demonstrate how plants transport water and nutrients up their stem to their leaves.

Experiment A: (1) Carefully cut the stem of a flowering plant (e.g., daisy, carnation, etc.) lengthwise from the bottom of the stem halfway to the flower. (2) Fill two cups with water and add a different color of food coloring to each cup making a concentrated solution of deep, dark color. (3) Place one half of the stem in each solution. (4) Report and explain your observations every 12 hours for the next 3 days.

Experiment B: (1) Fill two cups with water. (2) Pour a tablespoon of sugar into one cup and stir. (3) Place a celery stalk into each cup. (4) Wait 24–48 hours then taste the celery in each cup. (5) Report and explain your observations.

Assignment due: _____

_____	_____	___/___/___
Student's Signature	Parent's Signature	Date

PLANTS

Work Date: ____/____/____

LESSON OBJECTIVE

Students will compose a graphic organizer showing the relationships among algae, mosses, seedless, and flowering plants.

Classroom Activities

On Your Mark!

Prepare for the lessons in this unit by paying a visit to the local nursery, classroom aquarium/bog/pond, and pet/fish store. A vast variety of algae can be obtained from a fresh water aquarium or the soupy green water of bogs or freshwater ponds. A collection jar left in a warm, aerated sunlit place serves well as a sufficiently cultured reservoir of collected samples. Mosses can be obtained in sufficient amounts adhering to the soil and roots of fungi and ferns. The local nursery should be able to supply sufficient numbers of ferns and inexpensive flowering plants.

Begin Lesson #1 by displaying the **labelled samples** of "Algae," "Mosses," "Ferns," and "Flowering Plants." Use the information in the Teacher's Classwork Agenda and Content Notes to give a brief lecture about the descriptions used by the Ancient Greek philosopher **Theophrastus** (b. 372 B.C.; d. 287 B.C.) to classify plants. Have students define the following terms according to the definitions used in the Teacher's Classwork Agenda and Content Notes: **botany, gymnosperm, angiosperm, cotyledon, monocotyledon, dicotyledon**.

Get Set!

Give students the opportunity to read the Fact Sheet before briefly testing their knowledge of what they have read. Discuss and list some of the horticultural, agricultural, and medicinal uses of plants and have students copy your list on Journal Sheet #1. Instruct students to begin composing a graphic organizer that will summarize the information in their Fact Sheet.

Go!

Give students ample time to complete the activity described in Figure A on Journal Sheet #1. Circulate around the room to insure that students are creating a logical graphic organizer that breaks down the characteristics of nonvascular (e.g., algae and mosses) and vascular (ferns and seed-producing) plants.

Materials

pre-prepared samples of algae, mosses, ferns, and flowering plants

LS11 JOURNAL SHEET #1

PLANTS

IMPORTANT PLANT TERMS

botany: _____

gymnosperm: _____

angiosperm: _____

cotyledon: _____

monocotyledon: _____

dicotyledon: _____

NONVASCULAR PLANTS   **VASCULAR PLANTS**

SEED   SEED

LEAF   LEAF

two cotyledons   cotyledon

FIGURE A

Directions: (1) Read the FACT SHEET. (2) Start with the arrows to create a graphic organizer that has as many facts as you can gather about each group of microorganisms. (3) Identify the schematic drawings above.

PLANTS

Work Date: ____/____/____

LESSON OBJECTIVE

Students will examine the basic characteristics of algae and mosses.

Classroom Activities

On Your Mark!

Display the pre-prepared cultures of "Algae" and "Mosses". Begin with a review of the graphic organizer composed in Lesson #1, concentrating on the characteristics of algae and mosses described in the Fact Sheet. Display the containers of commercial products that include any of the following ingredients: seaweed, kelp, brown algae, algin. Explain that **algin** is a water-soluble, cream-colored powder that is harvested from a number of species of seaweeds, kelp, and brown algae. With chemical treatment algin is used commercially as a thickener and emulsifier (e.g., meaning to "make creamy") of a variety of products including ice cream, whipped, cream, paint, and cosmetics.

Get Set!

Point out that algae and moss are green plants containing chlorophyll which allows both organisms to carry on photosynthesis. Students should be able to identify the dark green chloroplasts present in the species of algae using a microscope under medium to high power. Explain that algae frequently exist in colonies of attached cells adhering to leaves and other surfaces in fresh-water ponds and streams or floating on the surface of the ocean. Ocean **phytoplankton**—mainly unicellular golden or brown pigmented diatoms and dinoflagellates—manufacture most of the oxygen present in the atmosphere. Mosses are partially adapted to land, living in moist soil and on fungus. Mosses have both male and female reproductive organs (e.g., **male/female gametophytes**) which produce male sperm cells and female egg cells that fuse as part of the moss's reproductive cycle.

Go!

Give students ample time to complete the activity described in Figure B on Journal Sheet #2.

Materials

pre-prepared samples of algae and mosses, microscope slides and cover slips, water, eyedroppers, tissues, microscopes, magnifying lenses or dissecting scopes

LS11 JOURNAL SHEET #2

PLANTS

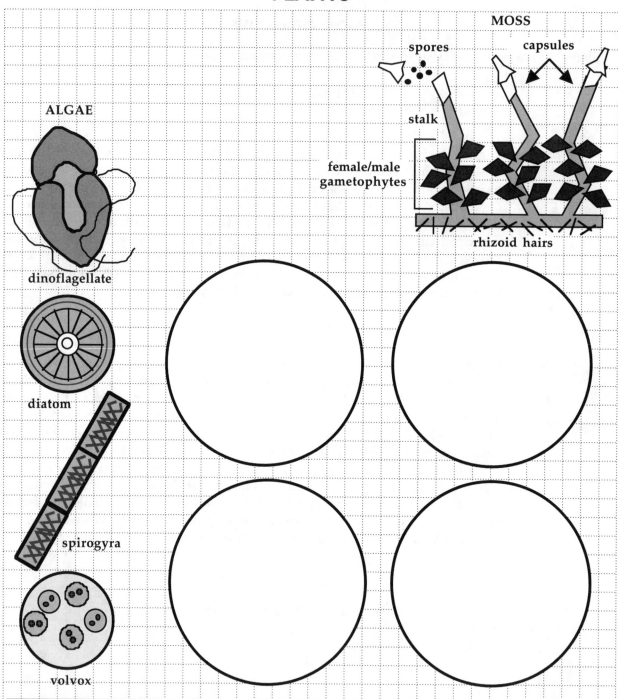

FIGURE B

<u>Directions</u>: (1) Use an eyedropper to obtain a sample drop from the "ALGAE" culture. (2) Place the drop on a microscope slide and gently cover the drop with a cover slip. (3) Place the corner of a tissue into the excess water leaking from the sides of the cover slip. This will draw up any excess water from under the slide. (4) Observe and draw the sample under the microscope beginning with a low power objective. (5) Obtain a "MOSS" sample. (6) Examine the moss under a magnifying glass or dissecting scope. (7) Draw what you obeserve.

PLANTS

Work Date: _____/_____/_____

LESSON OBJECTIVE

Students will examine the roots, stems, and leaves of seedless plants.

Classroom Activities

On Your Mark!

Display the samples of ferns and flowering plants obtained from a local nursery. Ask students to comment on the obvious difference between the two types of plants: the ferns lack the flowers present in the flowering plants. Inform the students that unlike flowering plants ferns do not have seeds. They reproduce by releasing spores in much the same way as molds and mosses.

Get Set!

Refer to the diagram on Journal Sheet #3 to explain the life cycle of a fern. Fern leaves produce **sporangia** which make **spores**. Spores develop into **prothallus** having **archegonium** (e.g., female gametophyte) and **antheridium** (e.g., male gametophyte). Archegonium produce **eggs** and antheridium produce **sperm**. Sperm fertilize eggs to produce a **zygote**. The zygote doubles, quadruples, etc., and develops into a new plant having a new prothallus with **roots**, a **stem**, and **leaves**. Explain that while ferns having a vascular system (e.g., roots and stems) to transport water throughout the plant are better adapted to land than mosses, the survival of their spores requires a watery environment.

Go!

Give students ample time to examine the roots, stems, and leaves of a fern using a magnifying glass or dissecting scope. Have them draw their observations as directed in Figure C on Journal Sheet #3.

Materials

samples of ferns, tweezers, magnifying lenses or dissecting scopes

LS11 JOURNAL SHEET #3

PLANTS

LIFE CYCLE OF A FERN

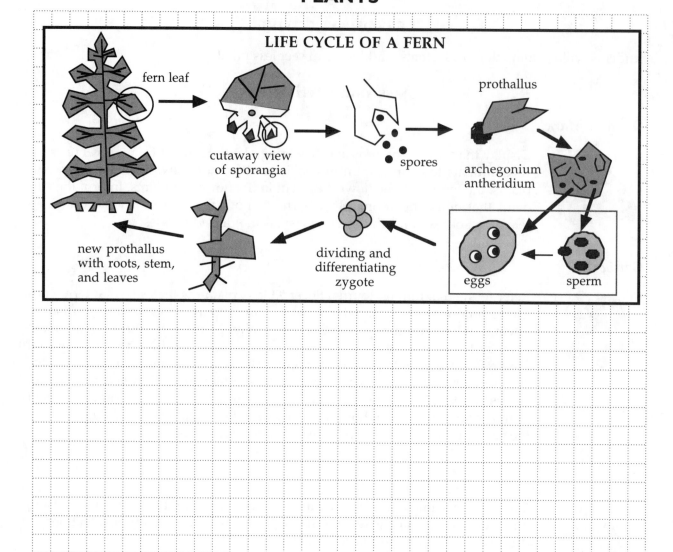

fern leaf

cutaway view of sporangia

spores

prothallus

archegonium antheridium

eggs

sperm

dividing and differentiating zygote

new prothallus with roots, stem, and leaves

FIGURE C

Directions: (1) Obtain a section of "FERN". (2) Examine the roots, stem, and leaves of the fern using a magnifying glass or dissecting scope. (3) Draw and compare your observations to the schematic diagram of structures above.

PLANTS

Work Date: ____/____/____

LESSON OBJECTIVE

Students will examine the roots, stems, leaves, and reproductive organs of flowering plants.

Classroom Activities

On Your Mark!

Display the samples of ferns and flowering plants obtained from a local nursery. Review the obvious difference between the two types of plants to assess students' recollection of the parts of the fern and to point out that flowering plants have flowers. Flowers produce seeds that are protected by fruit. Flowering plants (e.g., angiosperms) are the most sophisticated organisms in Kingdom Plantae.

Get Set!

Refer to the diagrams on Journal Sheet #4 identifying the main parts of the plant's structure and the reproductive organs of the flower. Explain that the **stamen** is the male reproductive organ. The **anthers**—supported by **filaments**—produce **pollen** (e.g., analogous to sperm). The female reproductive organ is called the **pistil**. The pistil has a sticky **stigma** that "catches" pollen and a **style** that leads down to the **ovary**. The ovary stores the unfertilized **ovules** (e.g., analogous to eggs) that become **seeds** after fertilization. The **sepals** are the tiny green leaves that surround the flower before it blooms. The aroma of the open **petals** attracts birds and insects that pick up and spread pollen to other plants. The process of spreading pollen to foreign plants results in **cross-breeding** (e.g., hybridization) within a species.

Go!

Give students ample time to examine part of the flower using magnifying glass or dissecting scope. Have them draw their observations as directed in Figure D on Journal Sheet #4.

Materials

samples of flowers, tweezers, magnifying lenses or dissecting scopes

LS11 JOURNAL SHEET #4

PLANTS

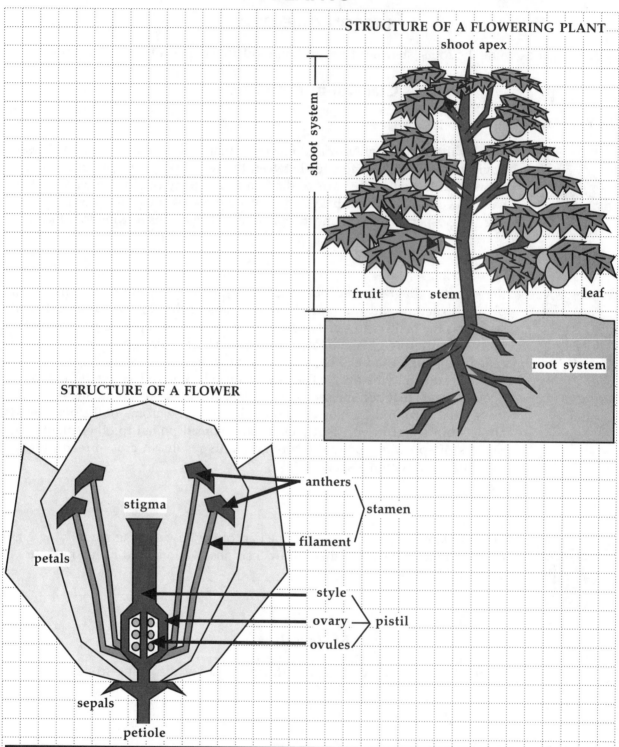

STRUCTURE OF A FLOWERING PLANT

shoot apex

shoot system

fruit   stem   leaf

root system

STRUCTURE OF A FLOWER

petals

stigma

anthers

stamen

filament

sepals

petiole

style

ovary → pistil

ovules

FIGURE D

<u>Directions</u>: (1) Obtain a "FLOWER". (2) Examine the parts of the flower using a magnifying glass or dissecting scope. (3) Draw and compare your observations to the schematic diagram of structures above.

LS11 REVIEW QUIZ

Directions: Keep your eyes on your own work.
Read all directions and questions carefully.
THINK BEFORE YOU ANSWER!
Watch your spelling, be neat, and do the best you can.

CLASSWORK	(~40): _____
HOMEWORK	(~20): _____
CURRENT EVENT	(~10): _____
TEST	(~30): _____
TOTAL	(~100): _____

(A ≥ 90, B ≥ 80, C ≥ 70, D ≥ 60, F < 60)

LETTER GRADE: _____

TEACHER'S COMMENTS: _____
_____

PLANTS

TRUE–FALSE FILL-IN: If the statement is true, write the word TRUE. If the statement is false, change the underlined word to make the statement true. *20 points*

_____ 1. <u>All</u> plants are autotrophs.

_____ 2. Organisms use <u>chlorophyll</u> to trap the energy radiated by the sun.

_____ 3. The term <u>tropism</u> means "making things with light."

_____ 4. <u>Algae</u> were the first organisms on the planet to contain chlorophyll.

_____ 5. Organisms that reproduce "asexually" <u>do not</u> require a mate to complete the process.

_____ 6. Nonvascular plants <u>have</u> specialized organs to transport water around their body.

_____ 7. Algin found in <u>kelp</u> is used to make ice cream, puddings, cosmetics, paints, and insecticides.

_____ 8. <u>Mosses</u> were probably the first "chlorophyll-containing" organisms to live on land.

_____ 9. Mosses <u>do not</u> need lots of water to survive.

_____ 10. Ferns have a <u>vascular</u> system for transporting water and nutrients to the different parts of their body.

_____ 11. Ferns <u>have</u> seeds.

_____ 12. <u>Roots</u> absorb water from the soil.

_____ 13. <u>Leaves</u> move the water and nutrients up and down the plant.

_____ 14. <u>Stems</u> take in carbon dioxide, release oxygen, and catch the rays of the sun.

_____ 15. Ferns require lots of water to spread their <u>spores</u>.

_____ 16. Organisms that reproduce "sexually" <u>do not</u> require a mate to complete the process.

_____ 17. <u>Xylem</u> carries water and dissolved materials up from the roots to the leaves.

_____ 18. <u>Phloem</u> carries food up and down the plant.

_____ 19. Movement in plants are called <u>reflexes</u>.

_____ 20. Fertilization in plants is called <u>photosynthesis</u>.

ESSAY: Write several sentences to describe the main differences among angiosperms and gymnosperms. *5 points*

_____

_____

_____

_____

_____

_____

ESSAY: Write several sentences to describe the main differences among annual, biennial, and perennial plants. *5 points*

_____

_____

_____

_____

_____

_____

_____   _____   ____/____/____
Student's Signature   Parent's Signature   Date

INVERTEBRATES

TEACHER'S CLASSWORK AGENDA AND CONTENT NOTES

Classwork Agenda for the Week

1. Students will draw a schematic diagram of an organism in each of the eight major invertebrate phyla.
2. Students will examine the basic characteristics of porifera and coelenterata.
3. Students will examine the basic characteristics of platyhelminthes, nematoda, and annelida.
4. Students will examine the basic characteristics of mollusca, echinodermata, and arthropoda.

Content Notes for Lecture and Discussion

The survival of any group of animals depends on how well it has evolved to solve basic biological problems. All organisms must obtain food and oxygen, free themselves of the wastes produced by their own metabolic actions, maintain water balance, sense and respond appropriately to environmental change, and successfully reproduce offspring having the same beneficial adaptations. While it is convenient to use terms such as "lower" or "higher," "primitive" and "advanced," or "simple" and "complex" to describe organisms of different phyla, it is important to remember that all living species are successful at what they do in solving life's most essential problems. If they are not, then they are doomed to extinction. A well-adapted organism is a successful organism regardless of the "esteem" paid it by its human categorizers; and its value to the ecosystem of which it is a part can only be fully determined after the species is gone.

Zoology was originally of concern to ancient and medieval farmers and physicians for its value in obtaining foods and medicinal remedies from the organs and secretions of animals. It was not until the 16th century that the study of comparative anatomy and physiology by biologists such as the English physician **William Harvey** (b. 1578; d. 1657) that anatomical and physiological relationships between animals were appreciated for their purely scientific value. The study of comparative anatomy played an important role in the discovery of how organ systems such as the circulatory system work and in the development of the modern taxonomy. In the early 18th century **Carolus Linnaeus** (b. 1707; d. 1778) and others systematically categorized living organisms according to their anatomical traits, giving zoology and botany the foundations required to expand with the frontiers of seafaring explorers.

The vast variety of **invertebrates** are distinguished from animals of the **vertebrate** phyla by their lack of an internal skeleton and backbone (e.g., notochord). They are largely restricted to moist watery environments: the major exception being the tens of thousands of insect species belonging to phylum arthropoda whose diverse adaptations have made them successful in the air, at sea, and on land.

The study of external structure always gives a worthwhile impression of an organism's physical adaptations and preserved specimens should be displayed for student consideration whenever available. While there is no substitute for the careful and systematic dissection of preserved organisms as a means of visualizing the similarities and differences between them, students can still become familiar with the basic distinguishing characteristics of different animals without it.

In Lesson #1, students will draw a schematic diagram of an organism in each of the eight major invertebrate phyla.

In Lesson #2, students will examine the basic characteristics of porifera and coelenterata.

In Lesson #3, students will examine the basic characteristics of platyhelminthes, nematoda, and annelida.

LS12 Content Notes *(cont'd)*

In Lesson #4, students will examine the basic characteristics of mollusca, echinodermata, and arthropoda.

ANSWERS TO THE HOMEWORK PROBLEMS

Students' sentences should summarize the pertinent information supplied in the Fact Sheet.

ANSWERS TO THE END-OF-THE-WEEK REVIEW QUIZ

1. true	11. echinodermata	21. I
2. true	12. arthropoda	22. F
3. vertebrates	13. H	23. H
4. invertebrates	14. E	24. F
5. true	15. D	25. H
6. true	16. B	26. G
7. true	17. A	27. H
8. true	18. B	28. I
9. annelida	19. H	29. H
10. mollusca	20. C	30. H

LS12 Fact Sheet

INVERTEBRATES

CLASSWORK AGENDA FOR THE WEEK

(1) Draw a schematic diagram of an organism in each of the eight major invertebrate phyla.
(2) Examine the basic characteristics of porifera and coelenterata.
(3) Examine the basic characteristics of platyhelminthes, nematoda, and annelida.
(4) Examine the basic characteristics of mollusca, echinodermata, and arthropoda.

Kingdom Animalia is traditionally divided into two major groups: animals that have a backbone and animals that do not have a backbone. Animals that have a backbone are called **vertebrates**. Animals that do not have a backbone are called **invertebrates**. Both of these groups of organisms are further divided into smaller and smaller groups (e.g., phylum, class, order, family, genus, and species) depending upon their **anatomy** (e.g., structure of body parts). Vertebrates include animals such as fish, amphibians, reptiles, birds, and mammals all having an internal skeleton. Invertebrates include animals that lack a skeleton but may have a hard outer shell to protect their soft internal organs. Invertebrates include sponges, jellyfish, worms, snails, starfish, insects and crustaceans (e.g., crayfish and lobster).

The **phylum porifera** includes sponges. Sea sponges can be found in warm coastal waters attached to rocks on the shallow bottom. Freshwater sponges attach themselves in summer to the submerged roots or branches of freshwater streams and ponds. Unlike other animals a sponge does not have a variety of organ systems that accomplish particular life functions (e.g., circulatory system, nervous system, etc.). Sponges are composed of a few different types of cells held loosely together to form layers of tissue. They feed by filtering bacteria and other microscopic organisms through pores in their outer layer of tissue.

The **phylum coelenterata** includes hydra, coral, and jellyfish. These organisms dwell in sea or freshwater environments. Tiny tentacled hydra can be found attached to the underside of rocks and fallen leaves submerged in freshwater rivers, lakes, and ponds. Sea coral live in colonies, each individual organism secreting calcium carbonate to form a hard outer "skeleton" that protects the colony. Millions of individual coral about 1–3 millimeters in size form gigantic structures called coral reefs off the coastlines of warmwater islands. Large tentacled jellyfish such as the umbrella-shaped "aurelia" and the "Portuguese man-of-war" float free on the surface of the ocean. The identifying characteristic of all coelenterates is their central body cavity or gut connected to a single opening or mouth. Most eject poisonous spines that can paralyze and immobilize prey.

Simple flatworms belong to **phylum platyhelminthes**. There are more than 20,000 species in the phylum including planaria and tapeworms. There are fresh and sea water varieties of platyhelminthes and others such as the parasitic tapeworm that live inside an animal host. They range in size from the microscopic to more than 20 meters in length. Unlike flatworms, roundworms of **phylum nematoda** have long cylindrical bodies with clearly defined digestive, excretory, and reproductive organs.

Earthworms and leeches belong to **phylum annelida**. These are "segmented" worms whose body appears to be made of "stacked" ringlike sections. The common earthworm can be found near the surface of moist grassy soil mostly on warm rainy nights during the spring and summer. Leeches attach themselves to animal hosts that live among the weeds of ponds and freshwater streams. Annelids have well defined organ systems such as a digestive, circulatory and nervous system.

The **phylum mollusca** includes scallops, clams, snails, and squids. All mollusks have a strong muscular "foot" used for creeping or swimming, holding onto surfaces, or grasping prey, and a hard outer shell to protect their soft inner bodies. There are more than 50,000 species of mollusk inhabiting either fresh or sea water habitats.

The **phylum echinodermata** includes starfish, sea urchins, and sea cucumbers. They can be recognized by their hard "spiny" skin and the "radially symmetrical" shape of their body. The body of an organism that has **radial symmetry** such as a starfish can be cut from its middle of center point into sections that are exactly alike.

All insects, spiders, and crustaceans are members of **phylum arthropoda**. There are over 1,000,000 species belonging to this group. They live on land, in water, and in the air. The have a well-developed **head, thorax,** and **abdomen**. The two most obvious distinguishing characteristics of all arthropods is their hard exoskeleton (e.g., outer skeleton) and their agile jointed legs.

Homework Directions

Write one sentence for each major invertebrate phylum that summarizes the identifying characteristic(s) of organisms in that phylum.

Assignment due: _____

_____   _____   ____/____/____
Student's Signature   Parent's Signature   Date

INVERTEBRATES

Work Date: ____/____/____

LESSON OBJECTIVE

Students will draw a schematic diagram of an organism in each of the eight major invertebrate phyla.

Classroom Activities

On Your Mark!

Display preserved specimens of invertebrates if available.

Using the information provided in the Teacher's Classwork Agenda and Content Notes begin Lesson #1 with a brief review of the biological problems that all organisms must solve in order to survive. Define an **invertebrate** as an animal that lacks a backbone. Distinguish this group of animals from **vertebrates** (e.g., humans) that have a backbone. Emphasize that all organisms have evolved specialized adaptations suitable for the environments in which they live.

Get Set!

Explain that a "schematic drawing" is not an exact representation of an object like an artist's depiction of reality. A schematic drawing merely has the essential qualities of the object. Illustrate this by drawing two "stick figures" on the board of a human being and a dog. Ask students to describe the major distinguishing characteristic(s) between the two animals represented by these two schematic drawings. Obviously, the human being stands erect on two appendages. The dog stands on all four appendages. Give students the opportunity to read the Fact Sheet before you test their knowledge of what they have read. Tell them to carefully study and discuss the distinguishing characteristic of each phyla of invertebrates.

Go!

Give students ample time to complete the activity described in Figure A on Journal Sheet #1. Circulate around the room to insure that students are creating simple schematic drawings to represent the "ideal" organism of each invertebrate phyla and not a complicated "artist's" rendition.

Materials

preserved invertebrate specimens (if available), Journal Sheet #1, Fact Sheet

LS12 Journal Sheet #1

INVERTEBRATES

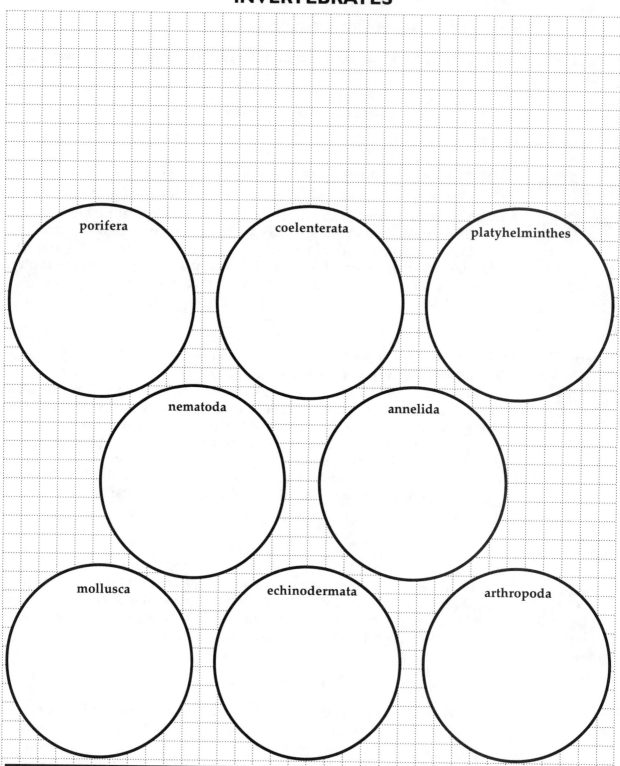

porifera

coelenterata

platyhelminthes

nematoda

annelida

mollusca

echinodermata

arthropoda

FIGURE A

<u>Directions</u>: Using the information on the FACT SHEET make a simple "schematic" drawing to show the most important characteristic(s) of an animal in each of the invertebrate phyla.

INVERTEBRATES

Work Date: _____/_____/_____

LESSON OBJECTIVE

Students will examine the basic characteristics of porifera and coelenterata.

Classroom Activities

On Your Mark!

Display preserved specimens of porifera (e.g., sponges) and coelenterata (e.g., jellyfish) if available. Have students refer to their schematic drawings of sponges and coelenterata completed in Lesson #1. Have students compare their drawings to the illustration on Journal Sheet #2.

Get Set!

Point out that sponges live in colonies while jellyfish tend to float away from other members of their species. Members of both groups of organisms have an outer layer of **epidermal** (e.g., meaning "skin") cells and an inner layer of cells that absorbs nutrients. The **mesoglia** of coelenterates gives the organism added buoyancy. Give students time to discuss and come to agreement on one or more characteristics that distinguish the two groups of organisms (e.g., sponges have multiple incurrent pores to admit water and food while jellyfish have a single mouthlike opening). Have them agree upon a single characteristic common to these two types of organisms (e.g., both groups have a central body cavity where food and water accumulate before being filtered by cells lining the cavity).

Go!

Give students ample time to complete the activity described in Figure B on Journal Sheet #2.

Materials

Journal Sheet #2

LS12 JOURNAL SHEET #2

INVERTEBRATES

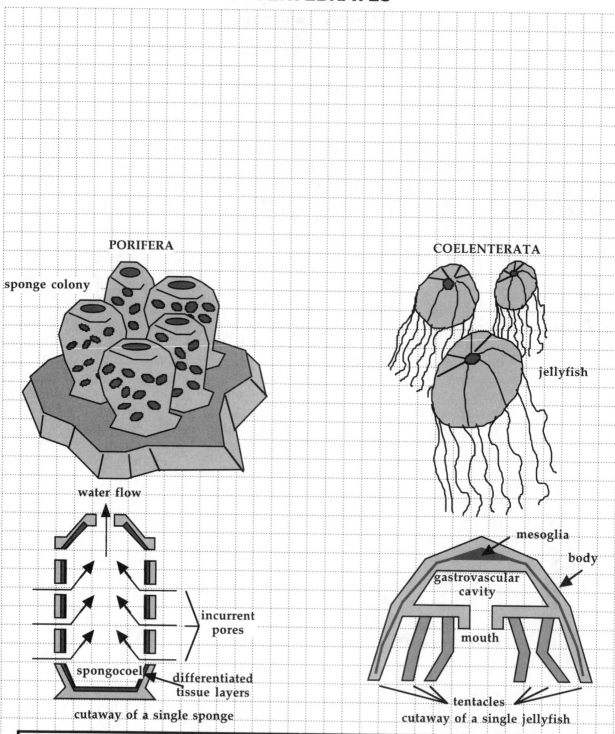

PORIFERA

sponge colony

water flow

incurrent pores

spongocoel

differentiated tissue layers

cutaway of a single sponge

COELENTERATA

jellyfish

mesoglia

body

gastrovascular cavity

mouth

tentacles

cutaway of a single jellyfish

FIGURE B

<u>Directions</u>: (1) Compare the diagrams of PORIFERA and COELENTERATA. (2) Write a sentence describing a common characteristic of both sponges and jellyfish. (3) Write a sentence describing a feature of sponges that is not present in jellyfish. (4) Write a sentence describing a feature of jellyfish that is not present in sponges.

INVERTEBRATES

Work Date: ____/____/____

LESSON OBJECTIVE

Students will examine the basic characteristics of platyhelminthes, nematoda, and annelida.

Classroom Activities

On Your Mark!

Display preserved specimens of platyhelminthes (e.g., planaria), nematoda (e.g., ascaris), and annelida (e.g., earthworm) if available. Have students refer to their schematic drawings of these phyla completed in Lesson #1. Have students compare their drawings to the illustration on Journal Sheet #3.

Get Set!

Give students time to discuss and come to agreement on one or more characteristics that distinguish the three groups of organisms. Point out the increasing complexity in the cross sections for each organism as one compares platyhelminthes to nematoda, then nematoda to annelida. Ask: "Which phyla most probably evolved first?" Answer: Platyhelminthes is considered the most primitive because it is the least complex. Platyhelminthes consist of three tissue layers of differentiated cells called the **endoderm**, **mesoderm**, and **ectoderm**. The cells of nematoda are slightly more specialized. Explain that members of phyla annelida have a developed nervous system consisting of a **brain** situated near the mouth of the worm. It has a tiny **heart** in each segment along the **dorsal** and **ventral blood vessels**. Most annelida have a **clitellum** which is involved in reproduction. A pair of **nephridia** in each segment allows the organism to get rid of wastes. Have students note the **setae hairs** and two sets of muscles that give the worm mobility. **Longitudinal muscles** assist the animal in forward movement. The **circular muscles** give the worm the ability to constrict its width enabling it to "slip" through spaces between small pebbles.

Go!

Give students ample time to complete the activity described in Figure C on Journal Sheet #3.

Materials

Journal Sheet #3

LS12 JOURNAL SHEET #3

INVERTEBRATES

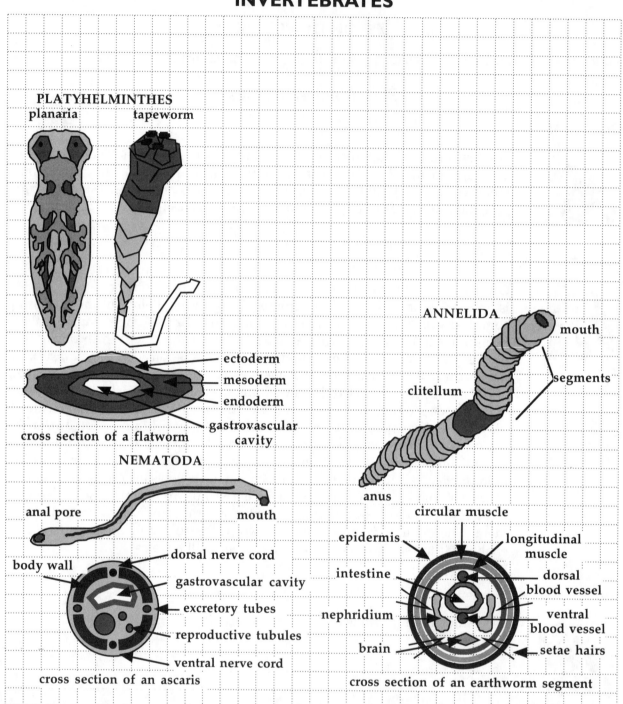

PLATYHELMINTHES
planaria   tapeworm

ectoderm
mesoderm
endoderm
gastrovascular
cavity
cross section of a flatworm

ANNELIDA
mouth
segments
clitellum
anus

NEMATODA
anal pore   mouth
body wall
dorsal nerve cord
gastrovascular cavity
excretory tubes
reproductive tubules
ventral nerve cord
cross section of an ascaris

circular muscle
epidermis
longitudinal muscle
intestine
dorsal blood vessel
nephridium
ventral blood vessel
brain
setae hairs
cross section of an earthworm segment

FIGURE C

Directions: (1) Compare the diagrams of PLATYHELMINTHES, NEMATODA, and ANNELIDA. (2) Write a sentence describing a common characteristic of all three phyla. (3) Write a sentence describing a feature of platyhelminthes that is not present in either nematoda nor annelida. (4) Write a sentence describing a feature of nematoda that is not present in either platyhelminthes nor annelida. (5) Write a sentence describing a feature of annelida that is not present in either platyhelminthes nor nematoda.

INVERTEBRATES

Work Date: ____/____/____

LESSON OBJECTIVE

Students will examine the basic characteristics of mollusca, echinodermata, and arthropoda.

Classroom Activities

On Your Mark!

Display preserved specimens of mollusca (e.g., snails), echinodermata (e.g., starfish), and arthropoda (e.g., grasshopper, ant) if available. Have students refer to their schematic drawings of these phyla completed in Lesson #1. Have students compare their drawings to the illustration on Journal Sheet #4.

Get Set!

Give students time to discuss and come to agreement on one or more characteristics that distinguish the three groups of organisms. Have students note that echinodermata have **radial symmetry** which is obvious in the starfish and apparent in the sea cucumber when viewed from the mouth down the long axis of the organism's body. Mollusca that live in water (e.g., squid and clams) have **gills** similar to those of fish which can absorb water-dissolved oxygen. All arthropoda, regardless of their number of legs, have jointed legs attached to their thorax. The **thorax** connects the **head** and **abdomen**. Arthropods have **spiracles** along the sides of their abdomen which allow the passage of air. The spiracles are connected to tubules that make up the respiratory system of the organism. Students should note that all of these organisms have a hard or spiny epidermis to protect their soft internal organs.

Go!

Give students ample time to complete the activity described in Figure D on Journal Sheet #4.

Materials

Journal Sheet #4

LS12 JOURNAL SHEET #4

INVERTEBRATES

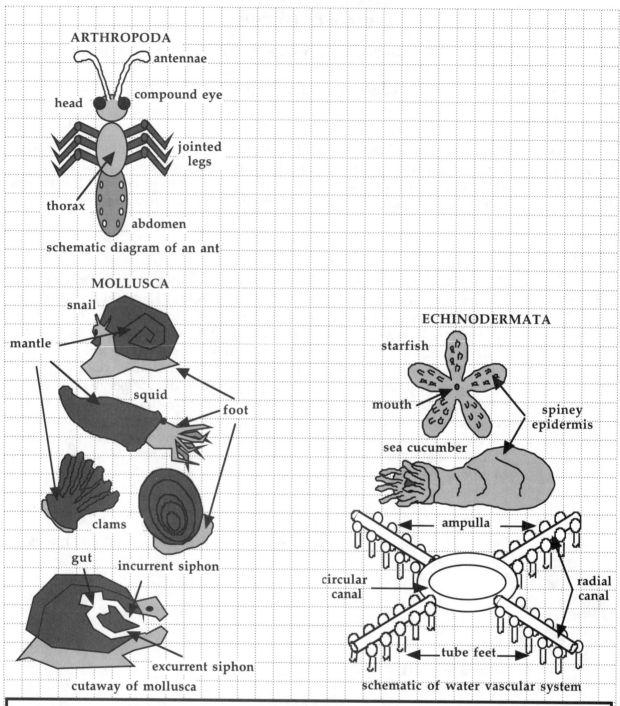

ARTHROPODA
antennae
compound eye
head
jointed legs
thorax
abdomen
schematic diagram of an ant

MOLLUSCA
snail
mantle
squid
foot
clams
gut
incurrent siphon
excurrent siphon
cutaway of mollusca

ECHINODERMATA
starfish
mouth
spiney epidermis
sea cucumber
ampulla
circular canal
radial canal
tube feet
schematic of water vascular system

FIGURE D

<u>Directions</u>: (1) Compare the diagrams of MOLLUSCA, ECHINODERMATA, and ARTHROPODA. (2) Write a sentence describing a common characteristic of all three phyla. (3) Write a sentence describing a feature of mollusca that is not present in either echinodermata or arthropoda. (4) Write a sentence describing a feature of echinodermata that is not present in either mollusca or arthropoda. (5) Write a sentence describing a feature of arthropoda that is not present in either mollusca or echinodermata.

LS12 REVIEW QUIZ

Directions: Keep your eyes on your own work.
Read all directions and questions carefully.
THINK BEFORE YOU ANSWER!
Watch your spelling, be neat, and do the best you can.

TEACHER'S COMMENTS: _____

_____

INVERTEBRATES

TRUE–FALSE FILL-IN: If the statement is true, write the word TRUE. If the statement is false, change the underlined word to make the statement true. *12 points*

_____ 1. Animals that have a backbone are called <u>vertebrates</u>.

_____ 2. Animals that do not have a backbone are called <u>invertebrates</u>.

_____ 3. <u>Invertebrates</u> include animals having an internal skeleton.

_____ 4. <u>Vertebrates</u> include animals that lack a skeleton but may have a hard outer shell to protect their soft internal organs.

_____ 5. Animals of phylum <u>porifera</u> do not have a variety of organ systems that accomplish particular life functions.

_____ 6. Animals of phylum <u>coelenterata</u> have a central body cavity or gut connected to a single opening or mouth.

_____ 7. Animals of phylum <u>platyhelminthes</u> include parasitic worms that can live inside an animal host.

_____ 8. Animals of phylum <u>nematoda</u> are worms with long cylindrical bodies and clearly defined digestive and excretory organs.

_____ 9. Animals of phylum <u>mollusca</u> have bodies that look like sections of rings stacked together.

_____ 10. Animals of phylum <u>annelida</u> have a strong muscular "foot" used for creeping and a hard outer shell to protect their soft inner bodies.

_____ 11. Animals of phylum <u>arthropoda</u> have bodies with radial symmetry.

_____ 12. Animals of phylum <u>echinodermata</u> have a hard exoskeleton and jointed legs.

LS12 Review Quiz (cont'd)

MATCHING: Choose the letter of the phylum to which each animal belongs. *18 points*

_____ 13. mosquito

_____ 14. earthworm

_____ 15. roundworm

_____ 16. coral

_____ 17. sponge

_____ 18. jellyfish

_____ 19. bumblebee

_____ 20. tapeworm

_____ 21. snake

_____ 22. snail

_____ 23. spider

_____ 24. clam

_____ 25. lobster

_____ 26. starfish

_____ 27. centipede

_____ 28. rabbit

_____ 29. beetle

_____ 30. horsehoe crab

(A) porifera

(B) coelenterata

(C) platyhelminthes

(D) nematoda

(E) annelida

(F) mollusca

(G) echinodermata

(H) arthropóda

(I) is not an invertebrate

_____   _____   ____/____/____
Student's Signature   Parent's Signature   Date

168

VERTEBRATES

TEACHER'S CLASSWORK AGENDA AND CONTENT NOTES

Classwork Agenda for the Week

1. Students will compose a graphic organizer showing the relationships among fish, amphibians, reptiles, birds, and mammals.

2. Students will compare and contrast the adaptations of fish and amphibians.

3. Students will compare and contrast the adaptations of reptiles and birds.

4. Students will compare and contrast the adaptations of mammalian orders.

Content Notes for Lecture and Discussion

At the end of the 19th century taxonomists turned their attention to **phylogeny**: the study of the evolutionary history of species. Comparative anatomists were at the forefront of the discipline and animal specimens were the most frequently studied. The hard bones and skeletons of ancient invertebrates and vertebrates are the best preserved in the fossil record. Such specimens as *Archeopteryx*—an intermediary species relating reptiles to birds—served to substantiate the "links" between related species further supporting the theory of evolution. Gaps in the fossil record were not of serious concern to **Charles Darwin** (b. 1809; d. 1882) as the preservation of organisms requires a specific set of environmental conditions. The vast majority of organisms are completely decomposed after death. Nevertheless, the logical prediction that "missing links" did at one time exist—and that their remains might be found in the fossil record—revitalized the science of paleontology. The German evolutionists **Fritz Müller** (b. 1822; d. 1897) and **Ernst Heinrich Haekel** (b. 1834; d. 1919) suggested that the ancestral history of an organism is "recapitulated" during its embryological stage. The **theory of recapitulation** launched investigations in the field of embryology aimed at identifying that ancestral history. The theory is presently appreciated more for its ability to generate embryological research than for its contribution to the understanding of phylogeny. Today, the structure of proteins and the sequence of nucleic acids in the genetic code are of greater

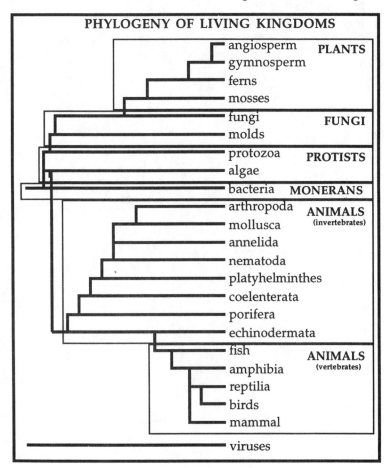

value in assessing the similarities and differences between living organisms with respect to their phylogenetic origins. The *Phylogeny of Living Kingdoms* shown on the previous page shows the generally accepted relationships between the organisms studied in this set of activities. The "common ancestor" of any given group is indicated by the nearest convergence of a horizontal and vertical line. It is therefore incorrect to say that reptiles are the ancestors of mammals. More precisely, the two groups have a common ancestor that may or may not be represented by an extinct organism represented in the fossil record.

In Lesson #1, students will compose a graphic organizer showing the relationships among fishes, amphibians, reptiles, birds, and mammals.

In Lesson #2 and Lesson #3, students will compile information to create a poster that displays the adaptations of a variety of organisms in a particular class of vertebrates: fish, amphibians, reptiles, birds, or mammals.

In Lesson #4, students will study the posters of other groups to learn more about animals in phylum chordata (e.g., vertebrata).

ANSWERS TO THE HOMEWORK PROBLEMS

Students' sentences should summarize the pertinent information supplied in the Fact Sheet.

ANSWERS TO THE END-OF-THE-WEEK REVIEW QUIZ

1. B	6. C	11. B
2. B	7. C	12. F
3. E	8. A	13. E
4. B	9. E	14. D
5. D	10. F	15. E

LS13 FACT SHEET

VERTEBRATES

CLASSWORK AGENDA FOR THE WEEK

(1) Compose a graphic organizer showing the relationships among fish, amphibians, reptiles, birds, and mammals.
(2) Compare and contrast the adaptations of fish and amphibians.
(3) Compare and contrast the adaptations of reptiles and birds.
(4) Compare and contrast the adaptations of mammalian orders.

All **vertebrates** belong to **phylum chordata**, meaning that they have a backbone. Long before birth, a "cord" of cells located at the midline of the animal begins to form down the long axis of its body. The cord of cells is called a **notochord**. The notochord will eventually become the vertebrate's **nervous system** (e.g., brain and spinal cord) and the protective bones that surround it (e.g., the cranium or skull and the vertebrae or back bones). There are five classes of vertebrates: *fish, amphibians, reptiles, birds,* and *mammals*. Each class includes many orders, families, genera, and species that have evolved a variety of **adaptations** designed to help them succeed in their struggle for survival.

Fish are **cold-blooded**. The body temperature of cold-blooded animals changes with the temperature of the environment. The heart of a fish pumps blood to its **gills** where carbon dioxide waste in their system is exchanged for fresh oxygen dissolved in the water. A fish also has a swim bladder to help it control its depth in the water. The fertilized eggs of fish develop into adults in the water where they can be easily devoured by predators long before they mature. Lamprey, sharks and rays, rainbow trout and salmon belong to the different orders of fish.

Amphibians are also cold-blooded and have moist skin and no scales. They are adapted for life in water and on land. The heart of an amphibian pumps blood to its **lungs** where carbon dioxide waste in their system is exchanged for fresh oxygen in the air. The fertilized eggs of amphibians develop in water until they reach a **larval stage**. A tadpole is a frog in its larval stage. At the end of its larval stage an amphibian goes through **metamorphosis** to become an adult. The amphibian class includes frogs, toads, and salamanders.

Reptiles are scaly, have lungs, and live most of their lives on land. Like fish and amphibians, however, reptiles are cold-blooded. The fertilized eggs of reptiles develop out in the open protected by hard or leathery outer shells. Reptiles lay their eggs in **clutches** which they bury for added protection against predators. Snakes, turtles, and lizards belong to the reptilian class.

Birds are **warm-blooded** animals that can maintain their body temperature in either hot or cold weather. They have feathers, lightweight bones, and most species have wings adapted for flight. Birds—like reptiles—lay eggs. They protect their eggs in a nest until their newborn fledglings hatch and are ready to leave the nest. The structure of birds' skeletons and their ability to lay eggs suggests that birds may be descended from Mesozoic dinosaurs. Members of the avian (e.g., meaning "bird") class, include chicken, eagles, turkeys, penguins, and ostrich.

Mammals are warm-blooded animals, most having hair or fur. Whales, porpoises and dolphins lack hair but have a layer of blubber under their skin to protect them against the cold. Mammals have the most complex nervous system of all vertebrates and are the most "social" of all animals. The fertilized eggs of mammals develop inside the womb of the female parent; so, mammals give birth to live young. After birth, all young mammals feed on milk produced in the **mammary glands** of their mother. Mice, cats, horses, kangaroos, and humans are members of different orders of mammals.

Homework Directions

Write one sentence for each major vertebrate phylum that summarizes the identifying characteristic(s) of organisms in that phylum.

Assignment due: _____

_____   _____   ____/____/____
Student's Signature   Parent's Signature   Date

VERTEBRATES

Work Date: ____/____/____

LESSON OBJECTIVE

Students will compose a graphic organizer showing the relationships among fish, amphibians, reptiles, birds, and mammals.

Classroom Activities

On Your Mark!

Prepare for this unit by checking out 10–20 reference books containing information about the five major classes of vertebrates. Use the information in the Teacher's Classwork Agenda and Content Notes to give a brief description of the evolutionary relationships between the five kingdoms and the assorted phyla studied in previous units.

Get Set!

Explain that students will use the Fact Sheet in this lesson to compose a graphic organizer illustrating the general characteristics of each group of vertebrates. Then, in Lesson #2 and Lesson #3, they will compile information using library resources on the adaptations of animals in individual classes of vertebrates. They will create a poster that their classmates can study in Lesson #4.

Go!

Give students ample time to complete the activity described in Figure A on Journal Sheet #1. Circulate around the room to insure that students are creating a logical graphic organizer that illustrates the common characteristics of each group of vertebrates.

Materials

Journal Sheet #1, Fact Sheet

LS13 JOURNAL SHEET #1

VERTEBRATES

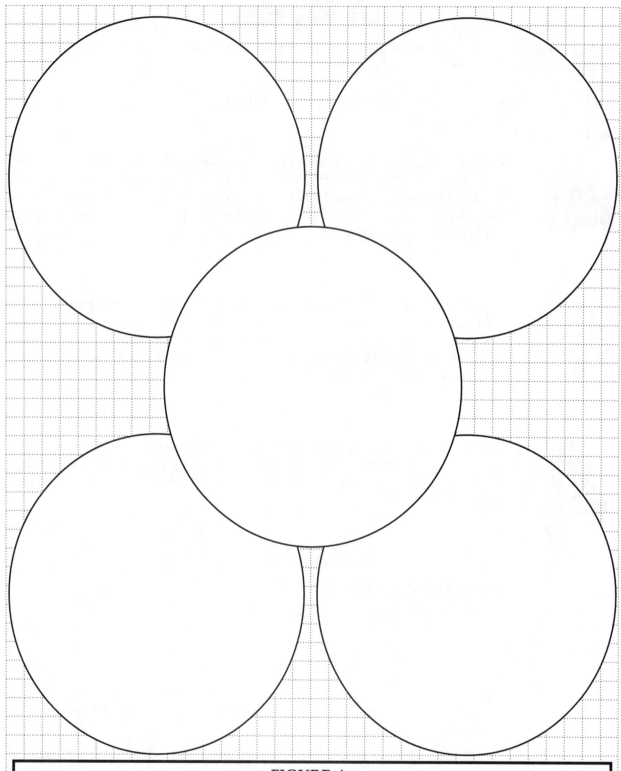

FIGURE A

<u>Directions</u>: Using the information on the FACT SHEET make a graphic organizer to describe the common characteristics of animals in each of the five vertebrate classes.

VERTEBRATES

Work Date: ____/____/____

LESSON OBJECTIVE

Students will compare and contrast the adaptations of fish and amphibians.

Classroom Activities

On Your Mark!

Prepare for this lesson by checking out 10–20 reference books containing information about the five major classes of vertebrates. Use old magazines to supply students with pictures of animals they can trace or cut out for use on their poster.

Get Set!

Assign groups of cooperative students the task of compiling as much information as they can about a particular class of vertebrates. Instruct them to use the correct Journal Sheet for the vertebrate class they are researching (e.g., Journal Sheet #2 is for information about fish and amphibians, Journal Sheet #3 is for information about reptiles and birds, Journal Sheet #4 is for information about mammals).

Go!

Give students ample time to plan and begin their poster describing the common characteristics and diverse adaptations of the class of vertebrates that has been assigned to them. Circulate around the room supplying additional facts that may be of interest to students, asking and answering questions that will help them to recognize the adaptations of the animals they are studying.

Materials

reference materials, crayons or colored pencils, magazine pictures of animals

LS13 JOURNAL SHEET #2

VERTEBRATES

Gather information about FISH in this section.

Gather information about AMPHIBIANS in this section.

VERTEBRATES

Work Date: ____/____/____

LESSON OBJECTIVE

Students will compare and contrast the adaptations of reptiles and birds.

Classroom Activities

On Your Mark!

Prepare for this lesson by checking out 10–20 reference books containing information about the five major classes of vertebrates. Use old magazines to supply students with pictures of animals they can trace or cut out for use on their poster.

Get Set!

Remind students to use the correct Journal Sheet for the vertebrate class they are researching (e.g., Journal Sheet #2 is for information about fish and amphibians, Journal Sheet #3 is for information about reptiles and birds, Journal Sheet #4 is for information about mammals). Explain that they will use the other sections in Lesson #4 when they will be given a chance to get out of their seats, circulate around the room, and collect information about the other classes of vertebrates from the posters of other students.

Go!

Give students ample time to finish their poster. Circulate around the room supplying additional facts that may be of interest to students, asking and answering questions that will help them to recognize the adaptations of the animals they are studying.

Materials

reference materials, crayons or colored pencils, magazine pictures of animals

LS13 JOURNAL SHEET #3

VERTEBRATES

Gather information about REPTILES in this section.

Gather information about BIRDS in this section.

VERTEBRATES

Work Date: ____/____/____

LESSON OBJECTIVE

Students will compare and contrast the adaptations of mammalian orders.

Classroom Activities

On Your Mark!

Have students display their posters on the wall or at their tables (e.g., joined desks) so that other groups have enough room to gather around one group at a time to do their research.

Get Set!

Remind students to use the correct Journal Sheet for gathering information about the different vertebrate classes as they circulate around the room in groups to collect information from the posters of other students. In addition to the information on their own poster, there are four more classes of vertebrates they will need to learn about.

Go!

Divide the time remaining in the period by four or eight (e.g., if there are duplicate posters for each vertebrate class) and permit students the allotted time to visit all posters to gather information on their Journal Sheets.

Materials

students posters, Journal Sheets

LS13 JOURNAL SHEET #4

VERTEBRATES

Gather information about MAMMALS in this section.

LS13 REVIEW QUIZ

Directions: Keep your eyes on your own work.
Read all directions and questions carefully.
THINK BEFORE YOU ANSWER!
Watch your spelling, be neat, and do the best you can.

CLASSWORK	(~40):	_____
HOMEWORK	(~20):	_____
CURRENT EVENT	(~10):	_____
TEST	(~30):	_____
TOTAL	(~100):	_____

(A ≥ 90, B ≥ 80, C ≥ 70, D ≥ 60, F < 60)

LETTER GRADE: _____

TEACHER'S COMMENTS: _____
_____

VERTEBRATES

MULTIPLE CHOICE: Choose the letter of the word or phrase that best completes the sentence or answers the question. *12 points*

_____ 1. All animals in phylum chordata have _____.
    (A) fur   (D) hard-shelled eggs
    (B) vertebrae   (E) lungs
    (C) scales

_____ 2. Which of the following pairs of animals is cold-blooded?
    (A) reptiles and birds   (D) reptiles and mammals
    (B) fish and amphibians   (E) fish and birds
    (C) amphibians and mammals

_____ 3. Which group of offspring feed on milk?
    (A) fish   (D) birds
    (B) amphibians   (E) mammals
    (C) reptiles

_____ 4. Which cold-blooded animals have no scales?
    (A) fish   (D) birds
    (B) amphibians   (E) mammals
    (C) reptiles

_____ 5. Which warm-blooded animals lay eggs?
    (A) fish   (D) birds
    (B) amphibians   (E) mammals
    (C) reptiles

_____ 6. Which animal buries its hard-shelled eggs to protect them?
    (A) fish   (D) birds
    (B) amphibians   (E) mammals
    (C) reptiles

MATCHING: Choose the letter of the class to which each animal belongs. *18 points*

_____ 7. alligator   (A) fish

_____ 8. ray   (B) amphibians

_____ 9. ape   (C) reptiles

_____ 10. venus fly trap   (D) birds

_____ 11. toad   (E) mammals

_____ 12. centipede   (F) not a vertebrate

_____ 13. dolphin

_____ 14. penguin

_____ 15. hamster

BIOMES

TEACHER'S CLASSWORK AGENDA AND CONTENT NOTES

Classwork Agenda for the Week

1. Students will use a map of the globe to identify the major biomes of the world.
2. Students will create imaginary organisms adapted for life in the tundra and desert.
3. Students will create imaginary organisms adapted for life in the forests and grasslands.
4. Students will create an imaginary organism adapted for life in the deep ocean abyss.

Content Notes for Lecture and Discussion

The geographical distribution of plants and animals was a major study of 17th century biologists owing to the Age of Exploration. But a proper theory to explain the obvious diversity was lacking until **Charles Darwin** (b. 1809; d. 1882) proposed his **theory of evolution** by means of mutation and natural selection. The idea that the oceans, continents, and climate had not changed since the Creation simply served to support the belief that the world's plant and animal populations had also remained stable. The Scottish geologist **Charles Lyell** (b. 1797; d. 1875), in his *Principles of Geology* published in 1830, showed that land features went through a constant metamorphosis. The land had changed under the influence of the same processes of erosion and weathering that transform its features today. Once it was shown that species could be modified following migration and isolation and—in the early 19th century—how mutation gave natural selection a variety of adaptive traits from which to choose, the study of biogeography was put on a firm theoretical foundation.

The English botanist **Joseph Dalton Hooker** (b. 1817; d. 1911) made trips to the Antarctic and India to classify and compare the diversity of species inhabiting the tundra and moutainous fresh-water and deciduous biomes. The German botanist **Adolf Engler** (b. 1844; d. 1930) classified organisms all over the world making several lengthy trips to Africa. Their work provided biogeographers with a voluminous database on which they could expand. The diversity of ocean organisms became apparent to seafaring explorers in the 16th, 17th, and 18th centuries but the ocean depths remained a mystery until the middle of the 20th century. The Swiss scientist **Auguste Antoine Piccard** (b. 1884; d. 1962) devised a **bathyscaph** that allowed his son **Jacques Piccard** (b. 1922) to explore the depths of the South Pacific in 1953. Piccard descended into the Marianas Trench near the island of Guam in 1960 observing organisms able to withstand the frigid cold and enormous pressures in the abyss. **Alfred Lothar Wegener**'s (b. 1880; d. 1930) theory of plate tectonics introduced an additional mechanism to explain biodiversity around the globe. The fact that the continents are adrift provides natural selection with additional selection pressures. Recent exploration of the ocean depths at midoceanic ridges rippled with seething volcanic vents has uncovered a sunless world inhabited by thriving tubular worms having a "talent" for chemosynthesis and a "taste" for hydrogen sulfide.

It is apparent to modern biologists that world biomes are in a continual state of change. World climates, land features, and oceanic conditions are not static. The organisms that reside in diverse habitats around the globe are under continual pressure to change.

In Lesson #1, students will use a map of the globe to identify the major biomes of the world.

In Lesson #2, students will create imaginary organisms adapted for life in the tundra and desert.

In Lesson #3, students will create imaginary organisms adapted for life in the forests and grasslands.

LS14 Content Notes (cont'd)

In Lesson #4, students will create an imaginary organism adapted for life in the deep ocean abyss.

ANSWERS TO THE HOMEWORK PROBLEMS

Students' graphic organizers should summarize the major characteristics and sample lifeforms inhabiting each of the biomes described in their Fact Sheet.

ANSWERS TO THE END-OF-THE-WEEK REVIEW QUIZ

1. biosphere
2. biome
3. true
4. true
5. true

6. tropical
7. grassland
8. grassland
9. true
10. true or oceanic

11. least
12. E
13. A
14. D
15. B

16. H
17. F
18. G
19. C

LS14 FACT SHEET

BIOMES

CLASSWORK AGENDA FOR THE WEEK

(1)   Use a map of the globe to identify the major biomes of the world.
(2)   Create imaginary organisms adapted for life in the tundra and desert.
(3)   Create imaginary organisms adapted for life in the forests and grasslands.
(4)   Create an imaginary organism adapted for life in the deep ocean abyss.

Living things inhabit a narrow zone of the planet's surface where conditions are just adequate to support them. Biologists call this zone the **biosphere.** The biosphere is limited to the watery environments of the world, a portion of earth's crust, and the lower elevations of the atmosphere. Because climate and land features differ around the world, the organisms that adapt and come to inhabit a particular geographical region can be very different from those of other regions. A large community of living things that inhabit a particular geographical region is called a **biome**. Biomes arise as a result of the interactions between climate, land features, and the activities of the plants and animals that must adapt to them. The major biomes studied by biologists include the *tundra, forests, grasslands, deserts, marine, mountain,* and *fresh-water* biomes.

About five million acres of **tundra** spreads across North America (e.g, Canada), northern Europe, and Northern Asia (e.g., Siberia). These regions are populated by many migratory species that move south during the harsh winter months. The tundra has low temperatures, a short growing season, and very little rainfall. Water is usually present in sufficient amounts, however, because the low temperatures slow down the evaporation process.

There are three major forest biomes: *coniferous, deciduous,* and *tropical*. South of the tundra—stretching across North America, Europe, and Asia—are the **coniferous forests**. Coniferous forests—also called the **taiga**—are inhabited by evergreen conifers (e.g., gymnosperms) that remain green all year long. A large variety of animals take advantage of the year-round shade and vegetation provided by the trees. Most of the lumber harvested by commercial loggers to provide wood for homes comes from coniferous biomes. The **deciduous forests** are found in more temperate climatic regions. These biomes are populated by fruit-and-nut-producing trees (e.g., maple, oak, and chestnut) that lose their leaves during the winter months. Animals present in those deciduous forests that have not been replaced by farms and cities include bear, deer, and foxes. The **tropical forests** have the widest variety of plants and animals. They are located along the equatorial regions of the world in Central and South America, Central Africa, Southeast Asia, and New Guinea. Animals that live in tropical biomes take advantage of heavy rainfall and dense vegetation that rises to a canopy layer more than 30 meters above the forest floor.

Grassland biomes comprise the prairies and grazing pastures of the Midwestern United States, Australia, Argentina, and southern Russia. The African **savannah** located north of that continent's central tropical rain forest and south of the Sahara Desert is also a grassland biome.

Desert biomes are scattered across the equatorial and temperate regions of the globe wherever rainfall falls below 25 centimeters per year. Vegetation is sparse and plants have thick and spiney outer layers to prevent water loss. Burrowing animals such as kangaroo rats and pocket mice who live in desert biomes have adapted ways to extract water from buried seeds and water-filled cactus.

The salty sea, or **marine biome,** is divided into an *oceanic zone* and a *neritic zone*. The **oceanic zone** refers to the open ocean off the continental shelf that surrounds every continent. It is the deep ocean, inhabited by a vast variety of organisms living near the surface and others adapted to the extreme pressures of the wide abyssal plain. The primary food and oxygen producers of the world called **phytoplankton** (e.g., photosynthesizing diatoms and dinoflagellates) inhabit the first few meters of ocean surface. All ocean-dwelling organisms feed directly on phytoplankton or on other organisms that do. The **neritic zone** refers to the shallow waters along the continental shelf. Boney fish, crustacea (e.g., crabs and lobsters), sea turtles, seals, and cetaceans (e.g., whales and dolphins) inhabit the neritic biome. These creatures are dependent upon the warm water, high salt content, and plentiful food on the shelf.

Mountain biomes are found in mountainous regions around the world such as the Rockies, Andes, and Himalayan mountain ranges. The extreme cold at high elevations limits plant and animal life. However, melting fresh snow during the spring and summer months produces **fresh-water biomes** where water flows from the mountains to the sea. Fresh-water biomes are diverse in plant and animal populations because they exist within the confines of other land biomes. They are also the least stable and change rapidly as temperature and rainfall change slightly from year to year.

Homework Directions

Create a graphic organizer that summarizes the major characteristics of each of the major world biomes.

Assignment due: _____

_____   _____   ____/____/____
Student's Signature   Parent's Signature   Date

BIOMES

Work Date: ____/____/____

LESSON OBJECTIVE

Students will use a map of the globe to identify the major biomes of the world.

Classroom Activities

On Your Mark!

Prepare for class by checking out atlases and reference books containing political/topographical maps of the world. Use the information in the Teacher's Classwork Agenda and Content Notes to give a brief lecture about the history of **biogeography**. Use the student Fact Sheet to explain the difference between the terms **biosphere** and **biome**.

Get Set!

List the major biomes of the world (e.g., tundra, conifer forest, etc.) and give a brief description of each. Point out that these are only general descriptions that summarize the major characteristics of some of the world's larger biomes. There are, in fact, two types of deciduous forests (e.g., temperate and tropical) and desert, mountain, and deciduous biomes in temperate climates are frequently bordered by chaparrals containing small thick-leaved shrubs. Salt marshes present at marine estuaries also comprise a distinctive biome.

Go!

Give students ample time to complete the activity described in Figure A on Journal Sheet #1. Clarify the abbreviations used in the activity: n. = north; s. = south; e. = east; w. = west; c. = central; u.s. = united states

Materials

political/topographical maps of the globe, crayons or colored pencils

LS14 JOURNAL SHEET #1

BIOMES

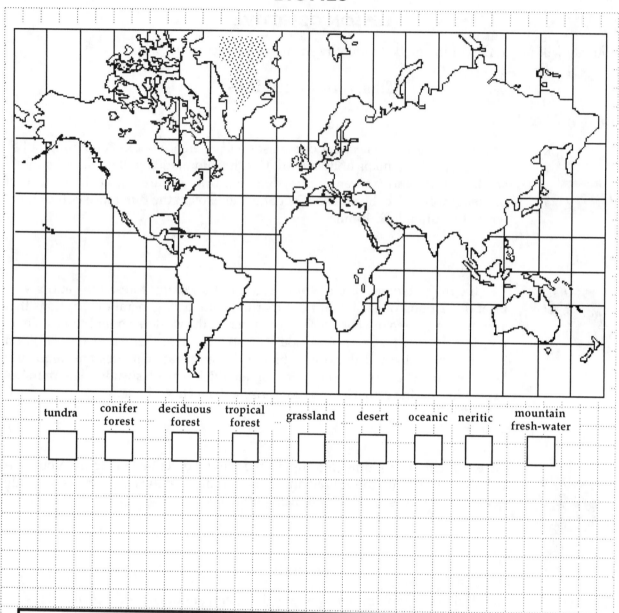

tundra   conifer forest   deciduous forest   tropical forest   grassland   desert   oceanic   neritic   mountain fresh-water

☐   ☐   ☐   ☐   ☐   ☐   ☐   ☐   ☐

FIGURE A

<u>Directions</u>: (1) Compare the map of the globe above to a political or topographical map of the world. (2) Color each rectangle beneath the map so that each biome is represented by a different color. (3) Locate the countries or regions listed below on the political or topographical map and color those areas correctly according to the information supplied. Note that Greenland is covered by a glacier.

tundra	conifer forest	deciduous forest	tropical forest	grassland	desert	oceanic	neritic	mountain fresh-water
n. alaska n. canada greenland n. asia	alaska canada siberia	eastern u.s. europe e. china japan e. australia	n. brazil w.c. africa thailand	s. canada midwest u.s. e.c. africa s. africa c. australia	n. africa arabia	atlantic pacific indian arctic	all coastlines	all mountain ranges

BIOMES

Work Date: ____/____/____

LESSON OBJECTIVE

Students will create imaginary organisms adapted for life in the tundra and desert.

Classroom Activities

On Your Mark!

Review the general descriptions of the conditions that exist in the tundra and desert.

Get Set!

Point out that students will need to discuss what they have learned about vertebrates in order to complete the activity described in Figure B on Journal Sheet #2.

Go!

Give students ample time to complete the activity described in Figure B on Journal Sheet #2. Circulate around the room to make sure that students are considering the questions asked in the assignment as they design and write about their imaginary creature.

Materials

Journal Sheet #2

Name: _____   Period:_____   Date: ____/____/____

LS14 JOURNAL SHEET #2

BIOMES

THE TUNDRA

The **tundra** is a cold, wet, treeless expanse of arctic grassland. The low temperature and short growing season make food scarce, especially during the late fall, winter, and early spring. More than 15 centimeters beneath the surface the ground is frozen most of the year, thawing for a month during the summer. The thin carpet of vegetation on the surface is comprised of small shrubs, mosses, and lichen.

THE DESERT

The **desert** receives less than 25 centimeters of rainfall per year. Temperatures in the desert frequently rise to more than 100 degrees Fahrenheit during the day but may drop to near freezing at night. There may be limited vegetation consisting of sagebrush and cactus or no vegetation at all.

FIGURE B

<u>Directions</u>: (1) Before designing an imaginary vertebrate adapted for life in the biomes assigned you must consider the characteristics of vertebrates and the conditions of the biome. How will your creations need to change their behavior, diet, or physical attributes as the seasons change? Will they need to migrate? If not, you must describe those adaptations that will enable them to survive seasonal change. (2) Draw and describe for each biome two imaginary animals each of which could be classified in a different vertebrate class (e.g., fish, amphibians, reptiles, birds, or mammals).

BIOMES

Work Date: _____/_____/_____

LESSON OBJECTIVE

Students will create imaginary organisms adapted for life in the forests and grasslands.

Classroom Activities

On Your Mark!

Review the general descriptions of the conditions that exist in the forests and grasslands.

Get Set!

Point out that students will need to discuss what they have learned about vertebrates in order to complete the activity described in Figure C on Journal Sheet #3.

Go!

Give students ample time to complete the activity described in Figure C on Journal Sheet #3. Circulate around the room to make sure that students are considering the questions asked in the assignment as they design and write about their imaginary creature.

Materials

Journal Sheet #3

LS14 JOURNAL SHEET #3

BIOMES

THE FOREST

A **coniferous forest** is rich with evergreen trees all year long, even in winter when the temperatures drop below freezing and the ground is covered with snow. Many animals migrate during winter, making food scarce for those that remain. There is dense shade throughout the year. A **deciduous forest** is rich with flowering trees that lose their leaves and fruits during the winter when the ground is hard and may be covered with snow. A **tropical rain forest** is rich with vegetation all year long. The air is warm and humid and rainfall can exceed 200 centimeters per year. The forest floor is covered in shadow by a high canopy of tall trees.

THE GRASSLAND

The **grassland** does not receive sufficient water to support a forest so vegetation consisting of shrubs and shortgrass is scattered and low to the ground. During winter, the plains are covered with snow making food scarce for the animals that live there.

FIGURE C

Directions: (1) Before designing an imaginary vertebrate adapted for life in the biomes assigned, you must consider the characteristics of vertebrates and the conditions of the biome. How will your creations need to change their behavior, diet, or physical attributes as the seasons change? Will they need to migrate? If not, you must describe those adaptations that will enable them to survive seasonal change. (2) Draw and describe for each biome two imaginary animals each of which could be classified in a different vertebrate class (e.g., fish, amphibians, reptiles, birds, or mammals).

BIOMES

Work Date: ____/____/____

LESSON OBJECTIVE

Students will create an imaginary organism adapted for life in the deep ocean abyss.

Classroom Activities

On Your Mark!

Review the general descriptions of the conditions that exist in the deep ocean abyss.

Get Set!

Point out that students will need to discuss what they have learned about invertebrates or vertebrates in order to complete the activity described in Figure D on Journal Sheet #4.

Go!

Give students ample time to complete the activity described in Figure D on Journal Sheet #4. Circulate around the room to make sure that students are considering the especially harsh conditions that exist in the deep ocean abyss as they design and write about their imaginary creature. Point out the difficulties a vertebrate might encounter as compared to an invertebrate. Remind students that vertebrates have an internal skeleton surrounded by relatively soft tissue.

Materials

Journal Sheet #4

LS14 JOURNAL SHEET #4

BIOMES

FIGURE D

Directions: (1) Before designing an imaginary invertebrate or vertebrate adapted for life in the deep ocean abyss you must consider the characteristics of both types of animals. The **deep ocean abyss** is characterized by enormous pressures that can exceed hundreds of pounds per square inch. Atmospheric pressure at sea level is only 14.7 pounds per square inch. Near volcanic vents located at midoceanic ridges, the temperature of the water is near boiling. In the middle of an oceanic plate the temperature at the bottom is freezing cold; but the water remains liquid because of the intense pressure. (2) Draw and describe two imaginary animals each of which could be classified as either an invertebrate (e.g., porifera, coelenterate, platyhelminthes, nematode, annelid, echinoderm, mollusk, or arthropod) or a vertebrate (e.g., fish, amphibians, reptiles, birds, or mammals).

LS14 REVIEW QUIZ

Directions: Keep your eyes on your own work.
Read all directions and questions carefully.
THINK BEFORE YOU ANSWER!
Watch your spelling, be neat, and do the best you can.

TEACHER'S COMMENTS: _____

_____

BIOMES

TRUE–FALSE FILL-IN: If the statement is true, write the word TRUE. If the statement is false, change the underlined word to make the statement true. *22 points*

_____   1. Living things inhabit a narrow zone of the planet's surface called the underline{biome}.

_____   2. A large community of living things that inhabits a particular geographical region is called a(n) underline{biosphere}.

_____   3. The coldest biome is the underline{tundra}.

_____   4. underline{Coniferous} biomes are inhabited by evergreen trees that remain green all year long.

_____   5. underline{Deciduous} biomes are populated by fruit-and-nut trees that lose their leaves during the winter months.

_____   6. underline{Grassland} biomes are located along the equatorial regions of the world.

_____   7. underline{Tropical} biomes comprise the prairies and grazing pastures of the Midwestern United States, Australia, Argentina, and southern Russia.

_____   8. The African savannah is a(n) underline{desert} biome.

_____   9. underline{Desert} biomes are located wherever rainfall falls below 25 centimeters per year.

_____   10. The primary food and oxygen producers of the world called phytoplankton live in the underline{marine} biome.

_____   11. Fresh-water biomes are the underline{most} stable biomes.

MATCHING: Choose the letter of the region that best describes the biome that inhabits it. *8 points*

_____ 12. tundra

_____ 13. coniferous forest

_____ 14. deciduous forest

_____ 15. tropical forest

_____ 16. grassland

_____ 17. desert

_____ 18. oceanic

_____ 19. freshwater

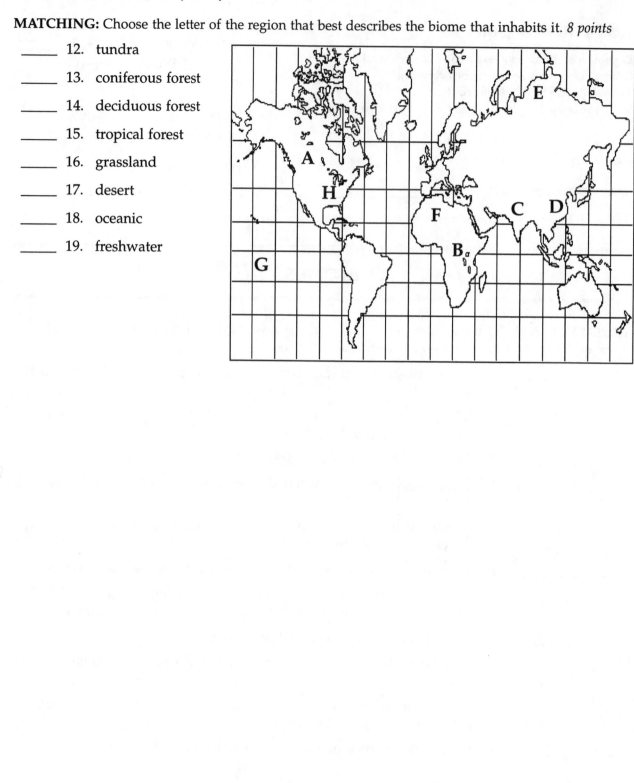

INTRODUCTION TO ECOLOGY

TEACHER'S CLASSWORK AGENDA AND CONTENT NOTES

Classwork Agenda for the Week

1. Students will diagram the relationships between organisms in an ecosystem.
2. Students will examine the food chains in aquatic and terrestrial communities.
3. Students will diagram the four major natural chemical cycles.
4. Students will examine the effects of pollution on the environment.

Content Notes for Lecture and Discussion

In 1749 **Carolus Linnaeus** (b. 1707; d. 1778) published *The Economy of Nature* in which he attempted to give a comprehensive view of the "fabric of life" on earth. In Linnaeus's view, Divine Providence assured each genus a particular place in the world. God had set aside a geographic range and set of resources for each group of living things so that different animals were dependent upon different food chains for their survival. In this way, the harmony and stability of living communities could be maintained. This view was seriously undermined by new evidence in the fossil record that more than a few species had become extinct in the course of geological history. **Charles Darwin** (b. 1809; d. 1882) showed in his publication *The Origin of the Species by Means of Natural Selection* that organisms competed for essentially the same resources and that those least adapted in their struggle for survival became extinct. While stability was apparent on the surface, the delicate balance of nature could be easily upset resulting in the extinction of individual species or whole biotic communities. The relationship between organisms was redefined in terms of "competition" rather than "harmony."

The German zoologist **Ernst Heinrich Haekel** (b. 1834; d. 1919) was the first to use the term **ecology** in 1866 to describe the relationships between living things. Haekel's works were preceded by that of German botanist **Friedrich Willhelm Heinrich Alexander Humboldt** (b. 1769; d. 1859) whose explorations of the Orinoco and Amazon Rivers of South America allowed him to delineate the geographic ranges of more than 60,000 species of plants. Humboldt—considered the "father of ecology"—correlated each species with the prevailing climatic conditions of their geographical habitat. Thus, he laid the groundwork for a true study of biological communities within particular biomes. Ecology focussed on the study of plants rather than animals for decades after Humboldt.

Due largely to advances in chemistry toward the end of the 19th century, biologists concentrated their attention on the physiology of plants and animals. Research along physiological lines began to reveal the requirements of all living organisms. Laboratory studies of the responses of plants to sunlight, temperature variation, and the availability of nutrients in the soil were matched to the volumes of observations that had been accumulated by plant geographers. In 1895, the Dutch botanist **Johannes Eugenius Bülow Warming** (b. 1841; d. 1924) published *Plant Communities* in which he established crucial relationships between plants and their natural environments. By 1915, the establishment of the British Ecological Society and the Ecological Society of America allowed botanists and zoologists to meet and compare notes thereby leading the way to the modern ecological sciences.

In Lesson #1, students will diagram the relationships between organisms in an ecosystem.
In Lesson #2, students will examine the food chains in aquatic and terrestrial communities.
In Lesson #3, students will diagram the four major natural chemical cycles.
In Lesson #4, students will examine the effects of pollution on the environment.

LS15 Content Notes *(cont'd)*

ANSWERS TO THE HOMEWORK PROBLEMS

Students' opinions will vary but should note the fact that the resources used to make the revolutionary new packaging material have been eliminated from taking part in the natural chemical cycles upon which living organisms depend. The advantages of having the new material need to be weighed against the consequences of removing resources from the ecosystem for an extended period of time.

ANSWERS TO THE END-OF-THE-WEEK REVIEW QUIZ

1. ecology
2. true
3. true
4. true
5. true

6. true
7. community
8. primary producers
9. consumers
10. decomposers

DIAGRAM (from top to bottom of pyramid): shark, seal, tuna, shrimp, plankton

DIAGRAM (from top to bottom of pyramid): hawk, mouse, grasshopper, caterpillar, grass

LS15 FACT SHEET

INTRODUCTION TO ECOLOGY

CLASSWORK AGENDA FOR THE WEEK

(1) Diagram the relationships between organisms in an ecosystem.
(2) Examine the food chains in aquatic and terrestrial communities.
(3) Diagram the four major natural chemical cycles.
(4) Examine the effects of pollution on the environment.

Ecology is the branch of **biology** that studies the relationship between living organisms and their environment. All organisms interact with their environment and changes in the environment can affect the organisms that inhabit it. An **ecosystem** is a unit of **biotic** (e.g., living) and **abiotic** (e.g., nonliving) things that "share" environmental resources. The use of valuable resources is balanced in nature. Most resources are used over and over again for many years. They are recycled. However, the balance of nature is a complex and delicate system that can be easily upset. Removing a particular rodent species from an ecosystem, for example, might allow the insects normally eaten by the rodents to overpopulate. The increasing population of insects might destroy the vegetation in the ecosystem. Other insects and animals that depend on the vegetation would starve. The ecosytem could be destroyed.

The biotic portion of an ecosystem is a **community**. Each organism within a community interacts with the environment thereby affecting the lives of other members of the community. This relationship is sometimes called "the web of life." In every community, animals and plants are part of a **food chain**. In a food chain, energy is transferred from one organism to another. A **food pyramid** is a diagram that describes how energy is passed from one organism to another.

Organisms can be classified according to how they obtain food. Plants are the **primary producers** of food. Plants trap the energy of the sun and make their own food by photosynthesis using water and nutrients from the soil and carbon dioxide from the air. Animal **consumers** obtain the energy stored in plants by eating plants or other animals that eat plants. **Decomposers** such as bacteria cause the "breakdown" or decay of dead organisms and the excreted wastes of animals. The products of this decomposition are put back into the soil to be used again by plant producers.

The place where an organism lives is called its **habitat**. There are two major habitats in nature: the **aquatic** (e.g., water) habitat and the **terrestrial** (e.g., land) habitat. The "job" that an organism performs in the community is called its **niche**. Organisms that are hunters are called **predators**. Organisms that become the food of predators are called **prey**.

Human beings play an extremely important role in protecting the biosphere. Since all organisms depend on one another for their survival, it is important that human beings understand how changes in the environment can affect the ecological balance that exists in all biomes.

Homework Directions

Is there anything wrong with the following "success story?"

A chemist discovers a new wrapping material that is so strong it will revolutionize the way products, easily damaged in shipment, are packaged. He sells his idea to a manufacturing company that begins to produce tons and tons of the material. Within a year, many of the products that were once easily damaged in shipment are arriving at market undamaged. Because a greater number of the products are arriving at market in good condition, the price of each product is much less. More people can afford to buy them. After unwrapping the product, people discard the revolutionary new packaging material along with their other garbage. The new material is taken to the dump where it is buried along with the other waste. The new wrappers are so durable it will take 1,000 years for each kilogram of the material to decay.

Write a paragraph of about 100 words expressing your opinion about these facts.

Assignment due: _____

_____   _____   ___/___/___
Student's Signature   Parent's Signature   Date

INTRODUCTION TO ECOLOGY

Work Date: ____/____/____

LESSON OBJECTIVE

Students will diagram the relationships between organisms in an ecosystem.

Classroom Activities

On Your Mark!

Prepare for class by collecting 10–20 pictures from magazines or library/text resources depicting various outdoor scenes (e.g., biomes). Try to include plants, animals, rocks, and water in pictures of both aquatic and terrestrial habitats.

Begin the lecture by defining the following terms as they appear on the student Fact Sheet: **ecology, ecosystem, biotic, abiotic, community, food chain, food pyramid, primary producers, consumers, decomposers, habitat**. Review the role of the sun in providing the energy that land and ocean plants (e.g., primary producers) can turn into food for the rest of the world.

Get Set!

Distribute the pictures/library/textbook resources. Have students use Journal #1 to compile a list of the biotic (e.g., plant and animal) members of the ecosystem students would expect to find there—even if they are not pictured—as well as the abiotic elements (e.g., rocks for shelter, water for nutrition) they would expect to be present.

Define the term **biomass** as the total mass (e.g., a function of the total number of individuals) of a particular species or group of species present in a given ecosystem. The biomass of tree leaves must be greater than the biomass of caterpillars in order for the caterpillars to survive. Scientists make estimates of different biomasses in order to draw conclusions about the stability of an ecosystem. If a plant biomass, for example, is less than the biomass of the ecosystem's primary consumer, the scientist may predict the impending collapse of the system.

Go!

Give students ample time to perform the activity described in Figure A on Journal Sheet #1. They should reach the conclusion that insects and small animals comprise a larger biomass than that of larger animals (e.g., there are more field mice than hawks), the former being placed lower on the food (e.g., energy) pyramid.

Materials

magazine and library/textbook pictures of outdoor scenes

LS15 JOURNAL SHEET #1

INTRODUCTION TO ECOLOGY

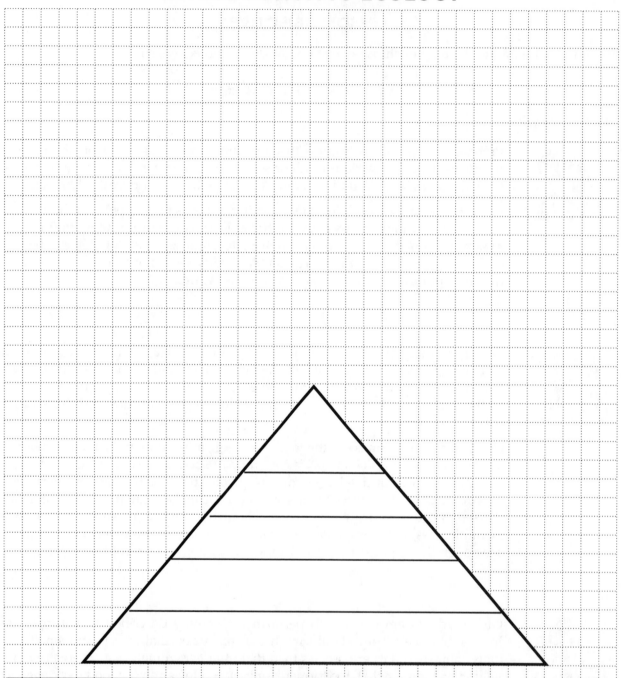

FIGURE A

<u>Directions</u>: (1) Study the picture(s) provided by your instructor with your groupmates. (2) Make a list of the biotic and abiotic elements you would expect to find in the ecosystem shown even if they are not pictured. (3) Make an estimate of the biomass (e.g., number of individuals) present for each type of living organism as compared to the biomass of organisms upon which it depends for survival. For example: If you think there are two eagles in the habitat, then you must guess the number of mice that would need to be present to support those eagles. Put the names of the organisms with the highest populations at the bottom of the pyramid starting with primary producers.

INTRODUCTION TO ECOLOGY

Work Date: ____/____/____

LESSON OBJECTIVE

Students will examine the food chains in aquatic and terrestrial communities.

Classroom Activities

On Your Mark!

Begin the lecture by asking students to help you compile a list of the things they have eaten in the last several days. As they contribute that information write the items on the board. Have students comment on the origins of each food. Did it come from the sea or land (e.g., aquatic or terrestrial)? Is it plant, animal, or does it belong to another kingdom (e.g., mushroom is a fungus)?

Get Set!

Define the term **predator** as any animal that must hunt and kill its food to survive. Define the term **prey** as any animal that is hunted or killed to become a food item. All plants are prey to animal predators; although not all animals can eat all plants. Some plants are poisonous to some animals. In addition, a few plants (e.g., the Venus fly trap) can trap and digest insects and small mammals. These types of plants are considered "carnivorous plants" rather than predators because they do not "hunt." Define an **herbivore** as an animal that eats mostly plants. Define a **carnivore** as an animal that eats mostly other animals. Define an **omnivore** is an animal that includes both plants and animals in its diet.

Go!

Give students ample time to perform the activity described in Figure B on Journal Sheet #2. Circulate around the room to make sure that each student is creating an actual "web" to show the relationships between these organisms. The arrows may even cross over from the aquatic to the terrestrial communities where appropriate.

Materials

Journal Sheet #2

LS15 JOURNAL SHEET #2

INTRODUCTION TO ECOLOGY

HIGHEST
ORDER
AQUATIC
CONSUMERS

HIGHEST
ORDER
TERRESTRIAL
CONSUMERS

PRIMARY
AQUATIC
PRODUCERS

PRIMARY
TERRESTRIAL
PRODUCERS

FIGURE B

Directions: (1) Choose from the list of organisms shown to create a "food web" of organisms present in both an aquatic (e.g., ocean) and terrestrial (e.g., land) community. (2) Remember that different predators may eat the same prey. So, it is fine to have more than one arrow directed at a single prey. It is also possible for two predators to consider each other a prey animal. The arrows shown should be used as a starting point in creating each "food web."

lady bugs	sharks	seals	whales	swordfish	tigers
monkeys	bananas	apples	oak leaves	shrimp	mice
plankton	penguins	grasshoppers	caterpillars	snakes	wolves
hawks	bass	lobsters	seaweed	starfish	salmon
sponge	squid	humans	wild pigs	zebra	grass

LS15 Lesson #3

INTRODUCTION TO ECOLOGY

Work Date: ____/____/____

LESSON OBJECTIVE

Students will diagram the four major natural chemical cycles.

Classroom Activities

On Your Mark!

Begin by pointing out that the earth has limited natural resources. Explain that any set of chemical events that is repeated over and over again is called a **cycle**. Draw Illustration A on the board and show students how atoms or molecules can be combined, separated, recombined, and reseparated to start the whole process again. List the four basic chemical cycles that occur in nature and have students compare the list to the illustrations on Journal Sheet #3: the **water cycle**, the **carbon cycle**, the **nitrogen cycle**, the **phosphorus cycle**.

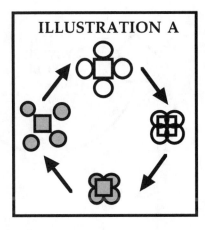

ILLUSTRATION A

Get Set!

Explain the major events that occur in each natural chemical cycle.

water cycle—(1) Liquid water **evaporates** into the atmosphere where it **condenses** to form clouds. (2) **Precipitation** (e.g., rain, sleet, snow) returns the water to the land or sea. (3) Water on land gets back to the oceans as surface **runoff** or can be **absorbed** into the ground where it **seeps** into underground **streams** that eventually return to the **oceans**.

carbon cycle—(1) Plants **absorb** carbon dioxide from the air and combine it with water in the soil to form sugar by **photosynthesis**. (2) Animals **consume** plants and **excrete** wastes. (3) Animal **respiration** returns the carbon dioxide to the atmosphere—or, the animals die. (4) **Decaying** dead animals or waste are fed on by **bacteria** that return the carbon dioxide to the atmosphere by respiration.

nitrogen cycle—(1) **Legume** (e.g., pea plants) plants absorb **molecular nitrogen** from the atmosphere (e.g., nitrogen **fixation**). (2) Animals or fungi (e.g., **mushrooms**) feed on the legumes and excrete wastes that have **ammonia salts** in them (e.g., **ammonification**). (3) **Nitrobacteria** in the soil use oxygen in the air to change the ammonia salts to **nitrate salts** (e.g., **nitrification**). (4) The nitrates are absorbed by plants that are eaten by animals and excreted as ammonia wastes. (5) Nitrobacteria return molecular nitrogen to the air by **denitrification**.

phosphorus cycle—(1) **Phosphate salts** in rocks are dissolved in water runoff that makes its way on the surface or undeground seepage to lakes and sea. (2) The salts are absorbed by plants and animals. (3) Animals eat the plants. (4) Animal and plant wastes return the phosphates to the soil. (5) **Volcanic eruptions** or other geological activity (e.g., upthrust) returns the phosphates to higher elevations where they are dissolved again in water runoff.

Go!

Give students ample time to perform the activity described in Figure C on Journal Sheet #3. Circulate around the room to make sure that students are applying the lecture material to the activity.

Materials

Journal Sheet #3

LS15 JOURNAL SHEET #3

INTRODUCTION TO ECOLOGY

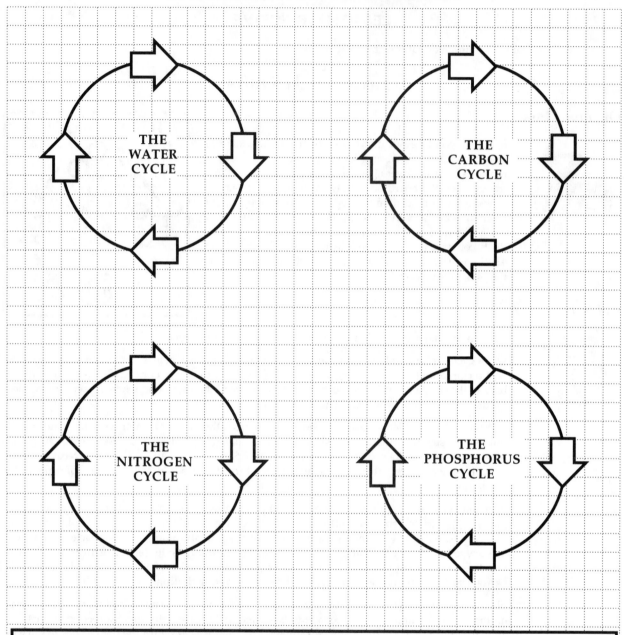

FIGURE C

<u>Directions</u>: (1) Choose from the list of terms shown to diagram the events taking place during each natural chemical cycle. (2) Write the terms along the curved lines or by the arrows to indicate the sequence in which events occur. Some terms may be repeated more than once while others are specific to a particular cycle.

green plants	clouds	nitrobacteria	precipitation	photosynthesis
animals	streams	mushrooms	respiration	ammonification
bacteria	ammonia	evaporation	decay	upthrust
transpiration	runoff	seepage	consumption	nitrates
fixation	excretions	denitrification	legumes	absorption
oxygen	molecular nitrogen	carbon dioxide	volcanoes	oceans

INTRODUCTION TO ECOLOGY

Work Date: ____/____/____

LESSON OBJECTIVE

Students will examine the effects of pollution on the environment.

Classroom Activities

On Your Mark!

Prepare for class by collecting 10–20 magazine pictures depicting various degrees of pollution: smoke from chimneys, crowded freeways, smoggy cities, dirty rivers, stained or eroded statues/monuments, rusted metal, garbage piling up at refuse facilities, etc.).

Display the pictures and select students one at a time to orally describe for the class each type of pollution.

Get Set!

Give students several minutes to brainstorm and decide how they would clean up some or all of the mess created in two of the pictures. Discuss their ideas by guiding a civil debate on the facility with which suggestions might actually be carried out. Ask them to consider the financial cost of accomplishing the task. Are their suggestions realistic? Mention that it might be better to "plan ahead" when dealing with potential pollutants.

Go!

Give students ample time to complete the activity described in Figure D on Journal Sheet #4 to demonstrate the difficulty inherent in "diluting" environmental pollutants.

Materials

food coloring, 500 ml beakers, water

LS15 Journal Sheet #4

INTRODUCTION TO ECOLOGY

FIGURE D

Directions: (1) Put one drop of food coloring (e.g., red, blue, or green) into the bottom of a 500 ml beaker. (2) Fill the beaker with clear tap water to the 500 ml line. (3) Consult with your groupmates to decide if the food coloring has disappeared. (4) If the solution has not cleared completely, then pour half the solution (e.g., 250 ml) into the sink and add clear water again to the 500 ml line. (5) Record the number of times you pour half the solution into the sink and repeat Step #3 through Step #4 until the solution is clear. (6) When the solution clears multiply 500 ml by 2 for every time you spilled half the solution down the sink. For example: If you spilled half the solution down the sink four times then you would multiply 500 x 2 x 2 x 2 x 2 = 8,000 ml. This is the volume of water you would need to completely dilute one drop of food coloring. (7) Write a paragraph expressing your answer to the following question: Does diluting a toxic pollutant until it cannot be seen, smelled, or tasted completely eliminate its harmful effects on the environment?

LS15 Review Quiz

Directions: Keep your eyes on your own work.
Read all directions and questions carefully.
THINK BEFORE YOU ANSWER!
Watch your spelling, be neat, and do the best you can.

CLASSWORK   (~40): _____
HOMEWORK   (~20): _____
CURRENT EVENT   (~10): _____
TEST   (~30): _____

TOTAL   (~100): _____
(A ≥ 90, B ≥ 80, C ≥ 70, D ≥ 60, F < 60)

LETTER GRADE: _____

TEACHER'S COMMENTS: _____
_____

INTRODUCTION TO ECOLOGY

TRUE–FALSE FILL-IN: If the statement is true, write the word TRUE. If the statement is false, change the underlined word to make the statement true. *20 points*

_____ 1. <u>Economics</u> studies the relationship between living organisms and their environment.

_____ 2. <u>All</u> organisms interact with their environment.

_____ 3. The biotic parts of an ecosystem <u>are</u> alive.

_____ 4. The abiotic parts of an ecosystem <u>are not</u> alive.

_____ 5. <u>Most</u> environmental resources are recycled.

_____ 6. An ecosystem <u>can</u> be destroyed by removing a single organism from that ecosystem.

_____ 7. The living organisms in an ecosystem make up a <u>family</u>.

_____ 8. Plants are the <u>consumers</u> of food.

_____ 9. Animal <u>decomposers</u> obtain the energy stored in plants by eating plants or other animals that eat plants.

_____ 10. <u>Primary producers</u> such as bacteria cause the "breakdown" or decay of dead organisms and the excreted wastes of animals.

DIAGRAM: Write the name of each organism below in the correct section of the food pyramid. *5 points*

shark   plankton   shrimp   tuna   seal

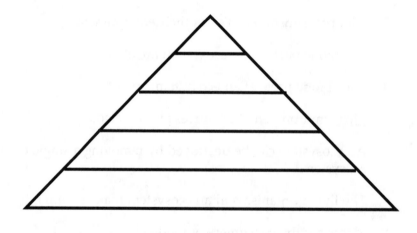

DIAGRAM: Write the name of each organism below in the correct section of the food pyramid. *5 points*

mouse   grass   grasshopper   hawk   caterpillar

_____   _____   ___/___/___
Student's Signature   Parent's Signature   Date

APPENDIX

NAME: _____ **PERIOD:** _____ **DATE:** ___ / ___ / ___

Keep this Grade Roster in the Science Section of your notebook

Date	Journal Points	Homework Points	Current Events Points	Quiz Points	Total Points	Letter Grade	Initials

How to Calculate Your Grade Point Average

Your Report Card grades in this class will be awarded to you according to your grade point average or GPA. You can calculate your GPA whenever you like to find out exactly how you are doing in this class.

First, award each of your weekly grades the following credits: each A is worth 4 credits; each B is worth 3 credits; each C is worth 2 credits; each D is worth 1 credit; and each F is worth 0.

Add your total credits earned. Then, divide by the number of packets listed on your Grade Roster and round the decimal result to the nearest tenths place. Your overall Letter Grade is assigned according to the following GPA values:

A+ ≥ 4.0	A ≥ 3.7	A– ≥ 3.4
B+ ≥ 3.1	B ≥ 2.8	B– ≥ 2.5
C+ ≥ 2.2	C ≥ 1.9	C– ≥ 1.6
D+ ≥ 1.3	D ≥ 1.0	D– ≥ 0.7
	F < 0.7	

FOR EXAMPLE:

John has completed five weeks of school and entered his grades from five packets on his Grade Roster. His grades are as follows: first week, A; second week, B; third week, C; fourth week, C; and fifth week, D.

John awards himself the correct amount of credit for each of his grades.

A	earns	4 credits
B	earns	3 credits
C	earns	2 credits
C	earns	2 credits
D	earns	1 credit
Total	earned is	12 credits

John divides his total credits earned by 5 (the number of packets on his Grade Roster).

12 divided by 5 equals 2.4

John's grade point average, or GPA, is 2.4. Referring to the grades shown above, John knows that he has a C+ in Science thus far, because 2.4 is greater than 2.2 (C+) but less than 2.5 (B–).

Name: _____ **Period:** _____ **Date:** ____/____/____

EXTRA JOURNAL SHEET

FACT SHEET TITLE: _____ **Lesson #** _____

Using Current Events to Integrate Science Instruction Across Content Areas

Science does not take place in a vacuum. Scientists, like other professionals, are influenced by the economic and political realities of their time. In addition, the ideological and technological advances made by science can influence the economic and political structure of society—for better or worse. It is therefore essential that students have an awareness of the day-to-day science being done at laboratories around the world, important work being reported by an international news media.

Most State Departments of Education, make **CURRENT EVENTS** a regular part of their state science frameworks. Science instructors can use newspaper, magazine, and television reports to keep their students informed about the advances and controversies stemming from research in the many scientific disciplines. Teachers can also use current events to integrate science instruction across the curriculum.

Set aside a class period to show students how to prepare a **science** or **technology** current event. They can do this on a single sheet of standard looseleaf. You may require pupils to read all or part of a science/technology article depending on their reading level. Have them practice summarizing the lead and one or more paragraphs of the article *in their own words*. Advise them to keep a **thesaurus** on hand or to use the dictionary/thesaurus stored in their personal computer at home. Tell students to find *synonyms* they can use to replace most of the vocabulary words used by the article's author. This activity will help them to expand their vocabulary and improve grammar skills. Show students how to properly trim and paste the article's title and first few paragraphs on the front of a standard piece of looseleaf. They should write their summary on the opposite side of the page so that the article is visible to their classmates when they present their findings orally to the class. Allow students to make a report that summarizes a newsworthy item they may have heard on television. The latter report should be accompanied by the signature of a parent/guardian to insure the accuracy of the information being presented.

Students' skills at public speaking are sure to improve if they are given an opportunity to share their current event. Current events can be shared after the end-of-the-unit REVIEW QUIZ or whenever the clock permits at the end of a lesson that has been completed in a timely fashion. You can select students at random to make their presentations by drawing lots or ask for volunteers who might be especially excited about their article. Take time to discuss the ramifications of the article and avoid the temptation to express your personal views or bias. Remain objective and give students the opportunity to express their views and opinions. Encourage them to base their views on fact, not superstition or prejudice. Should the presentation turn into a debate, set aside a few minutes later in the week, giving students time to prepare what they would like to say. Model courtesy and respect for all points of view and emphasize the proper use of the English language in all modes of presentation, both written and oral.

TECHNIQUES AND TIPS FOR LABORATORY DISSECTIONS

There are few laboratory activities that excite student interest more than dissection. Although this resource provides instructions for the dissection of a limited few organisms, teachers are encouraged to replace or supplement any convenient lesson or lessons with the appropriate dissection.

Students need to be informed that the art of dissection is as precise as it is ancient. The purpose of dissection is to carefully disjoin the identifiable organs of a specimen in order to (1) determine its anatomical (e.g., structural) relation to other organs and (2) to deduce its function if possible. Dissection is a painstaking separation of a specimen's anatomical structures, not a butchering process. Dissection tools are specifically designed for this purpose.

Prior to every dissection lab, students should be made aware of common sense health guidelines and the proper use of dissection tools.

Common Sense Health Guidelines

All preserved animal specimens should be washed in soap and water and rinsed thoroughly before dissection begins. Students should wear goggles, plastic surgical gloves, and an apron during dissection and cleanup. An eyewash consisting of clean tap water in a squeeze bottle should be placed at convenient locations around the laboratory and used immediately to rinse foreign organic substances splashed in the eyes. Students should take turns performing a dissection so that only one person at a time is handling sharp tools. The instructor should be informed immediately of any accidents. All gloves, broken tools, and biological materials should be discarded according to district biohazard guidelines. Aprons and goggles should be thoroughly rinsed with soap and water and dried. All surgical instruments should be sterilized under pressure in a steam-pressure cooker or autoclave. At the very least, instruments should be washed in dish soap and boiling hot water in an automatic dishwasher before being returned to storage in a secured cabinet. Students should wash their hands up to the middle of their forearms with antiseptic soap at the conclusion of the dissection period.

Use of Dissection Tools

paper towels   Paper towels are used to line the bottom of the dissection tray and for clean up.

dissection tray   The specimen should be placed in a metal or hard plastic tray having a synthetic rubber or wax bottom.

T-pins   Use T-pins (e.g., insect pins) to secure the specimen in the dissection tray. Pins are normally placed with the "T" pointed at an angle away from the specimen, the point piercing the flesh of the specimen and secured in the rubber or wax tray bottom. Pins can be removed and repositioned during dissection.

dissection needle   A dissection needle is used for probing or temporarily securing a flap of tissue.

plastic probe   A plastic probe is used to push aside organs or layers of tissue in order to temporarily examine underlying structures.

scissors   Scissors are used to cut away tissue in order to remove organs or expose underlying structures. The direction of a scissor cut should be horizontal to the underlying organs in an effort to avoid puncturing them.

scalpel   A scalpel is used to slice through tissue to expose underlying structures. Care should be taken to estimate the thickness of the tissue being cut in order to avoid damaging underlying structures. All cuts are straight cuts. Avoid "angle cuts" and do not change the direction of a cut as it is being made as the blade can slip or break. Connective tissue can be removed from between structures with a gentle sideways scraping action of the blade (e.g., perpendicular to the sharp edge of the blade).

forceps   Forceps are used to grasp organs and tissues in order to prepare them for pinning, cutting, or probing.

eyedropper   An eyedropper can be filled with water to keep tissues moist.

centimeter ruler   A centimeter ruler can be used to measure the sizes of structures for purposes of comparison.

BIO-DATA
CARDS

BIO-DATA CARD

ALCMEAON
(c. 500 B.C.)

nationality
Greek

contribution to science
first to document animal dissections
performed for scientific purposes

BIO-DATA CARD

ARISTOTLE
(born, 384 B.C.; died, 322 B.C.)

nationality
Greek

contribution to science
first to document a study of sea creatures in
their natural habitat for scientific purposes

BIO-DATA CARD

ROGER BACON
(born, 1214; died, 1294)

nationality
English

contribution to science
invented a hand-held glass lens to view
small objects used in his experiments

BIO-DATA CARD

WILLIAM BATESON
(born, 1861; died, 1926)

nationality
English

contribution to science
popularized Gregor Mendel's work on the
way traits are inherited by offspring

BIO-DATA CARD

LOUIS DE BROGLIE
(born, 1892; died, 1987)

nationality
French

contribution to science
discovered that electron beam behaved like
light waves making the invention of the
electron microscope possible

BIO-DATA CARD

MARTINUS WILLEM BEIJERINCK
(born, 1851; died, 1931)

nationality
Dutch

contribution to science
coined the term "virus" for the microscopic
germ that caused tobacco mosaic disease

BIO-DATA CARD

MARIE FRANÇOIS XAVIER BICHAT
(born, 1771; died, 1802)

nationality
French

contribution to science
investigated the effects of disease on more
than 20 types of living tissue

BIO-DATA CARD

STANLEY COHEN
(born, 1922)

nationality
American

contribution to science
performed the first genetic engineering
experiments on the plasmids of *Eschericia
coli*

INSTRUCTIONS TO TEACHERS
Xerox and cut out the Bio-Data Cards below and keep them in a handy file. Instruct students to choose one card and neatly glue it to the front of a 5" × 8" index card. They can use the school or public library to find out more about the scientist they have chosen. On the back of the index card they can draw a cartoon, write a poem or short paragraph that illustrates an important event in the life of this famous personality.

BIO-DATA CARD
FRANCIS H. C. CRICK
(born, 1916)

nationality
English

contribution to science
discovered the structure of DNA with James Dewey Watson and Rosalind Elsie Franklin

BIO-DATA CARD
GEORGES CUVIER
(born, 1769; died, 1832)

nationality
French

contribution to science
known as the "father of paleontology" for establishing the fact of extinction

BIO-DATA CARD
CHARLES ROBERT DARWIN
(born, 1809; died, 1882)

nationality
English

contribution to science
formulated the theory of evolution by means of natural selection and published *The Origin of the Species by Means of Natural Selection* in 1859

BIO-DATA CARD
HUGO MARIE DE VRIES
(born, 1848; died, 1935)

nationality
Dutch

contribution to science
rediscovered and helped to popularize Gregor Mendel's work on the study of genes

BIO-DATA CARD
HENRI DUTROCHET
(born, 1776; died, 1847)

nationality
French

contribution to science
outlined the process of osmosis in plant cells and described some of the respiratory parts of plants

BIO-DATA CARD
PAUL EHRLICH
(born, 1854; died, 1915)

nationality
German

contribution to science
developed the first techniques in chemotherapy using synthetic drugs to kill infections

BIO-DATA CARD
ADOLF ENGLER
(born, 1844; died, 1930)

nationality
German

contribution to science
made several trips to Africa to expand the field of plant geography by classifying thousands of new plants

BIO-DATA CARD
WALTER FLEMMING
(born, 1843; died, 1905)

nationality
German

contribution to science
first to describe the division of chromosomes as a prelude to cell division and coined the term "mitosis"

INSTRUCTIONS TO TEACHERS
Xerox and cut out the Bio-Data Cards below and keep them in a handy file. Instruct students to choose one card and neatly glue it to the front of a 5″ × 8″ index card. They can use the school or public library to find out more about the scientist they have chosen. On the back of the index card they can draw a cartoon, write a poem or short paragraph that illustrates an important event in the life of this famous personality.

BIO-DATA CARD

ROSALIND ELSIE FRANKLIN
(born, 1920; died, 1958)

nationality
English

contribution to science
assisted James Dewey Watson and Francis H. C. Crick in determining the structure of DNA

BIO-DATA CARD

GALEN
(born, 129; died, 200)

nationality
Greek

contribution to science
most respected European medical authority until the 1500s for his theories about blood circulation and disease

BIO-DATA CARD

ERNST HEINRICH HAEKEL
(born, 1834; died, 1919)

nationality
German

contribution to science
with Fritz Müller suggested that the ancestral history of an organism is "recapitulated" during its development

BIO-DATA CARD

WILLIAM HARVEY
(born, 1578; died, 1657)

nationality
English

contribution to science
advanced the study of comparative anatomy and explained the circulation of the blood in arteries and veins

BIO-DATA CARD

JACOB HENLE
(born, 1809; died, 1885)

nationality
German

contribution to science
first to make a logical argument that living organisms were responsible for diseases in animals and humans

BIO-DATA CARD

HIPPOCRATES
(born, 460 B.C.; died, 377 B.C.)

nationality
Greek

contribution to science
called the "father of medicine" for preaching moderation in life style and diet

BIO-DATA CARD

DOROTHY M. C. HODGKIN
(born, 1910; died, 1994)

nationality
English

contribution to science
pioneered the application of X-ray crystallography to determine the structure of biological molecules

BIO-DATA CARD

ROBERT HOOKE
(born, 1635; died, 1702)

nationality
English

contribution to science
coined the term "cella" to describe the tiny compartments seen in all living tissue under the microscope

BIO-DATA CARD

JOSEPH DALTON HOOKER

(born, 1817; died, 1911)

nationality
English

contribution to science
made lengthy trips to the Antarctic and
India to correlate plant diversity with
climatic conditions

BIO-DATA CARD

FRIEDRICH W. H. A. HUMBOLDT

(born, 1769; died, 1859)

nationality
German

contribution to science
called the "father of ecology" for relating
thousands of tropical plant species to their
environment

BIO-DATA CARD

JAMES HUTTON

(born, 1726; died, 1797)

nationality
Scottish

contribution to science
called the "founder of geology" and first to
argue against the then-popular notion that
earth was a few thousand years old

BIO-DATA CARD

THOMAS JEFFERSON

(born, 1743; died, 1826)

nationality
American

contribution to science
3rd President of the United States and
amateur scientist who popularized the
study of fossils

BIO-DATA CARD

EDWARD JENNER

(born, 1749; died, 1823)

nationality
English

contribution to science
developed the first effective vaccine against
smallpox but could not explain how the
vaccine worked

BIO-DATA CARD

HAR GOBIND KHORANA

(born, 1922)

nationality
Indian

contribution to science
performed genetic experiments that
established the positive role bacteria could
play in the treatment of disease

BIO-DATA CARD

HEINRICH HERMANN KOCH

(born, 1843; died, 1910)

nationality
German

contribution to science
developed techniques for culturing bacteria
used to replicate disease under controlled
laboratory conditions

BIO-DATA CARD

JEAN BAPTISTE LAMARCK

(born, 1744; died, 1829)

nationality
French

contribution to science
suggested the theory of acquired
characteristics—that later proved wrong—
to explain the diversity of species

INSTRUCTIONS TO TEACHERS
Xerox and cut out the Bio-Data Cards below and keep them in a handy file. Instruct students to choose one card and neatly glue it to the front of a 5" × 8" index card. They can use the school or public library to find out more about the scientist they have chosen. On the back of the index card they can draw a cartoon, write a poem or short paragraph that illustrates an important event in the life of this famous personality.

BIO-DATA CARD

ANTON VAN LEEUWENHOEK
(born, 1632; died, 1723)

nationality
Dutch

contribution to science
made the first drawings of microscopic bacteria and protozoa using a handheld microscope

BIO-DATA CARD

CAROLUS LINNAEUS
(born, 1707; died, 1778)

nationality
Swedish

contribution to science
developed the modern system of binomial classification to classify plants and animals

BIO-DATA CARD

JOSEPH LISTER
(born, 1827; died, 1912)

nationality
English

contribution to science
performed the first antiseptic surgery in 1867

BIO-DATA CARD

CHARLES LYELL
(born, 1797; died, 1875)

nationality
Scottish

contribution to science
first to deduce that the earth's age was in the millions or billions—and not thousands—of years old

BIO-DATA CARD

GREGOR MENDEL
(born, 1822; died, 1884)

nationality
Austrian

contribution to science
discovered the concept of the "gene" to explain how traits are passed from one generation to the next

BIO-DATA CARD

STANLEY LLOYD MILLER
(born, 1930)

nationality
American

contribution to science
with H. C. Urey demonstrated that the precursor molecules of life could be synthesized from nonliving matter

BIO-DATA CARD

HUGO VON MOHL
(born, 1805; died, 1872)

nationality
German

contribution to science
coined the term "protoplasm" to describe the jellylike fluid in cells

BIO-DATA CARD

THOMAS HUNT MORGAN
(born, 1866; died, 1945)

nationality
American

contribution to science
with H. J. Muller showed that X-rays could cause mutations in fruit flies

---

BIO-DATA CARD

FRITZ MÜLLER
(born, 1822; died, 1897)

nationality
German

contribution to science
with E. H. Haekel suggested that the ancestral history of an organism is "recapitulated" during its development

---

BIO-DATA CARD

HERMANN JOSEPH MULLER
(born, 1890; died, 1967)

nationality
American

contribution to science
with T. H. Morgan showed that X-rays could cause mutations in fruit flies

---

BIO-DATA CARD

LOUIS PASTEUR
(born, 1822; died, 1895)

nationality
French

contribution to science
developed "germ theory" and the pasteurization process to rid food of germs by slow heating

---

BIO-DATA CARD

AUGUSTE ANTOINE & JACQUES PICCARD
(born, 1884; died, 1962)   (born, 1922)

nationality
Swiss

contribution to science
father and son who designed and submerged the first deep sea bathyscaph

---

BIO-DATA CARD

PLATO
(born, 427 B.C.; died, 347 B.C.)

nationality
Greek

contribution to science
suggested that all forms of matter including living things were simulations of "ideal" forms called "archetypes"

BIO-DATA CARD

JOHN RAY
(born, 1627; died, 1705)

nationality
English

contribution to science
suggested that members of a given species could not arise "from the seed of other species"

BIO-DATA CARD

ERNST AUGUST FRIEDRICH RUSKA
(born, 1906; died, 1988)

nationality
German

contribution to science
invented the first practical electron microscope for viewing the details of cellular organelles

---

BIO-DATA CARD

MATTHIAS JAKOB SCHLEIDEN
(born, 1804; died, 1881)

nationality
German

contribution to science
with Theodor Schwann developed the theory that all living things were made up of cells

BIO-DATA CARD

THEODOR SCHWANN

(born, 1810; died, 1882)

nationality
German

contribution to science
with M. J. Schleiden developed the theory that all living things were made up of cells

BIO-DATA CARD

LAZZARO SPALLANZINI

(born, 1729; died, 1799)

nationality
Italian

contribution to science
discovered that some dessicated aquatic organisms could be reanimated by soaking them in water

BIO-DATA CARD

EDUARD ADOLF STRASBURGER

(born, 1844; died, 1912)

nationality
German

contribution to science
clarified the role of "haploid cells" in the process of fertilization

BIO-DATA CARD

THEOPHRASTUS

(born, 372 B.C.; died, 287 B.C.)

nationality
Greek

contribution to science
called the "father of botany" for his well organized and documented study of plants

BIO-DATA CARD

HAROLD CLAYTON UREY

(born, 1893; died, 1981)

nationality
American

contribution to science
with S. L. Miller demonstrated that the precursor molecules of life could be synthesized from nonliving matter

BIO-DATA CARD

ALFRED RUSSEL WALLACE

(born, 1823; died, 1913)

nationality
Welch

contribution to science
developed the theory of evolution by means of natural selection independently of Charles R. Darwin

BIO-DATA CARD

JOHANNES E. B. WARMING

(born, 1841; died, 1924)

nationality
Dutch

contribution to science
established crucial relationships between plants and their natural environments

BIO-DATA CARD

JAMES DEWEY WATSON

(born, 1928)

nationality
American

contribution to science
with Francis H. C. Crick and Rosalind E. Franklin determined the structure of the DNA molecule

BIO-DATA CARD

ALFRED LOTHAR WEGENER

(born, 1880; died, 1930)

nationality
German

contribution to science
developed the theory of continental drift adding an additional mechanism to explain the diversity of species

BIO-DATA CARD

AUGUST F. L. WEISMANN

(born, 1834; died, 1914)

nationality
German

contribution to science
suggested that every living cell contains a substance he called "germplasm" that carries hereditary information